THE PSYCHOLOGY OF CLOTHES

Series showing effects produced by a simple shawl

THE PSYCHOLOGY OF CLOTHES

by
J. C. FLUGEL, B.A., D.Sc.

International Universities Press, Inc.
NEW YORK

Copyright © 1930 J. C. Flugel
ALL RIGHTS RESERVED

First Paperback Edition 1969
Second I. U. P. Paperback Printing 1971

PRINTED IN THE UNITED STATES OF AMERICA

S'il m'était permis de choisir dans le fatras des livres qui seront publiés cent ans après ma mort, savez-vous celui que je prendrais? ... Non, ce n'est point un roman que je prendrais dans cette future bibliothèque, ni un livre d'histoire: quand il offre quelque intérêt c'est encore un roman. Je prendrais tout bonnement, mon ami, un journal de modes pour voir comment les femmes s'habilleront un siècle après mon trépas. Et ces chiffons m'en diraient plus sur l'humanité future que tous les philosophes, les romanciers, les prédicateurs, les savants.—Anatole France.

PREFACE

It is now a good many years since Herbert Spencer recorded the remark (not, of course, his own) that the consciousness of being perfectly well dressed may bestow a 'peace such as religion cannot give'. But though in the interval there have appeared quite a number of books on the psychology of religion, there have been very few on the psychology of clothes. Perhaps the subject has seemed too familiar, or perhaps again too frivolous, or perhaps the ghost of Teufelsdröckh has frightened later comers from the field; but the fact remains that, with one or two notable exceptions, psychologists have not concerned themselves with the matter, unless it be for a few observations here and there in passing. The result is that the approaches to clothes through the avenues of history or hygiene have alone been considered worthy of attention by the serious minded.

This must be my excuse, if excuse be needed, for the present modest volume. The incentive for writing it came largely (though of course indirectly) from the British Broadcasting Corporation, which in 1928 invited me to give a series of talks, several of which were devoted to the present subject. I am naturally much indebted to the few psychologists who have already contributed to our knowledge in this field (especially Dearborn, Flaccus, Knight Dunlap, and some members of the psychoanalytical school), also to some writers who have studied costume from the anthropological or social points of view (notably Fuchs, Selenka, Stratz and Webb). Among my personal friends, Professor N. J. Symons and Mr. Eric Hiller have made useful suggestions upon certain points. Miss Eve Macaulay has helped me, both in this way and by carrying out a special investigation, which has been published in full elsewhere. Dr. Henri Hoesli, M. André Friang, and M. Const. Pleský have most kindly rendered assistance in the collection and preparation of some of the illustrations. To my wife I owe much invaluable criticism and encouragement and also much aid in the indication of literary sources. To these, and to others who have assisted in a variety of ways, I am most grateful.

CONTENTS

	PAGE
PREFACE	7

CHAP.
I.	THE FUNDAMENTAL MOTIVES	15
II.	DECORATION—PURPOSIVE ASPECTS	25
III.	DECORATION—FORMAL ASPECTS	39
IV.	MODESTY	53
V.	PROTECTION	68
VI.	INDIVIDUAL DIFFERENCES	85
VII.	SEX DIFFERENCES	103
VIII.	TYPES OF DRESS	122
IX.	THE FORCES OF FASHION	137
X.	THE VICISSITUDES OF FASHION	155
XI.	THE EVOLUTION OF GARMENTS	167
XII.	THE ETHICS OF DRESS—ART AND NATURE	181
XIII.	THE ETHICS OF DRESS—INDIVIDUAL AND SEXUAL DIFFERENTIATION	198
XIV.	THE ETHICS OF DRESS—THE RATIONALISATION OF FASHION	216
XV.	THE FUTURE OF DRESS	227
	BIBLIOGRAPHY	239
	INDEX	243

LIST OF ILLUSTRATIONS

Frontispiece: Series showing effects produced by a simple shawl.

FIG.   TO FACE PAGE

1. A simple illustration of how a Skirt increases the feeling of size, importance, and beauty of line when the body is motionless   34
   (By permission of *The Dancing Times*.)

2. How a Skirt may add to the effect of movement   34
   (By permission of The Topical Press Agency.)

3. Loie Fuller in various dances   36
   (By permission of *l'Illustration*.)

4. Effects of 'Contrast' and 'Confluence'   37

5. Effect of Wind   38
   From the painting, 'The Peace of Spring', by Estella Canzani (by permission of the Medici Society).

6. Young African Girl, with ornamental scars   40
   From H. Hiler, *From Nudity to Raiment* (by permission of Messrs. W. and G. Foyle, Ltd.).

7. Minoan Snake Goddess, showing constricted waist   43
   From A. J. B. Wace, *A Cretan Statuette in the Fitzwilliam Museum* (by permission of the Cambridge University Press).

8. Coronation Robe of Catherine II. of Russia   48
   (By permission of The Topical Press Agency.)

9. A Native of Hawaii, showing 'dimensional' decoration   49
   From E. Selenka, *Der Schmuck des Menschen* (by permission of Vita Deutsches Verlagshaus).

FIG.		TO FACE PAGE
10.	A Native of New Pomerania, wearing shell collar	49

From E. Selenka, *Der Schmuck des Menschen* (by permission of Vita Deutsches Verlagshaus).

11.	Two Padaung Women with numerous metal collars	51

From W. M. Webb, *The Heritage of Dress* (by permission of the author).

12.	'Primitive' Costume, with elaborate head-dress, the typical hip-ring, and 'circular' (ring) ornamentation	51

From C. H. Stratz, *Die Frauenkleidung* (by permission of Herrn Ferdinand Enke).

13.	An Outdoor Costume from Tunis	61

From C. H. Stratz, *Die Frauenkleidung* (by permission of Herrn Ferdinand Enke).

14.	The Beginning of Costume	123

From C. H. Stratz, *Die Frauenkleidung* (by permission of Herrn Ferdinand Enke).

15.	'Primitive' Costume from Samoa, showing circular floral decoration and necklace of white whale's teeth	124

From E. Selenka, *Der Schmuck des Menschen* (by permission of Vita Deutsches Verlagshaus).

16.	Typical forms of (*a*) 'tropical' and (*b*) 'arctic' costume from Java and Siberia respectively	124

From C. H. Stratz, *Die Frauenkleidung* (by permission of Herrn Ferdinand Enke).

17.	Diana, from the Borghese Collection of the Louvre. A simple costume which enhances the beauty of the bodily form	156
18.	An elaborate stage costume, which frames rather than covers the body	156

LIST OF ILLUSTRATIONS

FIG.   TO FACE PAGE

19. Louis XVI., by Callet. An elaborate costume, the effect of which is independent of bodily form   158

    (By permission of Messrs. Levy and Neurdein.)

20. The shifting emphasis of fashion   160

    (*a*) Renaissance dress, with emphasis on the abdomen.

    (*b*) Empire dress, giving due weight to the lines of the body as a whole.

    (*c*) Crinoline, emphasising waist and hips, and enormously increasing the apparent total bulk of the body.

    (*d*) Bustle, emphasising the posterior parts (a tail-like appendage).

        From C. H. Stratz, *Die Frauenkleidung*, and Fischel and von Boehn, *Modes and Manners of the Nineteenth Century* (by permission of Herrn Ferdinand Enke and Messrs. J. M. Dent and Sons).

21. Illustrating evolution in dress   176

    (*a*) The red Hungarian cap which was the forerunner of the busby.

    (*b*) A busby (of the Honourable Artillery Company) in which the cap is a vestige only.

        From W. M. Webb, *The Heritage of Dress* (by permission of the author).

CHAPTER I

THE FUNDAMENTAL MOTIVES

> Should we be silent and not speak, our raiment
> And state of bodies would bewray what life
> We have led. *Coriolanus*, v. 3.

MAN, it has often been said, is a social animal. He needs the company of his fellows and is delicately reactive to their presence and behaviour. And yet, so far as the sense of vision is concerned, civilised man has but little opportunity of directly observing the bodies of his companions. Apart from face and hands—which, it is true, are the most socially expressive parts of our anatomy, and to which we have learnt to devote an especially alert attention—what we actually see and react to are, not the bodies, but the clothes of those about us. It is from their clothes that we form a first impression of our fellow-creatures as we meet them. The delicate discrimination of facial feature needs a somewhat intimate proximity. But clothes, presenting as they do a much larger surface for inspection, can be clearly distinguished at a more convenient distance. It is the indirect expression of an individual through his garments, that tells us, for instance, that the person whom we 'see' approaching is one whom we know; and it is the movement imparted to his clothes by the limbs within, and not the motion of the limbs themselves, that enables us to judge at first glance whether this acquaintance of ours is friendly, angry, frightened, curious, hurried, or at ease. In the case of an individual whom we have not previously met, the clothes he is wearing tell us at once something of his sex, occupation, nationality, and social standing, and thus enable us to make a preliminary adjustment of our behaviour towards him, long before the more delicate analysis of feature and of speech can be attempted.

But it is clearly unnecessary to enumerate the functions that clothing plays in all our social relations; it is only necessary to recall their general nature, lest their very familiarity should cause them to be overlooked. When we have once realised the social significance of clothes by this very simple process of recalling an everyday occurrence, we should need no further warning as to the importance of clothes in human life and human personality; indeed, the very word 'personality', as we have been reminded by recent writers, implies a 'mask', which is itself an article of clothing. Clothes, in fact, though seemingly mere extraneous appendages, have entered into the very core of our existence as social beings. They therefore not only permit, but demand, treatment from the psychologist; it is perhaps rather the absence of such treatment from our systematic handbooks of psychology that requires excuse and explanation.

The psychologist who approaches the problem of clothes enjoys one great advantage; an advantage which may save him a long and tedious preliminary chapter. There is general agreement among practically all who have written on the subject that clothes serve three main purposes—decoration, modesty, and protection. This important conclusion we may accept as fundamental for our own considerations. It is further agreed that the motives underlying all three purposes are pretty constantly operative in civilised societies. When it comes to the question which of the three motives is to be regarded as primary, there is indeed some dispute; though even here there is less difference of opinion than might perhaps have been expected. The primacy of **protection** as a motive for clothing has few if any advocates; students of humanity appear unwilling to admit that so important an institution as dress can have had so purely utilitarian an origin. Apart from the fact that the human race probably had its beginnings in the warmer regions of the earth, the example of certain existing primitive peoples, notably the inhabitants of Tierra del Fuego, shows that clothing is not essential, even in a damp and chilly climate. In this matter Darwin's often-quoted observation of the snow melting on the skins of these hardy savages, seems to have brought home to a somewhat startled nineteenth-century generation that their own snug garments, however cosy and desirable they might appear, were not inexorably required by the necessities of the human constitution. **Modesty,** apart from seeming to enjoy the authority of Biblical tradition, has been given first place by one or two authorities on purely anthropological grounds.[1] The great majority of scholars, however, have unhesitatingly regarded **decoration** as the motive that led, in the first place, to the adoption of clothing, and consider that the warmth- and modesty-preserving functions of dress, however important they might later on become, were only discovered once the wearing of clothes had become habitual for other reasons. We need not here enter into any detailed consideration of this speculative and somewhat arid discussion. It is a question that concerns the ethnologist rather than the psychologist, and there are other more important matters that await our own attention.

On the evidence available, it does not appear likely, however, that the psychologist will feel inclined to contradict the anthropologist when the latter regards the decorative motive as primary and in certain ways more fundamental than the motives of modesty and of protection. The anthropological evidence consists chiefly in the fact that among the most primitive races there exist unclothed but not undecorated peoples. Comparing ontogeny with phylogeny, it would likewise seem that in young children the pleasure in decoration develops earlier than the feeling of shame in exposure—though here observation is difficult because the child is, from the start, subject to the influence of its adult environment. Careful study seems to show, however, that, more primitive than either modesty or decoration, there exists a simple joy in the exercise and display of the *naked*

[1] Notably by Schurtz, 86.

body; this is a joy which the young child may feel intensely and which is often interfered with by the clothes which he is made to wear, so that, through the unpleasant associations thus acquired, the satisfactions of sartorial decoration often appear later than might otherwise be the case. Nevertheless the child sometimes does manifest simple decorative tendencies, not unlike those of the savage. Young children, says Sully,[1] 'like a lot of finery in the shape of a string of beads or daisies for the neck, a feather for the hat, a scrap of brilliantly coloured ribbon or cloth as a bow for the dress, and so on'.[2] The child thus resembles primitive man in that he is more interested in isolated ornaments than in whole costumes or coherent schemes of decoration; doubtless a corresponding trait to that which he manifests in his appreciation of pictorial art, in which, as experiment has shown, he enjoys the representation of single objects long before he can obtain pleasure from a total composition or the depiction of a complex scene. That we do not see more of this earliest decorative tendency is possibly due to the fact that, while emphasising the need of modesty and protection, we express in various ways our disapproval of the display tendency at an age when it still attaches mostly to the naked body, so that the whole impulse of display is, to some extent, nipped in the bud before it has time to develop to the stage of decoration.

Apart, however, from the question of the actually observable priority of the motive of decoration in the individual or the race, there are certain more *a priori* reasons of a psychological nature which make it improbable that modesty can be the primary motive for clothing. Modesty by its very nature seems to be something

---

[1] 95, p. 319.
[2] Much the same tendencies can be observed in the anthropoid apes, of whom Köhler says: 'Almost daily the animals can be seen walking about with a rope, a bit of rag, a blade of grass, or a twig on their shoulders. . . . Their pleasure is visibly increased by draping things round themselves. No observer can escape the impression that . . . the objects hanging about the body serve the purpose of *adornment* in the widest sense'—(W. Köhler, *The Mentality of Apes*, 2nd ed. pp. 92, 93).

that is secondary; it is a reaction against a more primitive tendency to self-display and, therefore, seems to imply the previous existence of this latter, without which it can have no *raison d'être*. Furthermore, the manifestations of modesty are of the most fluctuating and protean character. Not only do they vary enormously from place to place, from age to age, and from one section of society to another, but, even within a given circle of intimates, what is considered quite permissible on one occasion may, a few hours later, be regarded as veritably indecent. The actual manifestations of modesty appear, indeed, to be entirely a matter of habit and convention. This of itself does not show that the impulse of modesty in general is not innate ; on the contrary, it almost certainly is innate. Nevertheless, the arousal of modesty in connection with any particular part of the body, or indeed in connection with the naked body as a whole, can itself be scarcely more than a matter of traditional outlook—not a fundamental primitive tendency comparable to self-display, which, though also modifiable in its manifestations, seems much more rigidly determined with regard to its main forms. At any rate it has seemed to many thinkers extremely difficult to suppose that the general habit of wearing clothes can have been due to so variable and easily displaced a tendency as that which modesty everywhere shows itself to be.

As we have already said, however, it is fortunately unnecessary to enter upon a minute consideration of this question of priority. It is agreed that each of the three motives of decoration, modesty, and protection is important enough in its own way. And at that we may let the matter stand, merely expressing the pious hope that more exact observation under favourable conditions, both of primitive people and of young children, will before long enable us to evaluate more precisely the genetic significance of each motive.

Meanwhile it is of greater importance for us, from our present psychological point of view, to examine the relations between the three sets of motives—a task which has hitherto received far less attention, but which appears to lead straightway to the very heart of the clothes problem as it affects the psychologist, especially so in the case of the relation between modesty and decoration. It is clear that in some ways these two motives are opposed to one another. The essential purpose of decoration is to beautify the bodily appearance, so as to attract the admiring glances of others and fortify one's self-esteem. The essential purpose of modesty is, if not indeed the exact contrary, at least utterly opposed to this. Modesty tends to make us hide such bodily excellencies as we may have and generally refrain from drawing the attention of others to ourselves. Complete simultaneous satisfaction of the two tendencies seems to be a logical impossibility, and the inevitable conflict between them can at best be met by some approximate solution by way of rapid alternation or of compromise —a solution somewhat resembling that which some psychologists[1] have eloquently described under the term coyness.

This essential opposition between the two motives of decoration and of modesty is, I think, the most fundamental fact in the whole psychology of clothing. It implies that our attitude towards clothes is *ab initio* 'ambivalent', to use the invaluable term that has been introduced into psychology by the psycho-analysts; we are trying to satisfy two contradictory tendencies by means of our clothes, and we therefore tend to regard clothes from two incompatible points of view—on the one hand, as a means of displaying our attractions, on the other hand, as a means of hiding our shame. Clothes, in fact, as articles devised for the satisfaction of human needs, are essentially in the nature of a compromise; they are an ingenious device for the establishment of some degree of harmony between conflicting interests. In this respect the discovery, or at any rate the use, of clothes, seems, in its psychological aspects, to resemble the pro-

[1] *E.g.* W. McDougall, *Social Psychology*, 1st ed. p. 83.

cess whereby a neurotic symptom is developed. Neurotic symptoms, as it is the great merit of psycho-analysis to have shown, are also something of a compromise, due to the interplay of conflicting and largely unconscious impulses. Some symptoms of this kind seem indeed to serve as a compromise between almost exactly the same tendencies as those which find expression in clothes. Thus the attacks of psychological blushing, from which some patients suffer, are, on the one hand, exaggerations of the normal symptoms of shame, but, on the other hand, as psycho-analytic examination has demonstrated, at the same time involuntarily draw attention to the sufferer and thus gratify his unconscious exhibitionism. In terms of this very close analogy, it may indeed be said that clothes resemble a perpetual blush upon the surface of humanity.[1]

The circumstances that clothes can so well serve this double and, at bottom, contradictory function, is connected with the fact—at which we have already hinted —that the tendencies both of display and of shame originally relate not to the clothed but to the naked body. Clothes serve to cover the body, and thus gratify the impulse to modesty. But, at the same time, they may enhance the beauty of the body, and indeed, as we

[1] A fascinating study of a conflict between exhibitionism and modesty has been made by Arthur Schnitzler in his well-known novel, *Fräulein Else*. In this story the heroine is asked by an elderly roué to show herself to him naked, in return for some all-important financial assistance which he is, on this condition, prepared to give to her father. Instead of granting his request in private, she throws off her cloak and reveals herself completely nude in the crowded public room of a large hotel, committing suicide thereafter.

The poignancy of the emotional situation in this story lies in the fact that the request (to which the extreme urgency of her father's necessity bids her accede), though utterly at variance with her traditions of modesty, is nevertheless one which makes a very strong appeal to her repressed exhibitionistic tendencies. Such situations, in which ethical considerations at a higher level ally themselves with fundamental instinctive desires (this alliance being, in its turn, opposed by all the deeper and more ingrained moral elements), are among the most difficult that we can be called upon to meet. In the present case the conflict is solved in a manner that reveals very clearly the unconscious mechanism of 'overdetermination', in which antagonistic desires are gratified by one and the same act. By her exaggerated 'over-reaction' to the 'immoral' request, Else creates a situation which permits of a much more satisfying indulgence in exhibitionism than the circumstances require—a situation which is, however, at the same time one of public shame so great as to make the continuance of life impossible.

have seen, this was probably their most primitive function. When the exhibitionistic tendency to display is thus lured away from the naked to the clothed body, it can gratify itself with far less opposition from the tendencies connected with modesty than it could when it was concentrated on the body in the state of Nature. It is as though both parties were contented with the new development, the compromise involved becoming in consequence a relatively stable one. We shall see later on how the various changes manifested in successive fashions represent so many minor disturbances and readjustments of the equilibrium thus established—changes in the relative predominance of modesty and display, their direction to various parts of the body, and the degree of their displacement from the body itself to the clothes that cover it. In fact, the whole psychology of clothes undergoes at once a great clarification and a great simplification, if this fundamental ambivalence in our attitude be fully grasped and continually held in mind.

It is a relatively easy matter to see how, this great compromise between the conflicting motives of decoration and of modesty having once been reached, it would be strengthened by the third motive of protection. Clothes, having already shown themselves a remarkably successful means of reconciling two apparently irreconcilable attitudes towards the human body, were found to have still a third advantage—that of protecting the body against the disagreeable sensation of cold. Although purely hygienic considerations are alien to the primitive mind (since it is apt to consider that all disease is due to the agency of magic or of spirits), the biological advantages of reducing the heat loss of the body, and of thereby making possible a reduction of the energy to be supplied by food, may have gradually made themselves apparent, especially in so far as the pressure of population and the consequent struggle for existence induced certain sections of the human race to push forward into ever colder climes. Such ideas concerning hygiene as did affect clothing were, however, in recent centuries at any rate, largely based upon an exaggerated estimate of the danger to health accruing from cold air,[1] and were thus admirably suited to support the claims of clothing and to add to the satisfaction which clothing already gave to the motives of modesty and of display. Indeed, both of these latter tendencies have undoubtedly sometimes taken refuge behind the more purely utilitarian and therefore less emotional motive of protection. The latter motive was, in psychological terminology, used as a 'rationalisation' for the former, and in virtue of this process man appeared and considered himself to be obeying the purely reasonable motive of health protection when he was in reality being moved chiefly by the more primitive conflict between modesty and display—a process which, as we shall have occasion to see, is still to be observed in operation at the present day, though certain modern ideas of hygiene are less favourable to its occurrence than were those of a former generation. It is clear that in the last few years there has taken place a change in our ideas of hygiene, a change which has stressed the possibility of clothing affording not too little but too much protection, and which has even made it possible for us to sympathise with the view expressed by Herodotus of old that too complete a covering of the body is a cause of weakness. Such a change has clearly entailed corresponding modifications in our conceptions of modesty and decoration—of modesty in so far as there has come about a greater tolerance in certain directions of the bodily form, of decoration in so far as there have arisen strong tendencies towards simplicity and naturalness in dress. These correlated changes are matters of the highest interest, both to the historian and to the psychologist of dress, and in a later part of this book we shall return to deal with them in a manner more befitting their importance. Here it suffices to have drawn attention to them as a striking instance of the

[1] The reason for this exaggeration itself constitutes a psychological problem of much interest in the history of medicine. Cf. Ernest Jones, 55.

way in which the motive of protection interacts with the motives of modesty and of display. The three motives are, in their manifestations, so linked together that a change in one almost inevitably implies corresponding changes in the other two.

CHAPTER II

DECORATION—PURPOSIVE ASPECTS

Tanta est quaerendi cura decoris.
JUVENAL, *Sat.* vi. 501.

AFTER this brief examination of the principal motives of human clothing, it behoves us now to study each in somewhat greater detail. In the course of this study we shall, in so far as we are successful, acquire a more precise knowledge of the various ways in which each of the three motives achieves its satisfactions, both as regards the external means and situations which it uses and the internal urges which it satisfies and from which it springs.

In the present chapter and the next we shall deal only with the motive of decoration. This can be most conveniently considered under two chief heads. In the first place we shall deal with certain main purposes of decoration; here the accent will fall chiefly upon psychological or social factors. In our next chapter we shall consider certain forms or modes of decoration; the psychological category of purpose is, of course, implied there also, but, in the actual treatment, the accent will fall upon more definitely sartorial factors. That section will in fact consist to a great extent of a classification of the chief forms of decoration.

The Sexual Element.—It has been manifest to all serious students of dress that of all the motives for the wearing of clothes, those connected with the sexual life have an altogether predominant position. There is indeed agreement on this point, whatever view may be held as regards the relative primacy of decoration or of modesty respectively. The minority who consider that modesty was the primary motive, think that clothing originated as the result of an attempt to inhibit sex (the fig-leaf story in the book of Genesis is, of course, an example of this attitude). The great majority who believe in the primacy of the decorative motive hold that clothing originated largely through the desire to enhance the sexual attractiveness of the wearer and to draw attention to the genital organs of the body.

Among savage peoples clothing and decoration (like their antecedents, tattooing, painting, etc.) start anatomically at or near the genital region, and have very frequently some definite reference to a sexual occasion (puberty, marriage, etc.).[1] Among civilised peoples the overtly sexual rôle of many clothes is too obvious and familiar to need more than a mere mention. This is particularly the case as regards women's fashions in the last few hundred years. The designer who plans them, the dressmaker who sells them, the divine or the moralist who denounces them, the historian of dress who reviews them as they successively occupy the stage for such brief years or months as may be allotted to them—all are alike agreed that their ultimate purpose, often indeed their overt and conscious purpose,[2] is to add to the sexual attractiveness of their wearers, and to stimulate the sexual interest of admirers of the opposite sex and the envy of rivals of the same sex.

But though the general nature of the underlying sexual motive has been universally recognised, it is only in the last few years that there has been any clear realisation of the fact that clothes not only serve to arouse sexual interest but may themselves actually symbolise the sexual organs. Here again psycho-analysis has added considerably to our knowledge, and has shown that in the domain of clothes phallic symbolism is scarcely less important than, for instance, in the domain of religion. Indeed, we are still almost certainly as yet ignorant concerning the full extent of this symbolism in the case of clothes and of the exact nature of the rôle this symbolism plays in the history of the

---

[1] The clearest condensed treatment of this subject will be found in Bloch, 7, pp. 146 ff.
[2] Eduard Fuchs, 44, vol. iii. p. 212.

individual and the race.[1] We know, however, that a great many articles of dress, such as the shoe, the tie, the hat, the collar, and even larger and more voluminous garments, such as the coat, the trousers, and the mantle may be phallic symbols, while the shoe, the girdle, and the garter (as well as most jewels) may be corresponding female symbols.[2]

As a statement of this kind is apt to arouse the somewhat hostile incredulity that attaches to most psychoanalytic assertions concerning symbolism, two further sets of facts may be referred to, since they may help to make acceptance of the symbolism in question a little less difficult. In the first place, if we compare together observations from various sources and from various times, we can easily establish the existence of a continuous transition, from blatant exhibition of the actual genitals to the totally unconscious symbolisation of them by garments which resemble them but very little. Thus at one extreme we have the familiar enough perversion of localised phallic exhibitionism, in which an obsessive sexual satisfaction is derived from showing the naked penis, usually in its erect state. It seems psychologically but a slight modification of this (though one which entails the important step of 'displacement of affect' from the body on to clothes) when, as was the case with our ancestors for about fifty years during Tudor times, the tightness of male nether garments necessitated the housing of the genitals in a special bulging portion of the hose (the cod-piece)—a portion to which attention was sometimes gratuitously drawn by a vivid or contrasting colour, and which was further sometimes embellished by padding in such a way as to simulate a perpetual erection. Our next stage may be taken from a somewhat earlier period, when the

[1] For a brief summary of our present knowledge on the sexual symbolism of clothes, the reader is referred to the present writer's paper on 'Clothes Symbolism and Clothes Ambivalence', 36.
[2] The shoe, in this respect, is ambisexual. The female symbolism of the garter is prettily illustrated by some examples recently on sale in London, which were provided with a silver representation of a gate bearing such inscriptions as 'Go warily', 'This gate is private', 'Private ground'.

phallic substitute was found, not near the genital region itself but on a remote part of the body, namely the feet. There was at one time in the Middle Ages a tendency to fashion the long shoe, known as the *poulaine*, in the shape of the phallus, and this practice enjoyed a lengthy popularity in spite of the storm of indignation which it aroused.[1] At one stage further in the direction of disguise, the long point of the shoe has lost its actual phallic form, a beak or bird's claw being substituted. At the next stage[2] there is only the excessive and ridiculous length of the shoe to remind us of its underlying symbolism—but that this symbolism is still appreciated is shown by the moral disapproval and the charges of immodesty which it still encountered. As our final stage we may consider the modern shoe, in which there is still manifest a desire for a greater pointedness than is warranted by the shape of the foot, and in which objections to the unnatural shape have become almost entirely rationalised as motives of hygiene.

The other set of facts to which reference may be made are those relating to fetishism, *i.e.* a perversion in which sexual desire chooses as its exclusive and sufficient object some inappropriate part of the body (*e.g.* feet, hair) or some article of clothing (*e.g.* shoe, stocking, corset, handkerchief). Recent psycho-analytic work[3] has shown that the fetish also is often (perhaps always) a phallic symbol, though a phallic symbol of a specific kind, inasmuch as it represents the imaginary penis of the mother—a penis, the observed absence of which has had much to do with the development of the 'castration complex', of which we shall have more to say later.

This much may suffice for the sexual element in decoration, so far as our needs at the present moment are concerned. In what is to come we shall have ample opportunity for further realisation of its importance and (it may be hoped) for removing such impression of bald-

[1] Havelock Ellis, *Studies in the Psychology of Sex*, v. p. 25.
[2] The 'stages' here refer of course to clearness of erotic symbolism, not to chronology.
[3] *E.g.* Sadger, 82, pp. 327 ff.; Freud, 41, p. 161.

II DECORATION—PURPOSIVE ASPECTS

ness or dogmatism as the present somewhat bare and condensed statement may have created in the reader's mind.

We turn now to factors of less universal occurrence and more restricted scope, factors, however, which one and all play—or at least have played—a part of some importance in the development of clothes. But before embarking on their exposition we shall do well to bear in mind that, even here, there is often to be distinguished a certain sexual element in the satisfactions that they give—an element that is sometimes so clear and obvious that it needs no pointing out, but which in other cases may need a word of explanation before its full force and nature can be realised.

Trophies.—It has been suggested on good grounds (notably by Herbert Spencer[1]) that many of the decorative features of our clothing were originally connected with the wearing of trophies. When a hunter killed an animal, he would often carry home with him some part of the animal that seemed likely to be useful or decorative, or that would serve as a permanent memento of his prowess. Horns and antlers were particularly suited for decoration of this kind, and in one form or another horns have been very frequently used as ornaments, especially on headgear. The skins of animals, especially skins covered with fur, were both decorative and useful, and these also would serve as a sign of a successful hunter. But such symbols of success were coveted not only by the hunter. The warrior who went out to combat human foes would also desire a token of victory, and some part of the enemy he had slain would often be detached for this purpose. The scalps which the North American Indian cut from his victims served as one form of this decoration, and the practice of scalping is by no means confined to North America.[2] In other

[1] 91, vol. ii. pp. 128 ff.
[2] Nor to lower cultures. At any rate the present writer well remembers the pride with which a fellow-student exhibited (as the chief ornament of his study) a symbolic scalp in the shape of a policeman's helmet, seized and carried off during a college 'rag').

places necklaces have been worn that were made of the teeth of fallen foes, while in still others the bones of enemies have been carried as ornaments; thus, in some places, the jawbone has been worn round the arm like a bracelet. Even the hand or the phallus of a fallen foe has often been cut off, carried home, and looked upon as an important and valuable trophy.

This last example is calculated to bring home to us that phallic symbolism plays an important (though often more or less unconscious) part in the popularity of trophies. The trophy is often used as a sign of the power (ultimately the phallic power) of its wearer or possessor; it is as if the trophy provided the owner with a new and finer phallus. On the other hand, the removal of the trophy from the victim is often a symbolic process of castration, thus affording further evidence of the way in which the castration complex may influence clothes.[1] Indeed, the effects of the complex in this direction are probably far greater and more widespread than might at first be suspected. The removal of trophies from dead enemies is psychologically akin to the removal of weapons from captured enemies (cf. the ceremonial handing over of officers' swords as a symbol of submission). This again is closely related to the tendency, widespread among many primitive peoples, to undress or remove garments as a sign of respect: a tendency which still persists among us (*e.g.* removal of the hat) and to which we shall have occasion to refer again, when dealing with the differences between the sexes.

Terrorising.—Decorations consisting of the parts of fallen enemies easily become gruesome or awe-inspiring. And this brings us to another of the functions of decoration—though one that has only an occasional significance—namely, the wish to strike terror into the hearts of enemies or other persons whom it is desired to impress or alarm. Other examples of this kind of decoration are to be found in the use of 'war paint'—a natural accompaniment of war dances and other forms of mili-

---

[1] Cf. Marie Bonaparte, 9.

tary ceremonial—and of grotesque or ferocious masks; the latter used more often in connection with the proceedings of secret societies. We ourselves are still able to obtain some faint understanding of the aggressive use of masks through their employment at festivals of the carnival type, and, in general, military uniforms still perhaps to some slight extent perform this function, or did so until the conditions of modern warfare relegated to the parade-ground all but the plainest and most utilitarian forms of martial dress. It is supposed that the uniform of the Hussars was originally derived from an attempt to imitate the ribs, being thus (when completed by a representation of a skull upon the head-dress) doubtless intended to strike terror through the symbolisation of death. The influence of this dress is still to be traced in the apparently harmless uniform of page boys or 'buttons'.[1]

Sign of Rank, Occupation, etc.—The mention of military uniforms leads naturally to another function of decoration, namely, the indication of the wearer's rank or office. Certain special ornaments or special colours (*e.g.* crown, sceptre, royal purple) have always been the prerogative of royalty or of other high dignitaries—military, civil, or religious—and, with the establishment of military or ecclesiastical hierarchies, an elaborate system of ranks has found its counterpart in an equally elaborate system of sartorial or decorative differentiation, the general principle being that the higher the rank the more elaborate and the more costly is the ornamentation. Where, as in the majority of militaristic civilisations, differences of rank or office correlate pretty closely with differences of social standing, the same or a similar system of differences in clothing and ornament may come to distinguish different castes, classes, or professions. In the further course of evolution, some particular decorative feature of dress may come to be associated with almost any separate body of individuals bound together by certain common

[1] Webb, 103, p. 105.

interests. Of particular importance in this connection are the insignia of secret societies (*e.g.* Rosicrucians, Freemasons, Ku Klux Klan among civilised societies, the Duk Duk Society in the Bismarck Archipelago). Of lesser significance, because usually less fixed and more ephemeral, are the peculiarities of dress that become associated with political parties or tendencies (*e.g.* the association of red with revolution and of white with reaction).

Sign of Locality or Nationality.—Differing, so far as their psychology is concerned, only slightly from the last-named instances, are the special costumes that are associated with locality or nationality—the so-called 'national' (in reality more often 'local') costumes which indicate that the wearer belongs to a particular district, to a particular clan, or to a particular nation.

All the costumes or decorations falling within the last two categories possess one important feature in common—their tendency to immutability. The value of such costumes, as worn at any given moment, depends largely on the fact that they are similar to the garments associated with the same district, clan, etc., in the past. In this respect they contrast very strikingly with garments which are subject to changes imposed by fashion, whose value depends almost entirely on the fact that they are *not* the same as those worn in the past. This is a fundamental distinction to which we shall return later (in Chapter VIII.).

Display of Wealth.—Besides being related to class, rank, occupation, locality, etc., the decorative aspects of dress have very frequently had some connection with wealth. Richer individuals can afford to dress in more elaborate and costly materials than can their poorer brothers and sisters, and in societies where wealth is a matter of pride and a means of obtaining power and respect, it is natural that the wealthy should seek to distinguish themselves in this way. The distinctions of costume and ornament that thus arise have, however, the characteristic of being far less stable than those referred to under the last two headings. The acquisition of wealth is in some ways an easier matter than the acquisition of power, rank, or social standing (inasmuch as it depends more upon luck or individual ability and less upon social tradition and consent), and the distinctions between degrees of wealth are far less fixed and arbitrary than are the distinctions between rank. For this reason it usually proves impossible for the wealthier individuals or classes to maintain their particular sartorial distinctions for any length of time. It thus comes about that the distinctions of dress due to the varying wealth of the wearers have much more in common with the characteristic fluctuations of fashionable dress than have the distinctions based on rank or office.

Not only can an individual's wealth be indicated by the richness of his vestment, but wealth in a more readily exchangeable form may be carried in the shape of ornament. In civilised societies the most common approach to this is the wearing of precious stones as jewellery, though actual coins (for the most part, it is true, obsolete ones) may sometimes be seen fulfilling much the same purpose; while among primitive peoples wealth is often carried in the form of shells and teeth, which represent their currency. As economic life develops and the occasions requiring the actual use of currency become more frequent, the motive of display becomes merged in motives of a more purely utilitarian kind, and coinage, or its equivalent, may be carried, not only to show that the wearer is rich, but actually to enable him to buy what he requires.

Carrying Essential Articles.—This last consideration leads insensibly to another motive for clothing, namely, the need to carry with us what we require in our daily life. This factor has had a definite influence upon certain conventional costumes, especially military uniforms, where, for instance, sword and spurs may become part of a recognised whole and be worn for decorative and ceremonial purposes even on occasions when they are not required for actual use. The uniform of the boy scout, with its belt on which hang the knives and other instruments of scouting, constitutes a modern example of a costume that has obviously been much influenced by this same idea.

The necessity or custom of carrying essential articles is in reality a matter of considerable importance, and one which has been rather unduly neglected by the students of clothes. We shall return to it later when we come to deal with the practical considerations of clothes reform.

Extension of the Bodily Self.—There remains one motive connected with decoration which is rather more subtle in its operation, and for the first clear and explicit formulation of which we are indebted to Hermann Lotze (63). It is essentially a psychological motive and, reduced to its simplest terms, amounts to this: that clothing, by adding to the apparent size of the body in one way or another, gives us an increased sense of power, a sense of extension of our bodily self—ultimately by enabling us to fill more space. In the words of a writer who has made one of the most valuable of all contributions to the psychology of clothing,[1] 'Whenever we bring a foreign body into relationship with the surface of the body—for it is not in the hand alone that these peculiarities are developed—the consciousness of our personal existence is prolonged into the extremities and surfaces of this foreign body, and the consequence is—feelings, now of an expansion of our proper self, now of the acquisition of a kind and amount of motion foreign to our natural organs, now of an unusual degree of vigour, power of resistance, or steadiness in our bearing'. It will be observed that, according to this formulation, the principle is one that is by no means confined to clothes. Indeed, the simplest and clearest example of its application can be seen in the case of tools and implements. If you take a walking-stick and touch the ground with it as you walk along, you actually seem to feel the road as it

[1] Flaccus, 34.

Fig. 1. A simple illustration of how a skirt increases the feeling of size, importance, and beauty of line when the body is motionless

(By permission of *The Dancing Times*)

Fig. 2. How a skirt may add to the effect of movement

(By permission of The Topical Press Agency)

comes into contact with the bottom of the stick; it is as though the reach of your arm had become greatly extended. In a similar way, clothing enables us to extend our bodily self; indeed there are certain clear cases of transition between clothes and implements, and it is by no means plain whether skates and skis and boxing-gloves may be looked upon more appropriately as garments or as tools that have been fastened to the body. A very clear instance of this principle, in a sphere that is undoubtedly sartorial rather than instrumental, is afforded by that simplest and most obvious of all garments, the skirt. If the reader will glance at Fig. 1, he will be immediately reminded of the fact, with which he is, in reality, thoroughly familiar, that the skirt adds to the human form certain qualities with which nature has failed to endow it. Instead of being supported on just two legs with nothing but thin air between them, a skirted human being assumes much more ample and voluminous proportions, and the space between the legs is filled up, often with great increase of dignity. The simple pose of the dancer in the figure clearly exhibits this. By holding her skirt as she does, she creates an impression of bodily power and grace which could not possibly be achieved by the naked body, beautiful as this may sometimes be. The same principle is illustrated in the series of photographs shown in our frontispiece, in which the apparent extension of the bodily self produced by a shawl can be seen by comparison with an approximately similar pose of the same model clothed only in a tight-fitting bathing-dress.

As is indicated in the above quoted passage, however, it is not only when the body is stationary that it can undergo this sort of extension. In some respects this extension can be achieved even more easily and strikingly when the body is in movement. The movements of the body are imparted to the clothes, but, owing to inertia, the latter, unless they are tight-fitting, do not closely follow the bodily movements, and all sorts of remarkable effects may be produced in this way. To take another simple example: the pirouetting skater in Fig. 2 certainly seems to acquire, through the behaviour of her skirt, 'a kind and amount of motion foreign to our natural organs'. Such effects are capable of much development and certain forms of dancing depend very much upon them. In particular, the dancing of Loie Fuller was a remarkable instance of their utilisation for artistic ends (Fig. 3).

The effects here in question—effects which are undoubtedly of very great importance in the production of the various satisfactions that are derived from clothes—depend psychologically upon an illusion; the kind of illusion known to psychologists as 'confluence' In this illusion, the mind fails to distinguish two things which under other circumstances are easily kept apart, and attributes to A what really belongs to B, so that A appears to undergo an increase. Thus, in Fig. 4, the square W and the inner square of X are really of the same size. Nevertheless, the latter square is apt to appear larger because it partakes of the additional extension of the total figure provided by the surrounding outer square. This is analogous to what happens in the case of clothes. The extension of the total (human) figure, really due to clothes, is unconsciously attributed to the body that wears them, as being the more vital and interesting portion of the whole.

Here, as elsewhere, however, certain laws governing the illusion must be observed. Of these, the chief is that the difference between the two parts of the whole that are confused shall not be so great as to prevent the confusion. If the difference is too big, the process of 'confluence' gives place to the opposite process of 'contrast'; as is seen in Y, where the relatively very large surrounding square tends to make the inner square (which is in reality equal to the square W and the inner square in X) seem smaller. Similarly, there is a limit to the possible apparent increase of bodily extension by means of clothes. In particular, a garment that by its great size is totally incommensurate with the body of the wearer,

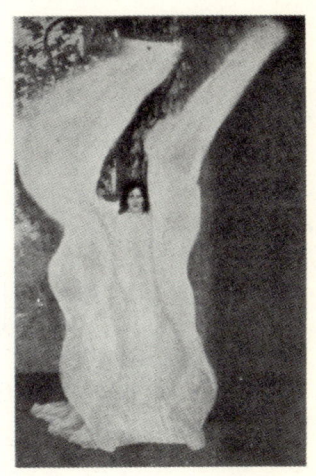

Fig. 3. Loie Fuller in various dances
(By permission of *l'Illustration*)

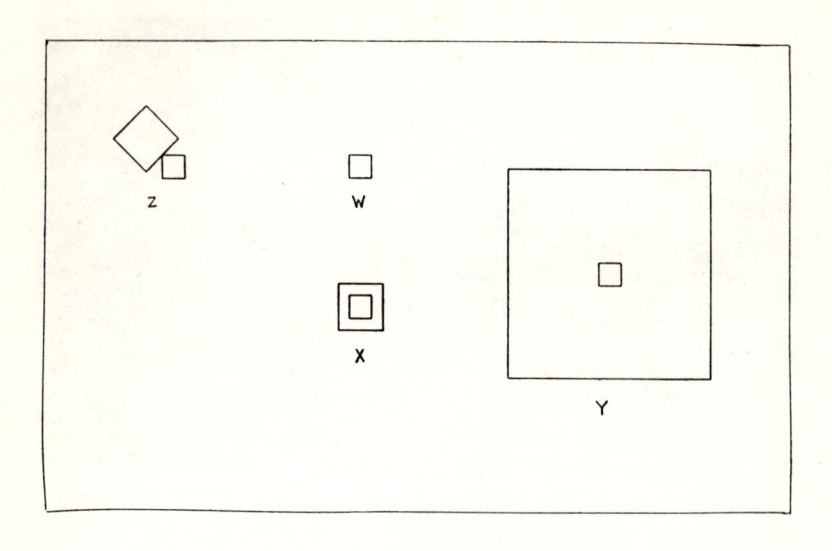

Fig.4. Effects of 'contrast' and 'confluence'

DECORATION—PURPOSIVE ASPECTS

may actually, through contrast, produce the effect of dwarfing the body. An example of this is referred to on page 48 and illustrated in Fig. 8.[1]

It should be noted, however, that excessive size of a garment is not the only factor of the kind that may interfere with the effect of confluence. In order for confluence to operate, the different parts of whole (here, body and clothes) must, to some extent, mentally fuse into a unity. A garment that by its apparent refusal to become part of an organic whole with the body (*e.g.* a large hat that threatens to fall off) may thus fail to undergo the necessary process of incorporation. The effect in such a case may be not unlike that of Z in Fig. 4, where the upright square (again of the same size as W) is not apparently increased in size by the juxtaposed inclined square (which is of the same size as the outer square in X).

As already implied, the effects of which we have been speaking are by no means confined to the sense of vision. By the actual wearer of a garment they are largely appreciated through the sense of touch. If the garment in question is liable to behave in a way that is not in accordance with the wishes of the wearer, it is apt to seem a troublesome foreign body rather than an agreeable extension of the self. A big hat, insecurely perched and liable to fly off at every gust of wind or incautious jerk of the head, exemplifies this in an extreme degree. On the other hand, a large head-dress that easily follows the movements of the head may give a very stimulating sense of upward expansion. This is perhaps true of the 'top-hat' (whatever its aesthetic faults as regards

---

[1] Both confluence and contrast may, of course, be used in many subtle ways in the details of costume. They may be employed, for instance, to emphasise the smallness of some part of the body, when this is desired, as is illustrated in the following passage: 'Souvent, c'est dans le volume de l'objet que le secret de la séduction se cache. Ce mouchoir de batiste n'intéresserait personne s'il n'était tellement exigu. Égaré, il semble à celui qui le ramasse un flocon de neige qui va fondre dans sa main. Ce mouchoir dit assez l'insignifiance de la rosée qu'il étanche: il sera remplacé demain, sans transition, par un énorme mouchoir de soie débordant la pochette, qui, par le moyen contraire, par la disproportion entre la cause et l'effet fait penser exactement à la même chose: à l'extrême petitesse du nez'.—(Bibesco, 4, p. 150.)

form and colour). The main point, however,[1] is that the 'extensive' function of garments should be such as to be in harmony with our conations rather than that they should be under our direct control. A plume or scarf or skirt blowing in the wind, or emphasising our movements through their inertia, may be very satisfying so long as they do not interfere with the carrying out of our desires. We then, quietly, as it were, annex the effects of wind and inertia, treat them as if they were produced by ourselves, and feel that our own bodily power is increased thereby.[2] This is illustrated (of course through vision) in Fig. 5, where the flowing garments, tugged at by the wind, seem only to emphasise or extend the gestures of the body and the implied attitude of mind. But if these effects of wind and inertia interfere with our movements (as when a skirt or coat impedes the free use of legs or arms), they at once begin to diminish rather than enhance our feeling of power and extension.

The determination of the conditions which produce the optimum extension is clearly a somewhat difficult and delicate matter, since these conditions obviously vary with circumstances and with individual tastes and habits. It is perhaps most often true, as Flaccus suggests, that 'the less the attention is distracted by irritating features in the surface of actual contact, the more perfect will be the illusion' (of extension). In this way unyielding materials, which make a series of rough contacts with the skin, may resist the necessary incorporation into the self. Nevertheless, there can be little doubt that, under certain circumstances and if used with due precautions, stiff fabrics are also capable of adding very considerably to this illusory extension of our personality. There is obviously here a field in which the experimental method may be very fruitfully applied.

[1] As Flaccus makes clear, *op. cit.*
[2] The considerations just brought forward by Cullis (18) make it seem possible that such effects of wind (over-determined by the associated ideas of intestinal gas) may have played a larger part in the development of voluminous and billowing garments than has previously been suspected.

Fig. 5. Effect of wind

From the painting, 'The Peace of Spring,' by Estella Canzani (by permission of the Medici Society)

CHAPTER III

DECORATION—FORMAL ASPECTS

*Each ornament about her seemly lies
By curious chance or careless art composed.*
    EDWARD FAIRFAX, *Godfrey of Bullogne.*

WE have now performed the first of the two tasks outlined at the beginning of the previous chapter; that is, we have examined the main psychological and social **purposes** of decoration. We may now proceed to the second task, *i.e.* the outlining of the chief **forms** of decoration through which these purposes (especially the last considered one) express themselves.

The forms of decoration may themselves be most conveniently classified under two main heads—the corporal and the external. Corporal decoration consists in actually moulding or manipulating the body itself; external decoration, in attaching clothes or other ornamental objects to the body. Corporal decoration does not strictly concern us here; nevertheless, a brief consideration of it may not be inappropriate, inasmuch as: (1) the motives prompting this form of decoration are very similar to those connected with the actual wearing of clothes; (2) the two forms of decoration may have in some cases a certain interdependence. Thus ear-rings or nose-rings imply some corresponding mutilation of the parts of the body concerned; while many forms of European dress have depended for their full effect upon some constriction (*i.e.* deformation) of the waist.

For our purposes the two main forms of decoration may be considered under various sub-headings as follows:

Corporal

Cicatrisation—embellishment by means of scars.
Tattooing.

Painting.
Mutilation.
Deformation ('Body-Plastic').

External

Vertical—tending to increase the apparent height.
Dimensional—tending to increase the apparent size.
Directional—emphasising the movements of the body.
Circular (ring-shaped)—drawing attention to the round contours of the body.
Local—emphasising a particular part of the body.
Sartorial—embellishment of already existing garments.

Cicatrisation.—This form of decoration consists of scars made purposely upon the skin of the body with a view to rendering it more beautiful. It is a practice which finds much favour among certain primitive peoples, notably among the native tribes of Australia. Fig. 6 gives a good idea of the strange appearance that these scars may give to the skin. Such a form of decoration seems indeed very remote from our own ideals of beauty. Nevertheless, there are a few instances in Western culture which may help us in certain ways to sympathise with those who admire scars. Among warlike peoples scars inflicted in battle have often been held to be a sign of honour, and therefore to add, rather than to detract, from a man's appearance. A distinction has even been drawn between 'honourable' scars in the front of the body—presumably acquired when boldly facing the foe—and 'dishonourable' scars upon the back—dishonourable because supposed to be evidence of flight. But the most striking case of the admiration of scars in modern times is afforded by the students of German universities. Duelling having long been regarded in these universities as an honourable form of sport, the scars inflicted in the course of duels have come to be admired as a sign that the possessor of the scars has enjoyed the distinction of

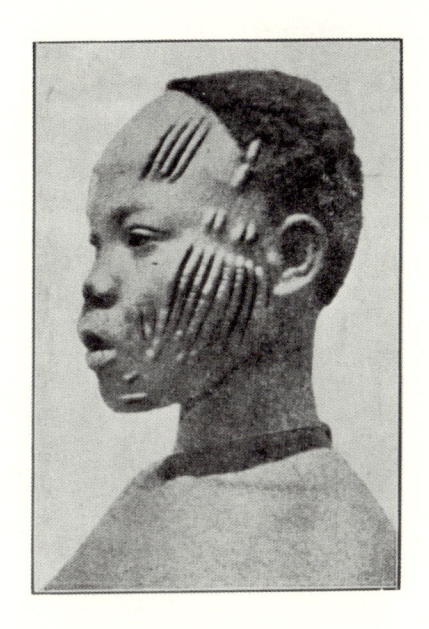

Fig.6. Young African girl, with ornamental scars

From H. Hiler, *From Nudity to Raiment* (by permission of Messrs. W. and G. Foyle Ltd.)

an academic training; a strange and perverted notion, it might seem, for if duelling is considered admirable, we should surely expect that the best duellers would receive the most honour, and the object of the duel is to inflict blows rather than to receive them.

Tattooing.—Another and much more widespread form of decoration is tattooing. This appears much less strange to us, and indeed is found in all ranges of culture. Of all forms of corporal decoration it may fairly be said to be the most artistic. Good tattooing may be really beautiful, and at the same time it undoubtedly has the effect of making the body seem less nude and less in need of covering than it would otherwise be: to some extent it can act as a psychological equivalent of actual clothes.

Painting is another form of embellishment that is to be found at all cultural levels. Indeed, remains have been discovered which indicate pretty conclusively that the practice of painting the skin was resorted to by prehistoric peoples. The complete painting of the body is sometimes carried out by savages on certain special occasions—for instance, during periods of mourning, when the body is often painted white. At other times the object of painting usually seems to lie in the desire to intensify the natural colour of the skin. This itself can be brought about in two ways. In the first place by actually applying paint of a similar colour to the whole surface, so that the natural hue is intensified; this is the case with regard to the present-day use of rouge and lipstick, by means of which reddish portions of the body, such as the cheeks and lips, are made redder. In the second place, natural colour may be increased by contrast. If a part of the skin be painted in a way that contrasts strongly with the natural colour, this natural colour will appear more striking in those parts that are left unpainted. For this reason white paint is used to cover parts of the body among certain dark-skinned peoples, on the same principle that the white races use black beauty-spots to intensify the whiteness of their skins.

The methods hitherto described are only skin deep. The two remaining methods of corporal decoration are more thoroughgoing.

Mutilation consists in the actual removal of some part of the body. There are innumerable instances of such mutilation among primitive peoples. Holes may be made in the lips and cheeks and ears; finger-joints may be removed or teeth knocked out. Operations, such as circumcision or subincision, may be performed upon the genital organs. In many cases, such mutilations are connected with the initiation ceremonies to which boys and girls are submitted at adolescence, and recent psycho-analytic studies[1] indicate that in unconscious psychological intent they are closely related to the 'castration complex'. Be this as it may, mutilation is often regarded as a sign that the age of manhood or womanhood has been attained. In general, however, it would appear that mutilation appeals less and less to us as we grow more civilised.[2] The only remnant of it that is to be found among European peoples is the boring of women's ears in order to attach earrings, but even this practice is declining in favour.

Deformation.—The last form of corporal decoration is deformation—or **Body-Plastic,** if we may use the more pleasing name that has been employed by some writers on the subject. The parts of the body that have been most subjected to deformation are the lips, the ears, the nose, the head, the feet, and the waist. The lips and the lobes of the ears may both be pulled down, and thus made long and pendulous by means of weights attached to them. The nose may be bored or flattened. The head may be made to assume all sorts of curious shapes by judicious pressure applied to the skull during the early days of infancy. The feet may be made shorter or narrower and the waist can be constricted.

[1] Reik, 'Die Pubertätsriten der Wilden' in 'Probleme des Religionspsychologie', p. 59; von Winterstein, 'Die Pubertätsriten der Mädchen und ihre Spuren im Märchen,' *Imago*, 1928, vol. xiv. p. 199.

[2] A tendency which the psycho-analyst would be inclined to regard as an increasing repression of the active tendencies underlying the castration complex.

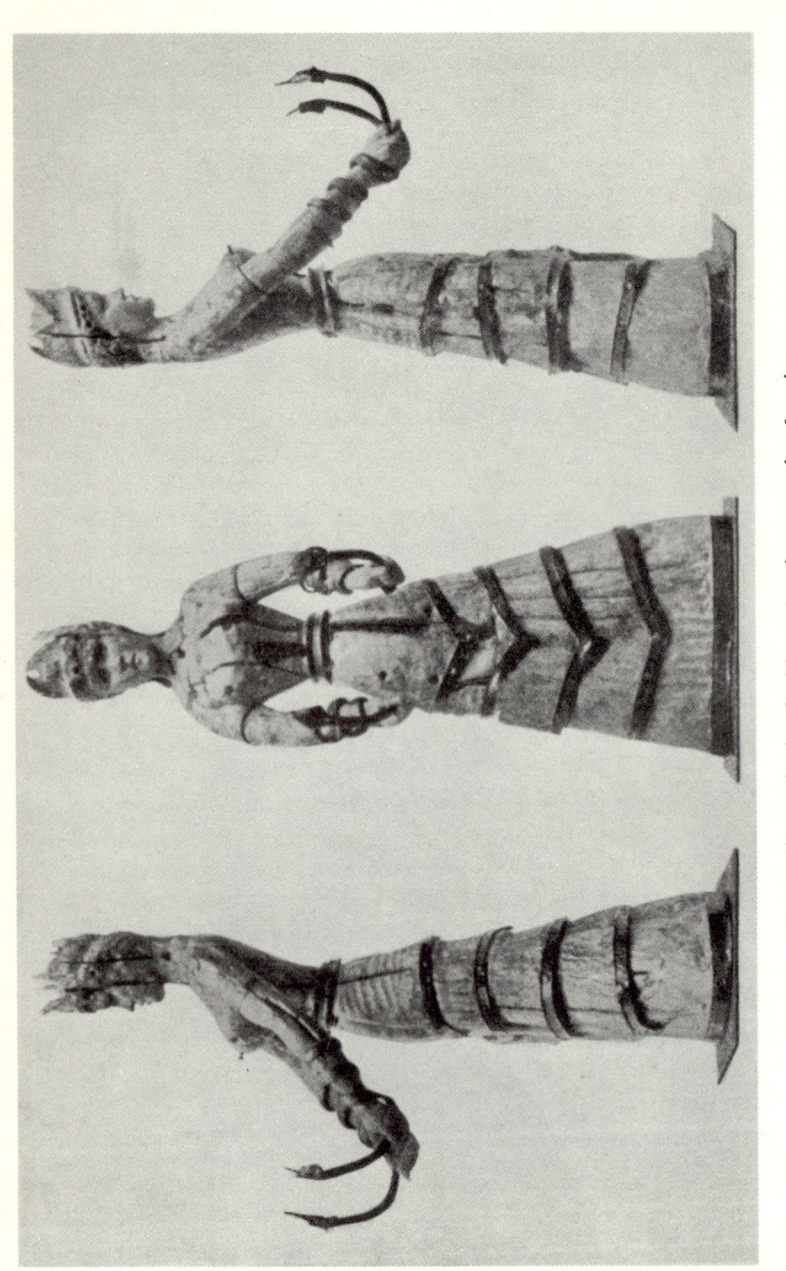

Fig.7. Minoan Snake Goddess, showing constricted waist

From A. J. B. Wace, *A Cretan Statuette in the Fitzwilliam Museum* (by permission of the Cambridge University Press)

It is only the two latter types of deformation that have been at all widely practised by civilised people. The most notorious example is to be found in the shortened feet of Chinese women. This deformation is produced by steady pressure applied to the toes and heels of little girls, as a result of which the feet become ever more arched, so that the heel is ultimately forced into a position quite close to the ball of the foot. Although no such extreme practices are indulged in by Western nations, the prevalent European ideal of a long and slender shoe is one that by no means altogether agrees with the natural form of the foot, and it also, therefore, has been responsible for a good deal of actual deformation. But the most striking case of deformation in the Western world is undoubtedly that which concerns the waist. Up to a few years ago, practically every book that dealt with women's dress from the moral or hygienic point of view had a section expounding, with the help of alarming diagrams and illustrations, the evil consequences of 'tight-lacing'—a section which now gives to all such books a curiously antiquated flavour. But the craze for the 'wasp waist', which we had with us not so many years ago, is one that is by no means new. The ancient inhabitants of Minoan Crete, who, as we now know, had developed a high civilisation more than two thousand years B.C., indulged in extreme waist constriction in both sexes—produced not by corsets but by tight metal belts (cf. Fig. 7); and the ideal of the slender waist has been responsible for a constantly recurring fashion among European women during the last few hundred years. On the whole indeed, in spite of certain striking exceptions, such as that of the Cretans, deformation is a type of embellishment that seems to have appealed more to women than to men, whereas tattooing and mutilation are more characteristic of the male sex.

With regard to the various forms of deformation that are practised in different parts of the world, it has been said that there is a general tendency to accentuate the natural characteristics of the race concerned. In the words of Darwin,[1] 'Man admires and often tries to exaggerate whatever characters nature may have given to him'. Where the lips are thick and large, they are made to protrude still further; where the nose is broad, it is further flattened. Chinese women, it would appear, have naturally small feet; but, not content with Nature's distinction, they seek to make them smaller still. The slender waist is undoubtedly a specifically European characteristic, and it seems to be only among Europeans that there exists the fatal attraction of the wasp waist.

As in the case of mutilation, there seems, as civilisation advances, to be a general tendency to abandon deformation as a means of embellishment, but the tendency has not gone so far in the case of deformation as it has done in that of mutilation. It is difficult for us to imagine how hands can be made more beautiful by the cutting off of a finger-joint, or a mouth by the knocking out of a tooth; but the frequent occurrence of the wasp waist in recent times makes it seem by no means impossible that we should return to some such ideal of the female form. Reviewing humanity as a whole, however, there would seem to be little doubt that, as culture advances, the more drastic, and, as one would feel inclined to say, brutal forms of corporal decoration tend to disappear.

There is one form of corporal decoration to which we have not specifically referred and which logically falls under the head of mutilation or deformation, although it seems to differ, in certain ways, so much from the other forms of these decorations that one is loath to place it in the same category. I refer to the removal or the dressing of hair and the trimming of nails. When hair is cut short or beards are shaved or nails are trimmed, there has taken place a forcible and artificial removal of certain parts of the body. When hair is 'dressed' (note the word as indicating the psychological equivalence of corporal and sartorial decoration) in various styles, either with the help of external instruments (combs, hair-

[1] *The Descent of Man*, p. 887.

pins, etc.) or by imparting some unnatural shape to the hair itself, there has taken place what is strictly speaking a deformation of this part of the body. The reasons why we tend to look upon these artificial manipulations as fundamentally different from the mutilations or deformations referred to above, would seem to be: (1) that to a large extent in these cases, art only anticipates nature; hairs would fall out and nails would be worn down even if we did not expedite the process by cutting or shaving the hair and paring the nails; (2) that the procedures adopted have no permanent or irrevocable effects. Even the most lasting of 'permanent waves' vanishes, as new, untreated hair takes the place of old; whereas finger-tips or teeth, once removed, are never regrown, and tight lacing, if indulged in regularly, produces a lifelong modification of the natural figure and of the relative positions of the internal organs.

This last distinction is one that also differentiates painting from the other (permanent) forms of corporal decoration. At any rate, whether this distinction be a pertinent one or not, there is no doubt that our present-day attitude towards painting and hair-dressing is different (in the sense of being more tolerant) from our attitude towards most of these other forms. Indeed, the popularity of painting and of hair-waving has considerably increased of recent years. Even here, however, there is perhaps a tendency to produce imitations of what we think to be Nature at her best, rather than to attempt a form of decoration that violently exaggerates or opposes Nature. The psychological implications of this general desire to avoid all the more extreme departures from Nature in corporal decoration (assuming that we are right in supposing the desire to exist) are worth noting here, although we shall deal with them more fully later on. This increasing satisfaction in the more natural forms of decoration and the corresponding distaste for the grossly artificial seem to imply that human beings, as they advance in culture, become, on the whole, more prepared to accept the human body as it is, more inclined to find beauty in its natural shape, and less liable to be pleased at violent distortions or modifications of it. This tendency seems to be a very important one for the whole history and development of clothing, and is one that should surely serve as a guide to those who hope, in a general way, to influence or to foretell the future course of human dress.

We now pass to the external forms of decoration.[1]

Vertical.—The first of these may be called the vertical. Its function is to accentuate the upright posture of the human body and to increase its apparent height. This effect can be achieved by all ornaments or garments that hang loosely on the body, such as chains and necklaces (particularly necklaces that hang right down over the bosom) and long drooping ear-rings; but the most striking of all such effects is, perhaps, that produced by the kilt or skirt. Most of us have had occasion to observe that if a woman exchanges her skirt for trousers or knickerbockers, she appears shorter than she did when wearing a skirt. The skirt, in fact, tends, very strikingly, to increase the apparent height of the body, and adds a corresponding dignity. But such an increase in the apparent height can also be brought about by other means. High-heeled boots and shoes, in a way, really add to our stature, while all tall headgear, such as the mediaeval hennin or the busby and top-hat of more recent times, produces the same effect. Probably the most daring form of decoration of this kind that has ever been invented is to be found in the immense head-dresses of the eighteenth century. The hair of women was then done up into a massive tower-like structure on the top of the head, the natural hair was added to when necessary, and freely powdered so as to become more prominent through its whiteness, and the whole was surmounted by little models of men, animals, ships, carriages, and other objects.

Dimensional.—The next form of decoration is the dimensional. Its purpose is to increase the apparent size

[1] The classification here adopted is that of Selenka, 89.

of the wearer, and it therefore has a general similarity to the Vertical form of decoration. Indeed, strictly speaking, the Vertical should be looked upon as only a particular species of the Dimensional—a species which, because of its peculiar importance, it is convenient to classify as a separate group.

Here again, from the point of view of conferring size, many of the most striking effects can be produced by the skirt. Indeed, this has been already implied by what we said about the skirt in the last chapter, when dealing with the 'Extension of the Bodily Self'. From time to time in the history of European fashion, the skirt has undergone enormous development. One of the most remarkable of these enlargements was during the crinoline period in the middle of the last century. Looking back upon them from our present-day point of view, such garments as were then in vogue are apt to appear ridiculous rather than impressive. But to a generation that valued pose and presence more than smartness or efficiency, they did —in virtue of their mere bulk—appear to confer a certain dignity upon the sex that wore them. Indeed, the crinoline has been looked upon as a symbol of feminine domination,[1] and there were many jokes of the period which related to the difficulty that men experienced in finding space to stand in a room that was occupied by a number of women thus attired. *Punch* indeed suggested that a very slight further increase in the size of these extravagant garments would make it necessary for a gentleman, confronted with the task of taking a lady downstairs to dinner, to climb perilously down outside the banisters, as the whole of the staircase itself would be taken up by the voluminous skirts of his partner. The relative sizes of men and women of that epoch inevitably suggest a comparison with certain species of insects, such as the *mantis religiosa*, the males of which appear extremely small and insignificant beside the much more magnificently developed females.

[1] Cf. Fuchs, 44, vol. iii. pp. 203-204; and Fischel and von Boehn, 32, vol. iii. p. 73.

Another way in which skirts can add to the apparent size and dignity of their wearers is by the use of trains, and long trains do indeed normally form part of ceremonial dress. I believe that the longest train on record was that worn by Catherine II. of Russia at her Coronation. It was no less than seventy-five yards in length, and required some fifty train-bearers to support it. A copy of this train was recently seen at a Chelsea Arts Ball at the Albert Hall in London, and is shown in Fig. 8. This garment was a curiosity rather than a sartorial success, for there can be no doubt that it failed to achieve its aim. It was too vast to allow us to regard it as a part of the wearer, and, so far from adding to her dignity, appeared to dwarf her by comparison with its own size. This illustrates the principle referred to in the last chapter, that there are limits to the successful use of all such forms of decoration. The human figure is only capable of a certain amount of apparent extension.

Another very frequent form of dimensional decoration aims at producing a broad-shouldered effect by the use of padding. This is especially found in men's dress. Men wish to appear broad-shouldered, as this is associated with muscular strength; hence most men's coats are padded at the shoulders, and many military uniforms have epaulettes, which very definitely increase the apparent width across the chest. A case of primitive decoration with the same aim will be seen in Fig. 9.[1] Padding may also serve on occasion to make good the real or imagined deficiencies of other parts of the body. Padded bosoms, padded hips, and padded legs have all played a part at one time or another in the history of European costume.

Directional.—Another form of external decoration for which the considerations at the end of the previous chapter have prepared us is the Directional. This aims at emphasising the movements of the body, in particular the direction in which the body is progressing through

---

[1] Notice also in this figure the unmistakably phallic suggestiveness of the loin-cloth.

Fig. 8. Coronation robe of Catherine II. of Russia
(By permission of The Topical Press Agency)

Fig.9. A native of Hawaii, showing 'dimensional' decoration

From E. Selenka, *Der Schmuck des Menschen* (by permission of Vita Deutsches Verlagshaus)

Fig.10. A native of New Pomerania, wearing shell collar

From E. Selenka, *Der Schmuck des Menschen* (by permission of Vita Deutsches Verlagshaus)

space, the effects produced being due principally to the inertia of the garment, but sometimes also to the influence of wind. Any loose or flowing garment or any hanging form of decoration may help towards this end. Most forms of decoration that may be classified as Vertical when the body is at rest may become Directional when the body is in motion. And this serves to remind us of what must inevitably be the arbitrary and provisional nature of the present, or any other, classification of decoration; many kinds of ornament may fall sometimes into one, sometimes into another of our classes, according to circumstances.

Some of the most striking Directional effects are—here once again—produced with the help of skirts, and the reader may be reminded of Figs. 1, 2, and 3 in this connection. Feathers and plumes, however, are also very useful in producing this effect, especially feathers worn on the head and down the back, as in the costumes of the North American Indians. The same applies to ribbons and sashes, and even to the hair, when it is worn long and loose. The typical Greek helmet, also, pointed like the prow of a ship, has a strong Directional effect in suggesting the forward movement of the wearer.

The principle has not only a positive, but also a negative, application. Not only movement itself, but the restraint or absence of movement may be suggested by suitable means. Clinging and flowing garments, garments that fall in ample folds about the feet, necessarily hinder movement and make rapid walking impossible. They compel the wearer to adopt a solemn, measured gait and impart dignity by suggesting that he has no need to hurry. The train obviously falls into this category, as does also the Roman toga; indeed there is often a certain incompatibility between the Directional and Dimensional forms of decoration, as was hinted at just now in speaking of the crinoline. But if the garment merely impedes without being voluminous, it does not achieve the effect here in question. The hobble skirt had little dignity, and obviously had no such aim, its purpose being, it would seem, merely to produce an effect of slimness—to some extent the opposite of that aimed at by the Dimensional form of decoration.[1]

Circular (Ring-shaped).—This very widespread form of ornamentation draws attention to the round contours of the human body, especially the human limbs, which differ in this respect rather strikingly from those of most other animals. Rings may be used on many parts of the body, but are found especially round the waist, the arms, the neck, the legs, and the fingers. The most extravagant forms of ring decoration are probably those which are placed round the neck. Many primitive peoples have worn ring decorations that, in magnitude or grotesqueness, utterly eclipse even the great ruffs worn by our Elizabethan ancestors. Figs. 10 and 11 illustrate some remarkable developments in this direction. In particular, the two ladies from Burmah, shown in Fig. 11, have affected a style of dress and ornamentation which, judged by our own present-day standard (all standards, we shall do well to remember, are subjective), must surely approximate to the high-water mark both of discomfort and of ugliness. Their heads peep out, as it seems, most painfully, from over the top of their great mass of collars; indeed they appear to have most successfully emulated the giraffe in their endeavour to wear as many rings as possible. But they are far from being the only sufferers from a mistaken idea of beauty of this kind. Stanley, for instance, tells us of a negro king who made his wives carry round their necks metal rings weighing in all between forty and eighty pounds![2] It may be mentioned that the discomfort of such metal rings in a warm climate is even greater than might at first appear, for, if exposed to the tropical sun, they get so hot that water has to be frequently poured over them in order to make them bearable.

Fig. 12 shows, in addition to numerous leg-rings, the

[1] It is interesting to note in passing that this garment is by no means new. Like the wasp waist, it can boast of great antiquity, for women dressed in hobble skirts very similar to those worn just before the Great War, are depicted in prehistoric cave drawings. [2] Quoted by Flaccus, 34.

Fig. 11. Two Padaung women with numerous metal collars

From W. M. Webb, *The Heritage of Dress* (by permission of the author)

Fig. 12. 'Primitive' costume, with elaborate head-dress, the typical hip-ring, and 'circular' (ring) ornamentation

From C. H. Stratz, *Die Frauenkleidung* (by permission of Herrn Ferdinand Enke)

hip-ring, which is found pretty frequently among primitive peoples, and which has a certain special importance for the development of dress, inasmuch as it has some right to be looked upon as the most primitive of all garments, as distinct from mere forms of decoration. We shall have occasion to return to this point in another chapter.[1]

Local.—The next form of external decoration, the local, has, as its name implies, little reference to the form of the body as a whole. It either draws attention to a particular part of the body, or else is used entirely on its own merits as an independent object of beauty, attractive in virtue of its intrinsic value (shape, colour, brightness) or of its meaning and associations. Among the forms of decoration that are classified under this heading are the use of needles, combs, and jewels in the hair, the precious stones that are found in rings, elaborate pins, clasps, etc. Badges and symbols of rank or dignity are also classified here. Masks are sometimes included, and, psychologically, these last are perhaps the most interesting of the whole group—but because of their social rather than of their aesthetic aspects. When we wear a mask, we cease, to some extent, to be ourselves; we conceal from others both our identity and the natural expression of our emotions, and, in consequence, we do not feel the same responsibility as when our faces are uncovered; for it appears to us that, owing to our unrecognisability and the alteration in our personality (*persona* = mask), what we may do in our masked state cannot be brought up as evidence against us when we resume our normal unmasked lives. The masked person is, therefore, apt to be freer and less inhibited, both in feeling and in action, and can do things from which he might otherwise be impeded by fear or shame. Hence the highwayman, the burglar, and the executioner have frequently worn masks, and a masked ball permits of less restrained expression of certain tendencies, notably the erotic ones, than is

[1] Notice also in Fig. 12 the directional effect of the elaborate head-dresses.

otherwise possible. If we are ourselves unmasked, we feel at a distinct disadvantage in talking to a masked person. To some extent the same effect may be produced by any garment (such as the veil) that tends to conceal the face, and even by spectacles or eye-glasses, since these make it more difficult to note the direction and movements of the gaze. The present writer must confess, too, that he always feels a little embarrassed and uncomfortable in talking to women whose hats are so low over their foreheads as more or less to hide the eyes.

Artistically, this local form of decoration is apt to be dangerous, just because it has no reference to the natural form of the body, and because, though the individual objects employed as ornaments may be pleasing in themselves, they may fail to harmonise with the general scheme of bodily adornment. Here, as in other spheres of art, development (individual or racial) implies an increasing interest in an aesthetic whole, be this whole a picture, a musical composition, or a costume. Hence, although the savage or the child may take an unrestrained delight in local ornament without reference to its effect upon the general appearance of the wearer and his dress, growing taste demands an ever greater subordination of local decoration to the claims of the *total* effect of the wearer's costume. Here again we have clearly to do with a general principle, which is of great importance for any consideration of the probable or desirable future history of human dress.

Sartorial.—The last form of external decoration, according to our present classification, is the Sartorial. It consists in the embellishment of already existing garments. Inasmuch as this embellishment mostly imitates the kinds we have already mentioned, the Vertical, Dimensional, Directional, Circular, and Local, there is no need for a separate treatment of it here.

CHAPTER IV

MODESTY

Lis est cum forma magna pudicitiae.
OVID, *Heroides*, xvi. 288.

HAVING dealt thus somewhat thoroughly with the motive of decoration, it is now our business to study more in detail the phenomena of modesty, in so far as they relate to clothes. If we take into account the pronouncement of moralists and preachers, it is probably true that more has been said and written on the subject of modesty than about any other aspect of the psychology of clothing. But, so far as the present writer is aware, there has been no serious attempt to classify the various manifestations of modesty, or to show the relations of one form to another. As it will be utterly impossible, in a book of small dimensions, to pass in review all the actual manifestations of modesty (which, as already noted, vary enormously both in time and space), it would seem more profitable here to indicate certain general principles, with the help of which the multitudinous actual manifestations can be classified and their interrelations made clear.

It would appear, upon consideration, that any given instance of modesty can be more or less satisfactorily described in terms of five (and not less than five) variables. This may sound a little alarming, but if the reader will persevere, he will, I think, soon realise that such an analysis, complicated as it may at first appear, is nevertheless a great step forward in the direction of producing order in a field that is still chaotic with the multitudinous confusion incidental to the stage of simple enumeration of instances. Moreover, the task is less formidable than it might seem, inasmuch as four out of the five variables range between two extremes, which may for most purposes be regarded as simple opposites;

indeed, in most instances, it will be sufficient to say that any given case of modesty exhibits predominantly the one or the other of these opposites.

Let us now proceed to enumerate these variables and to exhibit their use for purposes of classification by means of a simple diagram.

In the first place we must remember that, as was indicated before, modesty is itself in all cases a negative rather than a positive impulse. It bids us refrain from certain actions in which we might otherwise be prompted to indulge. Psychologically it seems to imply the existence of certain developmentally more primitive tendencies, and itself consists essentially of an inhibition of these tendencies. For our present purpose we may, therefore, regard modesty as an impulse, whose function is inhibitory; an impulse directed against the various forms of the opposite and more primitive tendency to display. Now this inhibitory impulse:—

(1) May be directed primarily against social or primarily against sexual forms of display;

(2) may be directed primarily against the tendency to display the naked body or primarily against the tendency to display gorgeous or beautiful clothes;

(3) may have reference, primarily, to tendencies in the self or, primarily, to tendencies in others;

(4) may aim, primarily, at the prevention of desire or satisfaction (social or sexual) or, primarily, at the prevention of disgust, shame, or disapproval;

(5) may relate to various parts of the body.

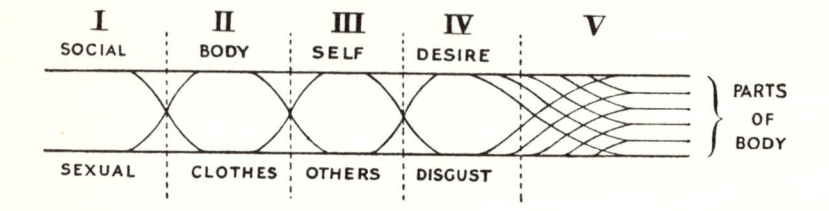

Now, imagine this inhibitory impulse flowing (say from left to right) like an electric current along the lines of the diagram. In its course it must pass through (in the terminology of the psycho-analyst it must 'cathect') each of the parts marked I. to V., but, in the case of each part, most of the current may pass through one or other of the alternative channels in any proportion. The different parts of the total course are, moreover, relatively independent of one another, so that if most of the current passes through, say, the lower channel in I., this is no reason why it should pass through either the upper or the lower channel in II.

Thus, to take an imaginary example, a particular instance of modesty may be directed primarily against sexual forms of display (lower line), against display of the naked body (upper line), its predominant object may be to avoid the arousal in other people (lower line) of the emotion of sexual desire (upper line), and it may relate primarily to the exposure of the legs (one particular line in V.).

Let us now consider the five variables rather more in detail.

I. The impulse of modesty may be aroused either by a predominantly sexual or a predominantly social situation, though, of course, the sexual and the social elements are both present, as a rule, in some degree. No doubt the sexual is usually the more important of the two and, in European civilisations at any rate, operates almost exclusively in the case of modesty relating to exposure of the naked body (II.). But situations of social modesty, in which there is at best only a more or less unconscious admixture of sexual elements, are not hard to find. Most people have occasionally felt the embarrassment incidental to appearing at some social function in an inappropriate costume, and the embarrassment may be equally great whether one is 'over' or 'under' dressed. Such a relatively small departure from 'correct' attire for a particular occasion, as is involved in finding oneself in a dinner jacket when most of the others are in 'tails', or *vice versa*, will reduce some men to a condition of extreme discomfort, and there will be few, if any, who will escape without some unpleasant feeling. Most people indeed in such a situation would look eagerly round in the hope of discovering some others attired similarly to themselves, and would be relieved in proportion as the search proved successful. A good many persons suffer from fairly frequent dreams (often accompanied by much emotion) in which they are inappropriately dressed, either through an unconventional combination of garments (*e.g.* 'bowler hat with evening dress', to quote from some examples which have been given me) or through the unsuitability of a particular costume for a particular occasion (*e.g.* 'lecturing to Trade Union officials in evening dress', 'attending a ball in a tailor-made costume and cloche hat'). All such situations, whether in real life or in dreams, bring out exquisitely the sense of shame and guilt that attaches to appearance or behaviour which is different from that of our fellows, unless such difference is manifestly of a kind that arouses their envy, admiration, or approval (or, on rarer occasions, our own approval). A detailed consideration of this important matter can, however, be appropriately delayed until we come to deal with fashion.

Among savages, social forms of modesty frequently require the actual removal of garments as a sign of respect.[1] In primitive societies relative or absolute nakedness is often a sign of inferior social status, subserviency, or submission; while there tends to be a positive correspondence between social rank and the quantity of garments worn. On approaching holy places or on coming into the presence of Royalty or other exalted persons, such garments as are normally worn may be removed; a tendency of which there are only a few survivals among civilised peoples (*e.g.* removal of the hat and, among Moslems, removal of the shoes).

[1] Schurtz, 86, p. 122.

II. This last point brings us to the consideration of our second variable. Among primitive peoples, who, for the most part, wear fewer clothes than do the civilised, modesty is more rarely affronted by the naked body than with ourselves. As regards Western culture itself, however, it is clear that a great increase of modesty took place at the collapse of Graeco-Roman civilisation. This increase—due probably for the most part to the influence of Christianity with its Semitic traditions—was doubtless reinforced by the customs and point of view of northern invaders coming from colder climates. Christianity upheld a rigorous opposition between body and soul, and taught that attention devoted to the body was prejudicial to the salvation of the soul. One of the easiest ways of attempting to divert thoughts from the body was to hide it, and, consequently, any tendency to exhibit the naked body became immodest. But the increase in the amount and complication of garments that this tendency brought about, itself provided the possibility of a new outlet for the exhibitionistic urges that were thus repressed. The interest in the naked body became, to some extent, displaced on to clothes, so that, in turn, a new effort of modesty was needed to combat this fresh manifestation of the tendencies to which modesty was opposed; and thus it came about that disapproval on the part of ecclesiastical authority of gorgeousness or extravagance in dress was expressed almost as vigorously as disapproval of the cult of the body itself. Hence the twofold direction of modesty as indicated by the double path in II. of the diagram. Taking actual examples from modern history, we meet, on the one hand, with denunciations of bare shoulders, bare bosoms, and bare arms (which latter were 'looked upon with horror and disgust' in Henry VIII.'s time),[1] of the general scantiness of attire that characterised the close of the eighteenth and the early years of the nineteenth century, and of the exposed legs of to-day, which, in Italy at any rate, have encountered both governmental

[1] Parsons, 71, p. 145.

and ecclesiastical condemnation.[1] On the other hand, we have had almost equally fiery denunciations of peaked shoes, high head-dresses, and long trains, and it has been maintained that the mere possession of numerous garments was a spiritual peril; for at least one woman, we are told, was taken to Hell by the Devil because she had 'tenne diverse gownes and as mani cotes'.[2] (One wonders what severer punishments were reserved for the Duke of Buckingham, the friend of James I., who had 1625 suits, and for the Empress Elizabeth of Russia, who had 8700 dresses.)[3]

We must beware of exaggerating the influence of such moral diatribes from the Church, which were probably no more effective than sermons on many other subjects. Whatever the cause, however, it is clear enough that, in the history of European dress, there have been successive waves of modesty which condemned what a previous generation had tolerated, both as regards exposure of the body and as regards elaboration of apparel. Thus we ourselves tend to regard as immodest both the exposure of the bosom, characteristic of the middle of the last century, and the accentuation of the buttocks that was implied in the bustles of a later period. The Puritans, also, disapproved both of the actual exposure of the upper part of the body and of the elaboration of dress itself which characterised Royalist society in the time of the Stuarts.

Since novelty of any kind (being itself, where clothing is concerned, a form of display) is apt to arouse not only curiosity but modesty, the covering of a part of the body that had habitually been exposed may itself arouse feelings of shame. Thus it has been reported that savage women who have been used to nakedness may become

---

[1] On the occasion of the great earthquake of July 1930, several Roman Catholic divines did not hesitate to put forward the view that this disaster was 'a scourge brandished by the merciful (!) hand of the Almighty', and as a divine corrective provoked by 'moral disorders and, in particular, shameful fashions', and to maintain that 'Naples had been saved from the catastrophe because (the Neapolitans) had resisted the present scandalous female fashions'.

[2] Parsons, 71, p. 43.   [3] Fuchs, 44, vol. ii. p. 205.

shy and embarrassed if a part of their body is suddenly clothed; and similar feelings have been aroused during the past year in some of our own young girls when they found themselves arrayed for the first time in their lives in (evening) dresses that hid their legs from view. It is as if the impulse of modesty had penetrated all disguise and understood the erotic element that constitutes an essential factor in all efforts at bodily concealment.

A case that at first seems to present some difficulty for our classification is that which occurs when modesty is directed, not so much against the naked body in itself, as against some very tight and close-fitting garment which reveals the form of the body, without actually exhibiting its surface. Instances of this kind would be supplied by the tight hose of the sixteenth-century men, by the figure-following women's modes of the 1890's, and the stockinged legs of women of to-day. It is clear, however, on a little reflection, that the objection in these cases is not against the garments as such, but rather against the exhibition of the natural form that is permitted by these garments. It is not because of their splendour, magnificence, or grotesqueness that modesty protests, but rather because of their exiguity and lack of independent form and development as garments, since indeed they are little more than artificial skins. In all such cases we can have no doubt that modesty is really directed against the scarcely veiled exhibition of the body itself and not against the displaced form of this tendency which manifests itself through clothes.

III. Our third variable concerns the relative dependence of modesty on psychological motives originating in the self and in others respectively. Of course, in a sense, all modest conduct (like all conduct whatsoever) must depend directly upon psychological factors in the self, but in some cases these factors may be not only necessary but sufficient; while in others they have a definite reference to the attitude of other persons, and depend for their very existence upon this reference.[1] In the one case, that is, the person feels that a certain kind of dress (or lack of it) is *in itself* immodest. His own feelings are a sufficient guide to him in the matter, and these may be independent of what other persons are feeling; indeed, they may be in conflict with the feelings of others, as when a puritanically minded person refrains from certain forms of display that are regarded by his neighbours as natural and harmless. The attitude of such a person may even remain unchanged when there are no other persons present, as in the extreme case of those who, acting on the recommendation of their religious advisers, have worn a garment even in their baths, fearing the effect of their own nakedness even on themselves. At the other extreme are cases where there is no private conviction of the immodesty of the form of dress or undress in question, but where the primary motive is to avoid the arousal of some undesired feeling in others. It may be felt, for instance, that certain forms of exposure would produce such an emotion in onlookers, and the exposure may be avoided, even though, apart from this reference to others, it might be regarded as harmless. There can be little doubt that such an attitude is often adopted; at the present day in England it can perhaps be observed more frequently in the lower than the upper social classes. And indeed it cannot be denied that the attitude is justified, so far as the actual fear of causing disgust is concerned; there are, for instance, persons who can be made to feel even 'physically ill' by the sight of unusually exposed bodies (while bathing, for instance); and this abnormal sensitivity is, after all, only an extension of feelings that are capable of being aroused in almost everyone, *e.g.* by disease or deformity.

[1] The vast majority of present-day psychologists hold that all our more specific 'moral' tendencies, including those connected with modesty, have originated in this latter way. Fortunately, however, it is not necessary for us to consider here the relative importance of inherited and acquired moral tendencies. It is, however, desirable to bear in mind that moral conduct which originally depended on outer sanction (the attitude of other persons) may come in time to depend upon an inner sanction (*i.e.* may become independent of other persons).

Fig. 13. An outdoor costume from Tunis

From C. H. Stratz, *Die Frauenkleidung* (by permission of Herrn Ferdinand Enke)

But disgust is not the only feeling in others which may affect our conduct in this way. The prevalent social contempt of the 'incorrectly' dressed person is another instance of an attitude in others which may make us refrain from certain forms of sartorial display and certain forms of liberty or individuality in dress to which we might otherwise feel drawn.

Still another emotion on the part of others that has probably played a part of great importance in the history of dress is that of jealousy, particularly the jealousy of husbands for their wives. A jealous husband does not want his wife to rouse too great admiration in other men, and the easiest of all ways of avoiding this is to keep her hidden. This may be done by actually excluding her from male society, as is of course to a large extent the custom in many Oriental countries. But the same object can be achieved to some extent by hiding her body from the view of men on such occasions as she does venture into public places. Those Eastern civilisations which have kept women in domestic retirement, away from all men but their husbands, have also, on the whole, most effectually hidden the bodily forms of women when they are outside their homes. In fact, it may be said that the whole Moslem theory of women's outdoor dress represents an attempt—sometimes desperate in its thoroughness—to avoid the arousal of sexual desire in men; a theory which is, of course, logically in harmony with a social system which stresses the view that all women are the property of some one man or another. A particularly striking instance of the working of this theory is shown in the outdoor dress from Tunis, illustrated in Fig. 13. It will be seen that the wearer is very amply hidden from the gaze of the curious. The only contact which her body has with the outside world is through the tiny slit about her eyes; otherwise one can only guess as to her form and features.

Although most strongly developed under the Mohammedan tradition, this motive of jealousy can often be observed elsewhere, especially perhaps in the fact that among a good many more or less primitive peoples, married women are accustomed to wear more clothes than those who are not married. Even among ourselves, husbands are often not too anxious that their wives should attract attention through the audacity of their costumes, though they might quite well appreciate costumes of equal boldness when worn by other women.

IV. We have just now spoken of the endeavour to avoid the arousal of two distinct and opposite emotions in other people—desire and disgust. This double attitude of modesty constitutes the fourth of the five variables in terms of which we are attempting to describe modesty. Since disgust, at any rate of the kinds with which we are here concerned, is itself in the nature of a reaction against desire, we may say that modesty can be directed—either against a primitive desire, which, if allowed to be gratified without inhibition, would give pleasure; or else against the conscious manifestation of the inhibition itself, which, if allowed to become strong, must necessarily give pain. In the latter case, it will be observed, modesty seems to function as an inhibition of the second instance, which protects from the pain that would be caused if the more primary inhibitions were brought into play at full force.[1] A few simple instances should make the meaning of this clear. A woman may, for example, refrain from going to a dance in a very *décolleté* dress: (*a*) Because, although she thinks it becomes her and she experiences a real gratification in the sight and feeling of her bare upper body, she yet experiences a sense of shame and embarrassment at the mere fact that she should do so. The modest impulse is here directed against desire rather than disgust (No. IV. in our diagram), and is connected with feelings aroused in herself rather than with feelings aroused in others (No. III. in our diagram), for she may feel ashamed in her own dressing-room when no one else is with her. (*b*) Because,

[1] In this respect the function of modesty is, in certain ways, comparable to a 'phobia', which, as psycho-analytic investigation seems to show, serves to protect the individual from the painful anxiety that would ensue if he were brought face to face with the (psychologically) 'dangerous' situation.

although she experiences none of the scruples just mentioned and freely enjoys the sight of herself in her mirror, she yet fears that she may unduly stimulate sexual desire in her prospective partners; in this case the modesty is still directed against desire, but now refers to feelings in others rather than to feelings in the self. (c) Because, on putting on the dress, she is immediately overcome by a feeling of repulsion at her own image. The vision of so much of her own bare flesh, instead of being pleasing but 'wicked', as in (a), is now definitely displeasing from the start, and she decides not to wear the dress, in order to protect herself from this displeasure. Modesty here works against disgust aroused in her own mind without reference to others. (d) Because, although she may herself be pleased at the effect of the low-cut dress, she thinks of the shock that her appearance in it will cause to certain puritanically minded friends, and, for their sakes, denies herself the pleasure which the free exposure of her own charms might otherwise afford her. In this case modesty is directed against disgust, rather than against desire (for she does not venture to suppose that the friends in question will allow themselves to find her nakedness alluring), and has reference to feelings in others rather than feelings in herself.

It is clear that in this antithesis between desire and disgust, we are really dealing with a particular form of the general antagonism between the tendency to display and the tendency to modesty that we spoke of in the first chapter. The complication with which we are here concerned is, as already indicated, that the inhibition of the display tendency may take place at various mental levels. If it takes place subconsciously, there is very likely to occur the conscious emotion of disgust. The function of the more conscious aspects of the tendency to modesty then becomes diverted from its original aim of combating desire (an aim which has already been achieved) to the secondary aim of preventing the development of the unpleasant emotion of disgust. If, on the other hand, the tendency to display is sufficiently strong (relative to the resistances) to force its way into consciousness, then these same conscious aspects of modesty remain at their original task and oppose themselves to the display.

The extent to which, and the level at which, the modesty impulses succeed in inhibiting the tendencies to display, are determined, of course, by a variety of factors—some probably depending upon an innately determined balance of forces, others upon the way in which circumstances, tradition, and upbringing have affected this balance. It would take us too far afield to investigate these factors in detail. There is, however, one circumstance which perhaps deserves some special consideration, viz., the natural beauty or ugliness of the individual concerned (according to the standards of beauty of her time and place). A high degree of beauty makes it easy for her to derive pleasure from the exhibition and adornment of her own body, and therefore tends powerfully to strengthen the tendencies to display and decoration. The possession of an aesthetically inferior body, on the other hand, limits the opportunity for such enjoyment, and, other things equal, fails to provide a corresponding stimulation and strengthening of the display tendencies. In this latter case, therefore, the impulse of modesty has an easier task. If we return to the example we were considering just now, it is clear that the woman trying on the low-cut dress will find it extremely difficult to be disgusted or ashamed at her own appearance, if she is in reality extremely beautiful; for her to do so would represent a *tour de force* on the part of modesty. It would, however, be relatively easy for modesty (or the subconscious inhibitions working on behalf of modesty) to achieve this result if her body should happen actually to be very far from perfect. Indeed, in this latter case, she might welcome a more ample covering to hide her bodily defects, or even (as is very often done) resort to an exaggerated modesty in order to save herself from the painful realisation of these defects. Thus Knight Dunlap is undoubtedly right when, in a recent most interesting contribution to the psychology of clothes,[1] he emphasises the importance of the desire to hide bodily defects as a factor making for the increase or retention of bodily coverings. In so far as the body is covered (provided the clothing is not skin-tight), the aesthetic differences between one individual and another tend to be hidden. We have really no means of judging of the degree of beauty possessed by the lady depicted in Fig. 13; and, in general, the wearing of clothes tends to put the well-favoured and the ill-favoured on an equal footing; whereas, abandonment or reduction of clothes allows the more beautiful to take fuller advantage of their natural gifts. It is probably true, as Knight Dunlap suggests, that there is in some ways a continual struggle between those who can advantageously show their bodies and those whose bodies are better hidden. A decrease in the amount of clothing habitually worn favours the one side, an increase favours the other. Thus, the reduction in the length of skirts in recent years, has conferred a great advantage upon those women who can profitably show their legs, while it has surely been a source of considerable embarrassment to others. Dunlap considers that the reason why men so strongly and persistently refuse to bare their arms is to be found in a fear, on the part of those with less adequate muscular development, that they will suffer by comparison with the more athletic members of their sex. He suggests too that, when there occurs a triumph for those who can afford to exhibit any portion of their bodies, this triumph is apt to be offset in some other way—a way which admits of equalising the advantages of the beautiful and the ugly as regards some other portion of the body. Thus it is perhaps, he thinks, no mere chance that, as regards women, increased exposure of the leg has been accompanied by increased use of cosmetics on the face. If the deficiencies of those who are endowed with less shapely lower limbs

[1] 24, p. 64.

have been freely exposed, this disadvantage has had to be compensated by the equalising of all complexions, good and bad, through the more general use of paint and powder.[1]

V. We have already remarked on more than one occasion how very variable are the manifestations of modesty. This variability is not merely quantitative, but also qualitative; it relates not only to the total amount of bodily exposure or sartorial display that is permitted, but also to the parts of the body that may be exposed or accentuated. Recently, for instance, there has taken place a revolutionary change in our ideas concerning the respectability of the feminine leg, and women now show freely what has, with very few exceptions, been draped since the dawn of Western civilisation. How great is the change that has taken place in a relatively few years can best be realised when we remember that, not so long ago, it was indelicate not merely to show the leg but even to refer to it—at least by its proper English name. Even during a period of exceptional undressing, Lady Brownlow, describing Parisian fashions in 1802, says that the dresses were 'held up so as to discover one *jambe*' (the French term being used, according to Mr. Cecil Brown, who quotes the passage in a recent letter to *The Times*, presumably because 'it was not polite to mention legs'). Ruskin's mother, when she broke her leg, referred to her damaged member (following her usual custom) as her 'limb';[2] while, in an earlier period, a would-be donor of silk stockings to a Royal bride was rebuked for the indiscreet implications of his intended gift by the statement, 'The Queen of Spain has no legs'.[3]

Our greater freedom as regards legs has, however, been accompanied by a great intolerance of certain other parts of the body, and a consequent greater disability to use them for purposes of erotic display than existed in

---

[1] Cf. below, Chapter XII.
[2] Amabel Williams-Ellis, *The Tragedy of John Ruskin*, p. 232.
[3] Havelock Ellis, *Erotic Symbolism*, p. 26.

some previous periods. The accentuation of the posterior regions brought about by means of the bustle now appears to us to be at least in very questionable taste,[1] while we now do all we can to make the breasts—for a long time the supreme attraction of the feminine anatomy—as inconspicuous as possible.

Modesty varies of course not only in time but in space. In parts of Central Africa, the buttocks are the region on which shame is concentrated, a shame which, with the inhabitants of those parts, far exceeds that attaching to the external genital organs.[2] Our own past sensitiveness to legs was not one that appealed to Moslems, who never tried to disguise from themselves the fact that women, like men, were bipeds. To them the face was the part of the body that demanded covering—an attitude which, in turn, met with but little understanding from Europeans, among whom the veil has never enjoyed more than a decorative or symbolic significance, and to whom the face, together with the hands, has usually been the region which is freest from the sense of shame.

Modesty thus varies enormously in its anatomical incidence, and a full description of its nature and operation in any given instance requires a statement on this aspect as much as on any of the other points we have dealt with in this chapter. The only difference is that, in the present case, the direction of modesty cannot be described in terms of a simple variation between two extremes (as in the case of our first four variables), but may, theoretically at any rate, be distributed in any proportions over the various surfaces of the body; while, in practice, it usually applies principally to one or two out of a small number of well-defined zones.

[1] That the bustle really symbolised, and served to draw attention to, the buttocks, was of course clearly evident to all who gave a little consideration to the modes of the time. Cf. the amusing rhyme then current:
Die letzte Kleidermode war
Noch immer nur so so;
Jetzt erst sind wir ganz und gar
Ein wandelnder P . . .
[2] Cf. Schurtz, 86, p. 50.

CHAPTER V

PROTECTION

Nay, now when the reign of folly is over, and thy clothes are not for triumph but for defence, hast thou always worn them perforce and as a consequence of Man's Fall; never rejoiced in them as in a warm, movable House, a Body round thy Body, wherein that strange THEE of thine sat snug, defying all variations of Climate? Girt with thick, double-milled kerseys; half-buried under shawls and broadbrims, and overalls and mud boots, thy very fingers encased in doeskin and mittens, thou hast bestrode that 'Horse I ride'; and, though it were in wild winter, dashed through the world, glorying in it as if thou wert its Lord. . . . Nature is good, but she is not the best; here truly was the victory of Art over Nature.—CARLYLE, *Sartor Resartus*, ch. ix.

THE protective function of clothes might seem at first sight to be simple enough. Nevertheless it shows itself, upon examination, to be much more diverse and complex than our casual and somewhat one-sided habits of thought upon this matter might lead us to expect.

The most obvious form of protection afforded by clothes is that against **cold**. Indeed, in a cold climate, there is considerable risk that it might be taken to be the only one. There seems little doubt that, in the later developments of dress, at any rate, it has played a more important part than any other protective function. It is probable that many of the higher developments of the tailor's art (such as that involved in the change from a loose-fitting 'gravitational' costume to a more tight-fitting and form-following 'anatomical' costume) would never have occurred in a warm climate, and that they owe their existence to the migration of certain portions of the human race from southerly into more northerly regions. Nevertheless it is possible, as we have seen, for human beings to exist in a practically unclothed state even in one of the most inclement portions of the inhabited world; and this should warn us against the danger of exaggerating the importance of the motive of protection as compared with the motives of decoration and of modesty. Especially so, since the motive of protection appears in certain ways more 'rational', more adapted to reality, than the other motives, and man is always inclined to indulge in 'rationalisation' of his motives. There is a good deal of unwillingness to admit the full force of the tendencies towards decoration and modesty, and, in consequence, man has probably exaggerated his need of covering himself to shut out the cold. At any rate, most medical authorities are to-day agreed that, from the point of view of hygiene, Europeans wear too many, rather than too few, clothes (though there has admittedly been a great improvement in women's clothes during recent years).[1] And the same applies *a fortiori* to clothing during the last few hundred years or so, when, except for brief periods, it was generally more ample than at present.

But clothing can protect not only against uncomfortably low temperature, but also against **heat,** in so far as this is due to the direct rays of the sun. Few Europeans, at any rate, could live in tropical countries without the protection to the head afforded by their sun helmets, and many of us have had occasion during a warm summer to regret dispensing for too long with the protection that our clothes afford against the rays of the sun upon other parts of the body; for sun-bathing, if indulged in too suddenly and without due habituation, can—as many have discovered—have very painful consequences.

Clothes can also protect us against enemies, both human and animal. The desire for protection against **human enemies** has led to the development of quite a special kind of clothing, known as armour. Armour, in western countries, has usually been of metal; in this form it underwent an immense development in the Middle Ages and, as the standard professional clothing of the knight, became intimately symbolic of the whole

[1] In the words of Knight Dunlap, 'Woman, long the worst offender, has suddenly outstripped man, both literally and in the line of progress'.

martial spirit of that time. The gradual disappearance of armour was doubtless due to the improvements in fire-arms, which eventually made it useless for its real purpose. But, as a ceremonial garment, a few vestiges of it have remained to the present day; for instance, the steel breastplate which forms a part of the uniform of the Guards, that most sumptuous of all military costumes. And, curiously enough, modern warfare, though in other respects it has made armour obsolete, has yet led to the revival of a very mediaeval-looking steel helmet, as well as to certain entirely new features of protective clothing, *e.g.* the gas mask.[1] In some places, however, materials other than metal have been used for armour, as in the case of certain African tribes who wear large woollen pads covering the whole body.[2]

Apart from regular warfare, armour or other special forms of protective clothing may, of course, protect against sudden or isolated attacks from fellow human beings. At one time a good many persons who had reason to suppose that their lives were in danger wore a metal tunic under their ordinary clothes, and, if report be true, quite a number of them succeeded in prolonging their lives in this way. Even ordinary clothing, if sufficiently thick or voluminous, may sometimes serve this purpose, and, quite recently, under the heading 'Passion and Petticoats', the *Observer* reported such a case. A girl in a Slovakian village was shot at with a revolver by a jealous lover, but fortunately she was wearing the traditional peasant costume of the district and, being in consequence 'armoured with some ten starched petticoats, the bullet only slightly injured her hip'.

Passing from deliberate attacks to unintentional injuries, certain forms of special clothing, mostly made of relatively soft and yielding material, are worn to protect from the **accidents** incidental to dangerous occupa-

---
[1] It has been plausibly suggested, though without adequate historical proof, that the influence of armour is to be traced in the starched stiffness that still characterises men's dress for formal occasions—(Baumann, 3, p. 16).
[2] Cf. Schurtz, 86, p. 114.

tions or sports. Witness the goggles of the stonebreaker, the padded costumes of dirt-track racers and baseball players, the protective face-covering of the fencer and leg-covering of the wicket-keeper. The top hat of the rider to hounds, though doubtless primarily used because it has become part of the correct equipment for this sport (just as most sports have become associated with a certain uniform which only permits of small individual variations), is often justified—how reasonably I know not—on the ground that it lessens the danger of injury to the head in case of a fall.

Of the **animal foes** against which man has sought to protect himself by clothes, insects are probably the most important, and indeed some writers (*e.g.* Knight Dunlap) consider that the wearing of clothes for protection against insects has played an important part in the origin of human dress. We ourselves sometimes clothe horses for protection against flies, and it seems not impossible that loose garments that would flap against the limbs when in movement, may have been of immense utility in many countries and led to the permanent adoption of garments of this kind.

All the functions of clothing which we have so far considered in this chapter are connected with protection against **physical** dangers and inconveniences. They are indeed, for the most part, sufficiently simple and obvious. Much more subtle in their operation and more easy to be overlooked are the ways in which clothing can reassure us against various real or imaginary dangers which are primarily **psychological** in origin and nature.

The most important of this second class of protective functions of clothing (especially in the early stages of the history of clothes) is undoubtedly that which has to do with the supposed influence of **magic** and of **spirits.** To the primitive mind the cause of all evils, whose source is not immediately obvious, is to be found, not in the physical properties and interactions of things, but rather in the influence of magical or spiritual agencies. To such a mind the whole universe is continuously permeated by these influences, and the disasters which befall human beings — such as accidents, disease, and death (for death is not attributed to 'natural causes')—are supposed to be due, either to hostile magic set into operation by other men, or to the working of ghosts or other discarnate psychical forces. The only protection that is possible against these multitudinous and maleficent influences is the use of counter-magic, and, as it is impossible to be perpetually engaged in exercising this counter-magic by actual magical practices (even supposing that the requisite procedure is known, for the more potent formulae are often the property of certain professionals or specialists), it is extremely convenient to carry about some amulet which can be trusted to ward off the evil influences without the necessity of active intervention. For this purpose various objects, supposed to possess magical properties, were hung or otherwise attached to the body, and some authorities[1] are inclined to believe that this magical purpose of articles carried on the person preceded even the ornamental purpose, and therefore constituted the real motive for the first beginnings of clothing. Such a view is of course in harmony with the opinion now coming to be widely held among anthropologists, that in general the earliest forms of art served utilitarian (*i.e.* magical) rather than purely aesthetic ends. If this is true with regard to clothes, it may be said that the motive of decoration in dress, in its earliest manifestations, gradually grew out of the magical utilitarian motive, in much the same way that, in later forms of art, instruments and other objects, originally constructed to serve some useful purpose, became decorative, and eventually, in certain cases, persisted as decorations, even when the advance of culture had reduced or abolished their utilitarian function. And, certainly, what we are able to trace of the later history of clothes supports this view, for there are numerous features in the clothes we wear to-day which are now purely orna-

---

[1] *E.g.* Wundt, 105, p. 219.

mental, but which were once useful; we shall find many instances of this in the chapter dealing with the evolution of garments.

If this view of the priority of magic over ornamentation be correct, the opinion held by the majority of writers that decoration was the original motive underlying clothing will need revision; not decoration but protection will have to be given the honour of first place —but, of course, protection against agencies other than those with which we chiefly associate it at the present day. Be this as it may, it is safe to assume that the magical and the decorative functions developed to some extent concurrently, both finding satisfaction in the same objects; and that the motive of decoration gradually acquired an increasing independence, so that eventually the magical purpose fell into the background and tended to disappear. But it never disappeared entirely, and even to-day we can appreciate something of the attitude of the savage in this matter, for we still use objects that are believed by the superstitious (and few of us can boast that we have entirely cast off the thralls of superstition) to bring good luck or avert ill luck. Not a few people have, at some time or other in their lives, worn a necklace, ring, jewel, or other decorative trinket which was supposed to have defensive properties, such as the ability to prevent disease or accident; indeed, there exists quite an extensive magical lore about some of the precious stones that are in use as ornaments to-day.

In somewhat more primitive cultures the function of such amulets is usually considered to be that of warding off 'the evil eye' (much as, in the Middle Ages, the cross was supposed to have the power of driving off the Devil and his minions). Now this belief may help us to realise something of the deeper meaning that would seem to underlie a great many (perhaps indeed all) of these superstitions concerning the protective value of certain ornaments. Psycho-analytic and anthropological observations have made it clear that one of the chief ways in which the 'evil eye' was supposed to harm its victims was by damaging their reproductive powers or reproductive organs. The doctrine of the evil eye seems in fact to be intimately connected with the castration complex.[1] In harmony with this view is the fact that most of the amulets used to ward off the evil eye appear to be symbols of the reproductive organs—male or female; the psychological principle involved being, apparently, in the nature of an assurance that potency and reproductive power are still intact.

Here we are brought back to the general subject of phallic symbolism that we referred to in Chapter II. It would appear that the general sexual symbolism of clothes, in virtue of which clothes seem to form an unconscious substitute for crude sexual display, is reinforced by the magical exhibition of sexual symbols as a defence against the fear of infertility. How far the actual widespread occurrence of genital symbolism is due to an active, aggressive tendency of sexual pride, how far it is a defence-mechanism against sexual fears connected with the castration complex, it is impossible to say with certainty in the present state of our knowledge. Here, as in many similar cases, the positive and negative elements are so intimately intertwined that it is difficult or impossible to disentangle them.

Closely similar, both in its ultimate psychological nature and in its tendency to become associated with phallic symbolism, is the function of clothes as a means of protection against **moral danger.** The monk protects himself in his plain, but all-enveloping, habit against the lures and temptations of this wicked world, and clothing is a help to many others in attempting to avoid distracting influences that might lead them away from the straight and narrow path of virtue. To be of service for this end, clothing must be ample, thick, tight, stiff, or unprovocative in colour; or, better still, possess several or all of these qualities. But these qualities (especially the

---

[1] See, *e.g.*, J. C. Flügel, 'Polyphallic Symbolism and the Castration Complex', *Inter. Jour. of Psycho-analysis*, 1924, vol. v. p. 188.

last four) are not purely negative in their protective value; they are in most cases at the same time a symbol of the resistive strength within. From the more simple and purely protective functions there is a continuous transition to a more positive reaction to moral dangers, through the assurance of moral strength that clothing can afford. Thus it is that certain garments can become symbolic of inflexibility of character, severity of moral standard, and purity of moral purpose—an ethical symbolism that plays a very considerable rôle in the more austere and formal of the costumes of modern men. In the thickness of material and solidity of structure of their tailored garments, in the heavy and sober blackness of their shoes, in the virgin whiteness and starched stiffness of their collars and of their shirt-fronts, men exhibit to the outer world their would-be strength, steadfastness, and immunity from frivolous distraction. Thus it is that garments of this kind have come to signify seriousness of mood and devotion to duty, and are associated with all the more responsible forms of professional and commercial work. Tightly gripping garments, also, have their moral significance; and women too have, at one time or another, enjoyed their share of this by means of corsets, bone collars, and bodices whose tightness was only matched by their rigidity.

All garments of this kind contrast with the gayer, looser, softer, and lighter clothes that are considered to befit a holiday. Soft collars are often thought unsuitable for business wear, the assumption being that their lack of rigid form betokens a corresponding 'slackness' in the wearer; while a dressing-gown and slippers, on the other hand, have become almost proverbial signs of ease and relaxation.

Various sources have contributed to the growth of associations of this kind, of which the most important seem to be:—

(1) **Colour.**—The universal connection (into the origin of which we cannot enter here) of black with seriousness

and white with innocence and moral purity, as distinct from the spectral colours—especially the brighter ones—which signify a freer play of the emotions.

(2) **Amplitude.**—The ascetic notion of the body as a source of evil passions, which can best be forgotten or controlled by as complete a covering as possible.

(3) **Thickness** (and stiffness).—The real protective value of thick clothes against certain physical dangers, this protection being unconsciously extended to the moral sphere. It is possible that the former use of armour and its associations with the moral traditions of chivalry have helped in this association.

(4) **Stiffness.**—The symbolic equation of physical stiffness and 'uprightness' (note the word) with moral probity and firmness, and of 'loose', 'slack', and 'sloppy' clothes with corresponding ways of life.

(5) **Tightness.**—The association is doubtless primarily due to the actual support of tightly fitting garments, a support which is largely physical, but which is easily and frequently transferred to the moral sphere.[1] Tightness, by its firm pressure on the body, may symbolise a firm control over ourselves (*e.g.* 'keeping a tight rein' on our passions), the opposite of that 'looseness' or 'dissoluteness' that we associate with immorality.[2]

Both stiffness and tightness are, however, liable to be over-determined by phallic symbolism. The stiff collar, for example, which is the sign of duty, is also the symbol of the erect phallus, and in general those male garments

[1] While on the way to his death (to be shot as a spy) Sergeant Grischa, in Arnold Zweig's well-known story, found that 'the only thing that comforted him was the feel of the broad leather belt round his middle, that kept him stiff and erect. Pride, sad, splendid liar, that forced him to preserve his honour in the face of his enemies by a brave death in a far country, was like that belt of his: it too held him together.'

[2] The moral protection of tight corsets, for instance, is interestingly brought out in the case of a lady who admitted that she 'would risk an encircling arm' when defended in this way, though she would not allow it under other circumstances; while the more active moral implications are shown by another lady who put on a stiff corset as soon as she became engaged. To the remonstrances of her somewhat disconcerted fiancé, she replied: 'I mustn't flop about now, but *you* can see me without them'. Actually the donning of this garment coincided with a change from a very free flirtatiousness to a distinctly rigid monogamous moral standard.

that are most associated with seriousness and correctness are also the most saturated with a subtle phallicism. Here, again, we find the compromise-formation between moral and instinctive factors which psycho-analysis has shown us to be characteristic, not only of so many neurotic manifestations, but also of so many aspects of our culture.[1]

There is, I believe, still one other and more general way in which clothes exercise a protective function. Like the last-mentioned functions of protection from magical and moral danger, it is psychological in nature; like these functions, too, it seems to depend in the last resort upon unconscious symbolism. The kind of protection to which we are now referring is, just because of its generality, more difficult to describe than are the previous kinds. Perhaps it can best be said to be a protection against **the general unfriendliness of the world as a whole;** or, expressed more psychologically, **a reassurance against the lack of love.** If we are in unfriendly surroundings, whether human or natural, we tend, as it were, to button up, to draw our garments closely round us. On a chilly day, when we leave our warm house and enter shudderingly into the inhospitable street, we turn up our collars and settle down as snugly as possible into our coats. Under the friendly influence of the sun, on the other hand, we throw off our outer coverings, or carry them more loosely, so that they no longer envelop us and isolate us from the external world. These influences are, I think, not to be accounted for entirely by the temperature. In the one case there is a sort of general unfriendliness which prompts us to withdraw our inner selves into the protection of our clothes, much as a tortoise may withdraw its head into the protecting armour with which Nature has provided it. In the other case there is a general kindliness with which we want to get intimately into touch, and to which we expand and open our arms (often literally) as if in welcome; there is

---

[1] Evidence for the existence of the moral influences here considered will be found in Flaccus, 34, and in Flügel, 35.

no need here of protective layers; on the contrary we feel a longing to bring our inmost being into contact with the friendly elements.

It is much the same with regard to our human environment. If we find ourselves among unsympathetic people—people to whom we feel ourselves superior, with whom we have nothing in common, or of whom we are afraid—in this case also we tend to draw our clothes tightly around us, as if they somehow kept us apart or protected us from these people with whom we desire no intimacy. Writers on clothes [1] have already noticed that certain forms of clothing, *e.g.* a high neckband or a high-cut coat collar, have, in the past, symbolised 'unapproachableness', 'stand-offishness', and resistance to democratic principles. Examples of this same general tendency from present-day life are not difficult to find. Thus, for instance, a man in a dress suit will often wear an overcoat while walking in the street, even in warm weather. He may not need it for protection against the climate, but he wears it because he feels that the other people in the street, who are probably most of them not in evening dress, are somehow different from himself, and, from the mere fact of being dressed as it were in different mood, will regard him with a certain degree of suspicion or hostility. He reserves the vision of his inner splendour for his own, similarly dressed, associates whom he will meet at the termination of his journey.[2]

With women similar tendencies are at work, though perhaps more tinged with an erotic element. Even more than with men (with whom it is often a mere sign of respect) the removal of outer garments signifies a con-

---

[1] *E.g.* Fuchs, 44, vol. iii. p. 176.
[2] In confirmation of this it may be noted that where there is less sense of a hostile or unsympathetic environment, there is less objection to walking abroad in evening dress. Thus, in a small region of the 'west end' of London, where it is understood that occasions demanding evening dress abound, men may sometimes be seen in the streets thus clad and without overcoats. The same holds true in even greater degree in the case of students at Oxford and Cambridge. Here the feeling is that the University forms the most important body of the population, a body for which, and round which, the other inhabitants exist; the undergraduate is therefore master of the situation and need fear no criticism from hostile outsiders.

dition of friendliness and of being 'at home'. Furthermore, there would seem to be a correspondence between democratic sentiments, sexual freedom, and the public exhibition of female beauty. In Mohammedan countries, where the sexual freedom of women was reduced to a minimum, women were apt to be carefully concealed from the public gaze, the very sight of their faces being jealously reserved for their husbands. In Europe, after the French Revolution, when 'liberty, equality, fraternity' was the slogan of the day, women wore the lightest of costumes in the street, where *décolleté* was regarded as no less appropriate than in the ballroom. In the period of prudishness and of greater social snobbery and differentiation that came later in the nineteenth century, such exposure became reserved for indoor occasions with friends and social equals. At the present day, when democratic views and greater sexual liberty are once more triumphant, women again unhesitatingly expose a larger portion of their bodies to the general view.

I am inclined to think that the same correspondence holds in individual cases, and that, for instance, the readiness with which a woman will remove her cloak when she is in evening dress at a theatre or other public function is to some extent diagnostic of her general friendliness and willingness to invite sexual admiration. If she throws off her outer wrap promptly, she is socially and sexually in sympathy with her environment; so long as she retains it, she preserves a certain aloofness, either because she is diffident about her own capacities or charms, or because she feels out of harmony with her surroundings and does not desire to invite the intimacy of those about her.

It will of course be said that, even supposing this is true, the situation here is complicated by the existence of individual differences in the sensibility to cold and in the consequent willingness to dispense with covering over bare arms and shoulders. I admit this to some extent; but, as I am endeavouring to show, this very matter of the sensitiveness to cold is itself far from being independent of the psychological factors here under consideration. The fact that we protect ourselves both from cold and from unfriendliness by clothing is surely not unconnected with the further fact that we naturally tend to symbolise love and friendliness by warmth and unfriendliness by cold. 'Coldness' is a universal metaphor for lack of love, as when we speak of sexual frigidity or of a person's manner being icy, just as, on the other hand, we speak of a fiery passion or a warm embrace. Now it seems probable that this connection, like so many other linguistic associations, is pretty deeply embedded in our mental structure, and that our reaction to, and even our feelings of, cold and heat are to a large extent unconsciously determined by these psychological identifications. I think it is even possible that some people are more generally sensitive to cold than others because they feel a lack of love in their lives. Others again perhaps dislike warmth, because they are afraid of giving free vent to their feelings of love. At any rate, there is definite evidence that in certain individuals periods of depression, anxiety, loneliness, or homesickness may coincide with a desire to be more warmly clad than usual. Thus a woman who, during the rest of her life, has made a special point of wearing the lightest clothes she could, continually wore a coat, even for playing tennis, at one particular period of adolescence, during which she passed through a phase of depression and was contemplating suicide. A boy who at home refused to wear an overcoat, at boarding-school, when he was homesick, would insist upon always going about in his overcoat, in spite of the teasing remarks of his companions. A student from America, studying in London, writes: 'It may be that homesickness calls for more clothes, for I have noticed that a steamer rug and gas fire . . . will do wonders for an attack of self-pity.' A special investigation on this point was recently carried out in a city of south-western England by Eve Macaulay. A group of fifty students were asked the question: 'Are there any circumstances (other than temperature) or states of mind in which you feel the need of more clothes than you usually wear?' Out of the fifty, twenty-four stated that purely mental conditions of the kind just mentioned did have this effect. Of course it is possible that this need for warmer clothing is entirely a secondary result of the influence of depression, anxiety, etc., upon the circulation. But it is noteworthy that only three of the twenty-four referred to 'lowered vitality' or other physical conditions in this connection, and in view of our general ignorance as to the real causal interrelations between body and mind in cases of this sort, and of the indubitable fact of the existence of a psychic association between cold and lack of love (as revealed, for instance, by the above-mentioned linguistic usages), it would be rash to neglect the possible existence of a purely (or primarily) psychic determinant of the need of more clothes. Thomas Carlyle—the writer of what is probably the most famous of all books on clothes—has admirably expressed in a few words the analogy between a protecting love and a protecting garment (an analogy which, by the way, was said by the above quoted homesick American student to be 'quite perfect'). Speaking of his dead wife, he says, 'She wrapped me round like a cloak to keep all the hard and cold world off me'.[1]

This last example gives, I think, the clue to the unconscious symbolism which (in some cases, at any rate) underlies the substitution of clothes for love. Carlyle's words almost irresistibly call up the thought of a mother. Deep down in the heart of mankind is the longing for a mother who will protect us, cherish us, and warm us with her love—a longing which seems to take us back to the very earliest stages of our being. One of the most astonishing discoveries of psycho-analysis was that concerning the importance and frequency of 'womb phantasies', *i.e.* phantasies of a return to the warm, enveloping, and protecting home, where we spent the first nine months of our existence. Concerning the precise significance of this phantasy, its causes, its importance for

[1] Quoted in *One Thousand Beautiful Things* (edited by Arthur Mee), p. 37.

normal development and for psycho-pathology, there is still much doubt and much dispute.[1] The fact that it has some considerable importance is beyond all reasonable doubt. The aspect of the phantasy that concerns us here is that the womb, or its symbol, is regarded as a refuge both from a generally hostile environment and from cold. That the womb is, in this phantasy, treated as a place of safety, to which one can retire from the dangers and difficulties of the world, has been very amply shown by many psycho-analytic studies. Recently Ernest Jones (55) has endeavoured to show that the unconscious foundation of the fear of cold is derived from the fear of separation from the mother. From this it is but one step to the idea that a return to the womb would constitute a refuge at one and the same time, both from cold and from the dangers incidental to separation from the beloved mother. Since clothes obviously protect us from cold, it is not surprising that they frequently become symbols of this aspect of the protective function of the mother, and then, by extension, of the other aspects also—the aspects in virtue of which she becomes a refuge from 'the hard and cold world' in general.

This extension is rendered easier by the fact that, with the majority of individuals, the mother is, for external reasons, associated with clothes from a very early age. It is she who usually dresses and undresses the child, or at least superintends these operations. And for many years after this (often indeed throughout her own life) the mother, as if prompted by an intuitive understanding of the symbolism here in question, tends to show her love by manifesting an anxiety lest her children should be inadequately clothed. It is seldom indeed that a mother warns her son or daughter against the danger of being overclothed—but how innumerable are the occasions on which she may be heard urging the putting on

---

[1] Cf. the present writer's *Psycho-analytic Study of the Family*, ch. viii. Otto Rank's interesting book, *The Trauma of Birth*, represents an extreme view of its importance that is not shared by the majority of psycho-analysts.

of warmer undergarments, or the taking of an extra wrap! Indeed, her anxiety in this matter often becomes a considerable source of worry and annoyance to her children, and may rouse in them a spirit of rebellion, which, by contra-suggestion, manifests itself in a desire to wear as little covering as possible. But this is a matter which we must reserve for the next chapter.[1]

We may close the present chapter by pointing out a parallelism, to which we shall also have to allude again in another connection, but which is peculiarly germane to the matter we have just been discussing. The parallelism in question—one to which many writers on clothing have drawn attention—is that between the protective functions of clothes and of the house respectively. Both protect against cold and other inclemencies of the weather. In fact their functions are to some extent complementary; in cold weather we divest ourselves of our outer garments on entering the house and put them on again when leaving. Clothes, like the house, are protective; but, being nearer the body and actually supported on it, they are (unlike the house) portable. With their help, we carry—like snails and tortoises—a sort of home upon our backs, and enjoy the advantages of shelter without the disadvantage of becoming sessile. We have even invented a number of objects which are in the nature of transitions between clothes and houses. The roofed-in car or carriage is, as Gerald Heard has pointed out,[2] one type of such an object. The umbrella is another. As regards this little instrument with its emergency roof, it is difficult to say whether it corresponds more to a miniature transportable house or to a temporary outer garment.[3]

---

[1] A somewhat more detailed treatment of the womb-symbolism of clothes will be found in an already-mentioned paper by the present writer, 36.
[2] 48 p. 154.
[3] If, as regards protection, clothes may be said to take over the functions of the house, as regards modesty, our houses, obviously to some extent, take the place of clothes. Within our own rooms, at any rate, most of us can divest ourselves of our clothes without feeling immodest Mohammedan ladies are, as we remarked in the last chapter, for the most part confined to their houses away from the gaze of the public, but, as a glance at Fig 13 will remind us, when they leave their houses the protection thus abandoned can, to a very large extent,

Now it is interesting to note that the house,[1] with which clothes have so much in common and with which they have so often been compared, has been shown by psycho-analysts to be a frequent symbol of the mother and of the mother's womb. In fact, it is one of the clearest and one of the most indubitable of this class of symbols. This must surely strengthen our conviction of the reality of the occurrence of this same symbolism with regard to clothes.

---

be made good by clothing. In this particular case, the lady from Tunis is almost as completely sheltered from the eyes of the indiscreet as she would be in the privacy of her own apartments. This shows us that the complementary function of house and clothes holds good in the sphere of modesty as it does in that of protection.

[1] And the room. Cf. the German word *Frauenzimmer*.

CHAPTER VI

INDIVIDUAL DIFFERENCES

The apparel oft proclaims the man.
Hamlet, i. 3.

WE have hitherto been dealing with the general psychological factors of dress—factors which are for the most part to be found at work in every individual mind. But of course these various factors are not all of equal relative importance in every mind. Here, as elsewhere in psychology, the differences between individuals are almost as important as the similarities, and it is time that we should devote some attention to these differences before going on to consider certain more specific aspects of clothing, such as the various types of dress and the nature of fashion. Accordingly, this chapter and the next will be devoted to this matter of differences. In the present chapter we shall deal with individual differences in the strict sense, reserving for the next chapter those special differences—perhaps more important here than in most other fields of psychology—which depend on sex.

As already indicated, it would appear that the young child in his earliest years has little interest in dress. Considerations of ornamentation and of modesty are alike foreign to him; at most there may exist for him something of the comfort of clothes as a protection against cold and as an unconscious means of the regression to the pre-natal state that we discussed at the conclusion of the last chapter. Gradually, however, there awaken certain tendencies, which, though they do not in themselves provide an interest in clothes, nevertheless are capable of being 'displaced' on to clothes, and, when thus displaced, become the main sources of the development of interest in dress in the individual—and therefore ultimately in the race. I refer to pleasures derived from the naked body—and in particular the exhibitionistic tendency.

Further analysis of these pleasures shows that they are derived from two main sources, which are of very unequal value for the development of clothes interest. In the language of psycho-analysis, one source is primarily Narcissistic, the other primarily auto-erotic. The Narcissistic element consists in the tendency to admire one's own body and display it to others, so that these others can share in the admiration. It finds a natural expression in the showing off of the naked body and in the demonstration of its powers, and can be observed in many children in the nude dancings and prancings in which, if allowed, they will indulge—preferably, but not necessarily, before the eyes of admiring adults. Much the same kinds of satisfaction are doubtless obtainable in later life from the exhibitionistic activities of the dancer and of the athlete, both of them clad as a rule in attire scantier than that which modesty allows for ordinary occasions. But the manifestations of this tendency are not of necessity permanently confined to the naked body; before long there arises the possibility of new (displaced) expressions connected with clothes or decorations. We saw in Chapters II. and III. how the various forms of dress and ornament may appear to extend and magnify the beauties of the body. It is natural that a tendency that finds satisfaction in the display of the body should, sooner or later, avail itself of such a ready means of increasing the attractiveness of the display. In this manner some of the original interest in the naked body becomes displaced on to the clothing or ornaments that appear to augment the aesthetic effect of the body, and this portion of the original interest may eventually come to be relatively independent of its first object, so that we may say that there now exists an interest in clothing which is relatively distinct from the interest in the body that is clothed; the original crude exhibitionistic tendency has been to some extent sublimated on to clothes.[1]

It would seem much more difficult to achieve any corresponding sublimation of the auto-erotic constituents of the pleasures connected with the naked body. These constituents are of two main kinds, which, again in psycho-analytic terminology, may be called skin- and muscle-erotism respectively.[2] The first of these two, so far as it concerns us here,[3] is concerned primarily with the pleasure of natural skin stimulation—the play of air, wind, and sun upon the surface of the body. Those who indulge in sun and air baths will realise that the pleasure to be derived from this source is very considerable. Indeed, in the replies to a recent questionnaire,[4] a number of persons described such pleasure of skin stimulation in very glowing terms, such expressions as 'heavenly', 'perfectly delightful', 'like breathing in happiness', being not at all uncommon. Now the wearing of clothes—especially any but the lightest and thinnest clothes—necessarily entails a great sacrifice of these pleasures, inasmuch as it largely prevents the essential stimuli from affecting the sensory surface of the skin. In return it can only offer two satisfactions: in the first place avoidance of unpleasant cold and the correlative pleasure of increased snugness, a source of gratification which, as we have seen, appeals primarily to tendencies of a different order (the really strong *sensory* pleasures of warmth, such as those produced by a warm bath, are, again, most readily enjoyed without a costume); in the second place, certain pleasant cutaneous sensations connected with the 'feel' of clothes-

[1] As already mentioned, it seems probable that we often impede the process of sublimation by interfering too soon and too strongly with the child's interest in his naked body and with his enjoyment of the more primitive forms of (for the most part 'local') ornament. Adults often attempt to impress upon the child the importance of the motives of modesty and protection before he is ready to appreciate them. Here, as in other cases, sublimation can often be prevented by a premature repression.
[2] Sadger, 82.
[3] Artificial stimulation of the skin (scratching, rubbing, tickling, etc.) may of course also be resorted to in order to gratify this skin erotism.
[4] Flügel, 36.

fabrics, the pleasures of contact with silk, velvet, fur, etc. These latter would seem to afford means for the genuine displacement of skin-erotism from natural stimuli, such as sun and air, to clothes; but at the same time there is evidence that the new pleasures to be derived from such clothes stimulation are rather limited, and, except perhaps in very cold climates, on the whole distinctly inferior to those that the natural stimuli can produce. Indeed, some further results of the questionnaire just referred to indicate that, for most people, unpleasant sensations connected with such stimulation are more frequent and intense than the pleasant sensations (though this is a matter that might perhaps be rectified if more care, and perhaps more money also, were devoted to the choice of underclothing). It is not surprising then that the skin-erotic components undergo but little sublimation on to clothes, and that persons in whom they are by nature strongly developed continue, as it were, to resent the wearing of clothes as a habit that robs them of a valuable source of pleasure.

The same considerations hold for the most part with regard to muscle-erotism. Here the pleasure is derived from the free play of the muscles. The sensory elements involved are partly derived from deep sensations directly caused by the muscular contractions, partly from cutaneous sensations due to the stretching and relaxing of the skin that necessarily accompanies such contraction. Both these classes of sensation can be best appreciated when the body is naked (hence an additional reason for the tendency to movement, that, as we noticed just now, is apt to accompany the Narcissistic exhibitionism of children). Clothes interfere with this appreciation, in the first place by deadening the natural skin sensations and adding irrelevant ones of their own (caused by the varying pressure of the garments as the body moves), in the second place by actually presenting obstacles to free muscular movement (as a man can easily verify by trying to swing his arms vigorously in an ordinary coat). The only compensation that clothes can offer for this loss of the satisfaction of muscle-erotism would seem to lie in the pleasurable pressure afforded by certain tight garments, such as a belt or corset, which appear to add to the strength of the body by producing sensations somewhat similar to those that accompany contraction of the abdominal muscles. Here, however, as in the case of skin-erotism, though the pleasures of clothing are real in so far as they go, they are for the most part inferior to those which are possible in a state of nudity; on the whole, therefore, muscle-erotism, like skin-erotism, loses rather than gains by the wearing of clothes.

It is, therefore, to displacements of the Narcissistic rather than of the auto-erotic elements that clothing must look for psychological support of a directly pleasure-giving kind. All the evidence points to the fact, however, that children get very little positive satisfaction from their clothes in the early years of life; they only wear them because their elders insist upon it, thereby making nakedness 'wrong' and the clothed condition 'right'. Later on, this vague sense of morality connected with the wearing of clothes becomes clarified by the acquisition of certain definite ideas of modesty—also of course acquired from elder persons, it would not be 'nice' to be seen without clothes or in too few of them, although it would undoubtedly often enough be pleasant to discard them, if it were not for this moral inhibition.[1] At the same time, however, the more aesthetic appreciation of clothes, derived from the sublimation of the Narcissistic tendencies, is beginning, and at first manifests itself in a relatively crude form in the desire for lots of ornament and for the gayest of colours. In fact, children, especially perhaps boys, who have less opportunity in this direction than have girls, frequently seem to suffer from a real but often half-suppressed longing for more colour in their clothes, and, if asked what costumes they would like to wear, are apt to propose some distinctly gaudy combinations; as in the case of one boy of nine whose choice consisted of 'red and yellow jersey,

[1] Eve Macaulay, 65, p. 157.

green belt, brown shorts, red and blue stockings, mauve cap.'[1] At this stage of development, there is little appreciation of the distinction that the sophisticated adult draws between festive clothes and working clothes; there is a desire to wear the finest and most elaborate clothes all the time (a desire which, when present in later years, is only found in backward children). The only alternative is to throw over the decorative principle altogether and to desire clothes that are as strong and plain as possible, so that play or romping may be undisturbed by the necessity of taking care lest 'best' or party clothes be torn or soiled—this last a point of very great importance in the life of the child, who, if at all boisterously inclined, is apt to come into frequent conflict with his elders in such matters. Only at a somewhat later age does the ideal of smart, well-cut, or 'suitable' clothes become one that appeals to the child. Like the savage, he is at first unable to appreciate the *finesses* of tailoring or dressmaking, as arts that have to take into account the *ensemble* constituted by the wearer, his costume, and his environment. Only when he is capable of this appreciation, however, is it possible for him to understand the point of view of the civilised and cultivated adult, and it is useless (and probably harmful) to try and force this point of view upon him prematurely.

Having thus indicated in briefest outline[2] the way in which the mental attitude to clothes develops in the early years of life, we will now proceed to our proper task of studying the individual differences among adults. Recent investigations[3] seem to make it possible to classify individuals into various 'types', so far as their attitude to clothes is concerned. Such a classification may greatly help to obtain a general idea of the nature of the chief individual differences concerned. But it must throughout be borne in mind—(*a*) that these types are pro-

[1] Eve Macaulay, 65.
[2] Further details concerning the development of children's attitudes towards dress will be found in Eve Macaulay's paper, 65.
[3] Particularly those reported in the above-mentioned paper by the present writer, 35.

visional, and that there may later on have to be a fresh and more elaborate formulation in the light of further knowledge; (b) that here, as often elsewhere in psychology, a 'type' means only a particularly striking combination of traits and does not imply that the majority of persons belong quite clearly and definitely to one type or the other. On the contrary, there are an indefinite number of intermediate stages between each type, and the majority of individuals exhibit the intermediate stages of the traits concerned. But, by arbitrarily picking out a few individuals here and there as constituting a 'type', we can bring some sort of order into what would otherwise be a chaos of individual variations. And we can, to some extent, 'place' the a-typical individuals by reference to the types between which they seem to stand. The establishment of types, therefore, seems to be a methodologically justifiable procedure, provided that the assumptions and limitations of the procedure are clearly kept in mind.

The most primitive type from the point of view of clothes-psychology is that which might be called the **rebellious type.** Persons of this type get little positive satisfaction from clothes and, at bottom, have never become fully resigned to the necessity of wearing them. They feel that clothes restrict and imprison them, and that to be truly free it is necessary to wear but the thinnest and lightest of clothes, or preferably none at all. With these persons the primitive interests attaching to the naked body have undergone but little displacement on to clothes—either because of the innate strength of these interests or because the circumstances connected with the development of the individuals concerned have been unfavourable to the formation of such displacement. In persons of this type the attractions of clothes, whether as satisfying the needs of decoration, modesty, or protection, are small as compared with the attractions connected with nakedness. Further research is needed before we can state with certainty the details which distinguish the mentality of the clothes-rebel. In the light of our present knowledge, however, it would seem that the following characteristics are very frequently to be found:—

(a) A strongly developed skin and muscle erotism,[1] which, as we have seen, is unfavourable to the development of clothes interests, since it does not easily admit of the required sublimation. There is some evidence that the skin sensitiveness in question is apt to affect the individual who possesses it in quite a number of ways—in making him, for instance, more sensitive to (and often more intolerant of) the 'feel' of clothes upon the skin, more liable to be worried by the weight and pressure of his garments, if these are at all tight or heavy, more desirous of having plenty of fresh air in his rooms, and more fussy about 'stuffy' and ill-ventilated places (though this latter trait may also depend upon other, relatively unconnected, factors).

(b) Relatively little pleasure in decoration. This seems directly due to the failure of exhibitionistic sublimation. Such a person will therefore tend as a rule to be indifferently or carelessly dressed; comfort with him is of far more importance than appearance. As regards the deeper levels of mentality, it seems probable that, in the case of men, the phallic erotism is relatively feeble in comparison with the more generally diffused skin and muscle erotism, and that, in consequence, there is difficulty in the formation of unconscious phallic symbols in clothes; or that such symbols, even if formed, provide little satisfaction as compared with the sacrifice of skin and muscle erotism that the wearing of clothes entails.

(c) Relatively little modesty. The clothes-rebel tends to regard modesty as an external, conventional matter, and has little shame about exposure of the body or

---

[1] It seems not unlikely that, in certain cases at any rate, some degree of anal erotism may also be involved—the anal elements being perhaps displaced on to the skin in the manner very recently reported by B. D. Lewin (*Int. Zeitschrift f. Psychoanalyse*, 1930, vol. xiv. pp. 47 ff.). These elements would then play a part in the general rebelliousness, and particularly in a certain defiant neglect or untidiness of clothes to which this type is often prone.

about wearing shabby, 'incorrect', or unconventional garments. It seems clear that his appreciation of modesty is not strong enough to make much headway against the powerful forces that impel him at bottom to despise and resent clothes as unnecessary restrictions.

(*d*) Relatively little feeling of the need for protection. Here again, the skin and muscle erotism easily triumphs —this time over the pleasures of warmth or of the other forms of protection. As regards the more unconscious aspect of this, it would appear that there is here in certain cases a tendency to get free from the sheltering, but often hampering, love of the mother, which, as we saw in the last chapter, may be symbolised by clothes. If, on the one hand, clothes represent the grateful refuge afforded by the mother, they also come to represent the trammels ('swaddling clothes') to movement and development that her influence creates. Hence the rebellious throwing off of clothes, and the scorning of their snug protection may come to be a vigorous symbolic assertion of independence, a freeing of the self from mother-fixation, and an adaptation to the outer (in symbolic thought, extra-uterine) environment; an environment that makes a strong appeal to the skin and muscle feeling with which individuals of this type are so well endowed.

It would seem highly probable (though I have had no opportunity to verify this assumption by personal investigation) that individuals of this type constitute the main body of supporters of the 'nude-culture' movement, in countries where such a movement exists. It is interesting to observe, however, that these apostles of nakedness have not succeeded in finally casting off the attachment to the mother. On the contrary, they find her again in what seems to them to be a greater and more noble form—in the form of Mother Nature; indeed, one of the chief attractions of the movement is that it brings its adherents into closer touch with Nature. In Germany, which is the real home of *Nacktkultur*, the chief society devoted to this end goes under the name of 'The Friends of Nature'.[1] 'Only utter nakedness', we are told by a well-known writer on the subject,[2] 'truly unites us for the first time with Nature.'[3]

Here, as in other cases, man seeks a rationalisation for conduct that is at bottom prompted by his less conscious motives, and such motives are often hidden under the more respectable and 'reasonable' guise of hygiene. Individuals of the present type naturally tend to stress the advantages of little clothing, and maintain that for the most part civilised man tends to over-clothe himself. They have not been slow to make all the use they can of the new knowledge concerning the beneficial effects of light; and, before this knowledge, they stressed the supposed greater strength and health of savage races, arguing that these advantages were largely due to the wearing of fewer clothes,[4] and that they were in consequence lost when European attire was adopted (though they admit that this attire was worn in very unhygienic fashion).

The next type, which may appropriately be called the **resigned type,** has much the same general make-up as the rebellious type, except that the habits and conventions of wearing clothes have become sufficiently strong to make it seem impossible to gratify the desire to throw off their clothes. They are like slaves who have not ceased to long for freedom, but who have ceased to struggle for it. Such a one, when asked (in the questionnaire already referred to) whether he enjoyed the feeling of sunshine and air on the skin, and whether he allowed this enjoyment to affect his clothes in any way, would reply sadly: 'Sun and air entirely excluded by my clothes, alas!' (whereas a member of the rebellious type might have replied with an account of sun and air baths,

---

[1] It is said that in the summer of 1928 it numbered between two and three hundred thousand members.
[2] Surén, 96, p. 107.
[3] When offered a cushion as a substitute for sitting on the ground (because there had been a thunderstorm the night before), a member of a 'gymnosophist' camp characteristically refused with the remark: 'Cushions seem all wrong here. I want to be as near as possible to Nature'.
[4] Cf., *e.g.*, Frederick Boyle, 12.

of shorts and open collars, of working in shirt-sleeves, of thin suits and underclothing, and, if a woman, of bare arms, exposed chest, and unstockinged legs). When asked if clothes can be improved as regards beauty, comfort, hygiene, or ease of putting on, he will reply, 'Not much to be done', 'I am used to the present method', 'It is almost impossible to answer, so ingrained in one's soul is the orthodox'. Such people may make complaints about the weight, texture, or appearance of their clothes, but have few, if any, suggestions for improvement. It is clear that in individuals of this type the elements impelling to nakedness are subject to a more powerful inhibition than in individuals of the rebellious type; but this inhibition is not maintained by *consciously* strong motives. There is, indeed, as in the rebellious type, but little conscious satisfaction in clothes; modesty, decoration, and protection alike make little appeal. It appears as though the inhibitions had occurred early in life and were now working at a relatively unconscious level, manifesting themselves to consciousness only in the resultant subservience to habit and convention. Only further, more intensive, study will enlighten us as to the intimate nature of the real motives that produced this inhibition.

In the third type, which may perhaps best be called the **unemotional,** the lack of strong conscious affect of any kind that is found in the resigned type is carried a stage further. Here the whole emotional and conative life of clothes seems reduced to a minimum. Clothes are chosen, put on and off, worn and discarded, with little satisfaction—but also with very little annoyance, worry, or discomfort. The whole clothes-life has become, as far as possible, mechanised; as with the resigned type, everything is a matter of course, but there is no sign of the underlying discontent that distinguishes this latter type. Thus, as contrasted with the sad inevitability with which, as it seems to the resigned type, clothes shut out light and air, this exclusion is regarded by the unemotional type as an obvious fact with scarcely any affective colouring. When questioned whether the appreciation of sun and air affect his clothes, a person of the unemotional type will reply, 'Of course not, I can't take off my clothes', and with that the matter ends. He neither struggles for the freedom which is the goal of the rebellious, nor longs for it as does the resigned; but at the same time he has little of the more positive needs for, and satisfactions in, clothing that distinguish the types hereinafter to be described; decoration scarcely appeals to him (though he is often, as it would seem, fairly neat and tidy in appearance), while the functions of modesty and protection are taken for granted and arouse little feeling or interest. He does not spend much consideration upon the appearance, comfort, or hygienic aspects of his clothes, but will often dress as quickly and efficiently as possible, in order to pass on to matters of greater interest and importance. It would seem as though, in this type, there were no strong auto-erotic elements to resist clothes, no strong exhibitionism to be displaced on to them, and, at the same time, no strong sense of modesty or need of protection. Hence the generally unemotional picture which this type presents.

We now pass to types which enjoy a more definite conscious satisfaction of one kind or another in their clothes. This satisfaction may itself be of two main kinds: in the one case, the satisfaction that attaches to a 'reaction-formation', *i.e.* to an impulse which is of an inhibitory nature; in the other case, the satisfaction that attends a 'sublimation'.

There would seem to be two chief types which are distinguished by the former (inhibitory) kind of satisfaction—the prudish type and the duty type.

In the **prudish type** there is a triumph of the impulse of modesty, which has definitely conquered the (often strong) exhibitionistic tendencies. Such individuals present a marked contrast to the rebellious type, inasmuch as the very thought of exposing their own naked bodies is embarrassing or disgusting; while exposure on the part of others arouses expressions of strong disapproval.

As a rule little distinction is made between the exposure of beautiful and of ugly bodies; the disapproval is usually expressed in general terms, such as—'the naked human body is unpleasant to look upon', 'bare arms and legs are ugly'. Occasionally, however, the disapproval may be rationalised as an aesthetic abhorrence of the imperfections of the majority of human forms—*e.g.* 'longer skirts are needed to hide English women's defective legs'. A more frequent form of rationalisation is the hygienic one, which—taking the opposite course to that adopted by the rebellious type—emphasises the dangers of insufficient covering. In the present day of comparatively simple and unornamental dress in both sexes, there is relatively little opportunity for persons of the prudish type to inveigh against the extravagancies and over-elaboration of costume (as distinct from the manifestations of undisplaced exhibitionism in exposure of the actual body); the more complicated and ornate dresses of past generations have, however, in their time, provided ample material for the moralisings of persons of this type, and in all recent periods it has been possible for them—indeed with much show of reason—to attack the unnecessary costliness and changeability of fashionable dress. At the present moment, moreover, objection is being raised to the increased and more unashamed use of cosmetics that has appeared of recent years.

Persons of the prudish type often exhibit also some characteristics of the **duty type**—a type in which certain features of costume (for the most part either those actually associated with uniforms or other working clothes, or those that are distinguished by a certain stiffness, tightness, or severity of line)[1] have become symbols of work and duty. In persons of this type the interests connected with clothes have come to represent not merely, as in the prudish type, a reaction-formation against self-display in any form, but an inhibitory tendency of a

[1] Often enough, of course, the two features are combined, as, for instance, in most military uniforms, in the uniform of a hospital nurse, or in starched collars, which by persons of this type are usually considered the only suitable neckwear for professional or office use.

much wider kind, directed against all manifestations of 'softness' or 'self-indulgence'. With them certain kinds of clothes have indeed become outward and visible signs of a strict and strongly developed 'Super-Ego' or moral principle. Such persons are apt to draw a sharp distinction between clothes worn for work and the less severe and more ornamental garments worn for rest or recreation, and (those of them at least who are capable of relaxation) tend to 'feel different', to adopt a less stiff and rigid view of life when themselves dressed in clothes of the latter type. Their view on this matter contrasts interestingly with that of many other persons (but especially it would seem with those of the rebellious and sublimated types), who think that working clothes should also be made as attractive as possible,[1] and that work itself is helped thereby. The views of persons of the duty type also conflict with those of many others (especially, but by no means exclusively, with those of the rebellious type), in that to these latter a stiff, conventional, working costume or uniform often suggests a rigidity or unadaptability that is contrary to the interests of work of the higher kind requiring breadth of outlook, bodily skill, and the power of accommodating oneself to varying conditions.

We now pass to types in which the conscious satisfactions in clothes are of a more positive sort, and which represent displacements of primitive tendencies rather than reaction-formations against such tendencies.

The first of these is the **protected type.** The outward manifestation of this type is the need of warm clothing to combat a very general tendency to chilliness. Such persons are as a rule warmly, rather than well or fashionably, dressed. With them the decorative function of clothes occupies a minor place; protection is all-important. Modesty may sometimes play a bigger rôle than might at first appear, since, in these cases, the imagined need for warmth may often have an important element of displaced and rationalised modesty behind it. The

[1] Usually with the proviso, 'so long as they are not extravagant or inconvenient'.

essential feature in this type, however, would seem to be the sensitiveness to cold. How far this is due ultimately to physiological conditions, or to such psychological conditions (felt want of love, etc.) as have previously been suggested, is a matter for future research. It may be that the elements that make for sensitiveness to cold have, necessarily or at least usually, an inverse relationship to the auto-erotic elements that distinguish the rebellious type; we have already seen how the two may conflict in the case of some of the psychological aspects of protection (p. 69). In any case, the protected type seems to have the auto-erotic skin and muscle elements but feebly developed, contrasting very strongly with the rebellious type in this respect. Persons of the protected type, however, will agree with those of the prudish type in emphasising the hygienic advantage of plentiful covering—at any rate so far as they themselves are concerned (they are less dogmatic and intolerant about others than are members of the prudish type). Indeed, this hygienic interest may in certain cases take on a distinctly hypochondriacal colouring, which is apt to make this type irritatingly fussy and timorous to those of contrasting types, *e.g.* the rebellious or the unemotional.

Next comes the **supported type.** Persons of this type feel pleasurably strengthened and supported by their clothes, especially by tight or stiff clothes. In so far as this support is moral (and such a moral element is often important), they have something in common with persons of the duty type. In so far as physical and sensory elements are concerned (and these after all appear to represent the most fundamental part of the 'support' in question), the pleasure seems to be derived, partly from a displacement of muscle erotism on to tight-fitting and 'supporting' clothes (belts, corsets, well-fitting boots, etc.) in the way described on p. 89, partly from an unusually strong emphasis upon the phallic symbolism of clothes and from the 'potency' associated therewith. If this analysis is correct, there are thus three main elements which go to the formation of this type—moral, muscular, and phallic. Persons of this type, it is interesting to note, are by no means necessarily devoid of appreciation of the Narcissistic or auto-erotic elements so characteristic of the rebellious type. Indeed, there may take place something of a struggle between the attractions of loose or little clothing on the one hand, and those of stiff, supporting clothing on the other, for it would appear that if full satisfaction is to be obtained from the 'support', the clothes must be so tight or so stiff as to be a little uncomfortable. The struggle here is between the unsublimated skin and muscle erotism on the one hand and the sublimated phallic tendencies upon the other. In typical examples of the supported type, the latter elements win—perhaps largely because they are reinforced, as we have just seen, by a certain amount of displaced muscle-erotism.

The **sublimated type**, as the name suggests, is the most satisfactory of all types from the point of view of pure clothes psychology. It is attained through an extensive sublimation of the Narcissistic elements from body to clothes. To individuals of this type the Narcissistic self-feelings ultimately fuse clothes and body into a harmonious unity, in a way that seems impossible of achievement in the other types, where there is usually some extensive and unresolved conflict of one kind or another. It is clear that this type demands a fairly strong original Narcissism. Probably, indeed, the Narcissistic elements are relatively strong as compared with the less easily sublimated auto-erotic elements. But absence of excessive inhibitions due to modesty is of course also essential. It is this type which is most fully capable of the satisfaction that sartorial display can give; and, where there is present aesthetic capacity also, it is to this type that we may look for the most satisfactory development of clothes. In fact, the only disadvantage to which this type is liable is that which may arise from its strong Narcissism, which may lead to an excessive interest in clothes display—*i.e.* an interest that unduly limits the time and energy available for other ends.

When such excessive interest occurs in persons of male sex, we may feel inclined to classify the individuals concerned as a separate type, which we might call the 'dandy' type. But this is perhaps hardly justifiable from the point of view of pure clothes psychology, since the difference between the dandy and the person of sublimated type is a quantitative rather than a qualitative one. From the point of view of general psychology and of sociology, however, the distinction may be legitimate, since the social value of the sublimation depends to some extent upon the clothes interest being 'normal', rather than excessive; and because the very high degree of Narcissism characteristic of the dandy is usually correlated with some degree of sexual abnormality (or at any rate a relative incapacity for normal hetero-sexual object love). In women we habitually expect and tolerate a higher degree of Narcissism than in men. Consequently, an amount of time and energy devoted to clothes that would be considered excessive in a man might be regarded as normal in a woman. Nevertheless, although the differences between the sexes in this respect is still generally accepted, it is admitted even by those who believe that 'it is women's mission to be beautiful', that here also there is a limit beyond which the concentration of effort and interest upon external appearance becomes harmful both to the individual and to society.

As a final category, we may distinguish the **self-satisfied type.** This type has something in common both with the unemotional and with the sublimated type. But questioned on the subject of clothes, this type exhibits a rather irritating smugness and self-complacency which are not found elsewhere; a person of this kind has no suggestions for improvements in clothes; the clothes he wears are the best possible ones; he knows what he wants and insists on getting it; by exercising a little care he can always dress comfortably, hygienically, and in good taste, and he is not a little contemptuous of those who have difficulties with simple matters of this kind. We might even be inclined to call such a person a clothes-prig. In the few cases which I have had the opportunity of investigating more closely, the excessive self-satisfaction of such a person has revealed itself as a defence mechanism against extensive feelings of inferiority. We are of course familiar, in general psychology, with the fact that inferiority may be hidden by an exaggerated assumption of superiority and self-confidence; in the present type, this exaggerated positive self-feeling seems to have attached itself especially to clothes. Why it should have taken this course is a question that I have, unfortunately, had no opportunity of studying in detail. Such little evidence as I possess points to the excessive satisfaction with clothes being a compensation for an extreme intolerance of the naked body, an intolerance that is itself founded on a strong castration complex. If this should prove to be generally true, it would seem that persons of this type (all that I have so far met are of the male sex) cling desperately to a satisfaction in clothes, because these, in virtue of their phallic symbolism, give reassurance against the fear of phallic loss.

In concluding this survey of types, let me repeat that the present list aims at being nothing more than a provisional classification. It is a list that has not been constructed *a priori*, but has been drawn up from a study of concrete cases. Further study—extensive and intensive—may result in a more reliable, more detailed, and more useful set of types.

CHAPTER VII

SEX DIFFERENCES[1]

> Forma viros neglecta decet.
> OVID, *Ars Amat.* i. 509.
> Fond of fun
> And fond of dress and change and praise,
> So mere a woman in her ways.
> D. G. ROSSETTI, *Jenny.*

PRIMITIVE **Sex Distinctions.**—If, as most authorities have maintained, sexual factors have been elements of great importance, perhaps of supreme importance, in the origin and development of dress, it is not surprising that the differences between the sexes should find expression in distinctions of habit and convention with regard to dress. And indeed, both among savage and among civilised peoples, distinctions of some sort are nearly always to be found, though their actual nature may vary greatly. Among the most significant of these distinctions are those which depend upon the relative importance of the two great motives of modesty and display. Among ourselves, at the present moment, the female sex is far more decorative than the male. Of savages in the main the opposite is true. With them, as with the majority of animal species, the male is more ornamental than the female; he is also (again the opposite of what we find among ourselves) the more enterprising and the less bound by tradition, as is shown for instance by his greater readiness to adopt articles of European dress when they come his way. Modesty, on the other hand, is more frequently to be seen among the women, and is probably connected, in a good many cases, with the various taboos which affect the female sex at certain times (*e.g.* child-birth, menstruation). This difference is apt to affect the relative quantity of clothing worn by

[1] Portions of this chapter were incorporated in a paper read before the Congress of the World League for Sexual Reform, September, 1929.

the two sexes. Where the motive of decoration is the chief one, men are, as a rule, more amply clothed than women; where modesty plays a larger part in clothes, women wear more than men.

Even with ourselves, however, there are what we may perhaps regard as vestiges of the more primitive state in which men were the more decorative, women the more modest, sex. Even the most gay feminine attire scarcely equals the gorgeousness of certain military uniforms. The same was true of academic robes until these were made available for women also. But the most striking difference that points in this direction is connected with the forms of respect which social convention prescribes for the two sexes. On entering a church a man must remove his hat, a woman must keep hers on, or at least (following Pauline precept) cover her head, if it be only with a shawl or handkerchief. The assumption is that clothes are a sign of disrespect in man, but nakedness a sign of disrespect in woman. The psychological reason for this distinction is probably that the displacement of exhibitionism from the body on to clothes has gone further with man than with woman. In virtue of this displacement, the wearing of a hat would be regarded as a proud piece of display on the part of man—a display that contravenes the essential elements of religious humility; whereas with woman the corresponding sign of disrespect would be the exposure of her naked head; a head-covering with her serves, it is supposed, the purposes of modesty rather than of decoration.[1]

---

[1] Jewish men do not remove their hats in the synagogue, probably because their ritual, being of more pure Semitic descent, partakes of the general Semitic unwillingness to expose the naked body. Their tradition bears witness to a lesser degree of displacement of exhibitionistic tendencies on to clothes than does that of Christianity. Therefore in the synagogue modesty is shown in both sexes by remaining covered.

The soldier also retains his head-dress, even in a Christian church. This is perhaps a little more difficult to explain. To some slight extent, perhaps, the psychology of it may be similar to that in the case of women; a military uniform is a whole, and the removal of any part of it gives the wearer an undressed, *i.e.* immodest appearance, so that the soldier without the complete uniform would be like a woman in an inadequate dress. But perhaps to a larger extent the explanation is of an opposite kind. The military uniform, with its sword and

The same general principles hold in social life. A man's ordinary greeting consists in temporarily removing a garment, the hat; a woman's in bowing the head. Similarly, when entering a friend's house, a man removes his hat, together, as a rule, with any outer garment (overcoat or cloak) he may be wearing. A woman, on the other hand, is required by convention to retain her hat and outer garments until asked to remove them. Here again the removal of garments is a sign of male respect, the retention of garments a sign of female respect; men's garments are treated as though they were used for purposes of display, women's garments as though they were used for purposes of modesty.[1]

Women's Sartorial Emancipation.—If, as seems to be the case among primitive peoples, men are more inclined to decoration and women more inclined to modesty, and if there are certain traces of the corresponding attitude still to be found in contemporary European society, we have to ask the question: what are the influences that have brought about so very different a state of affairs at the present day, in which—so far as ordinary civilian clothes are concerned—women's dress is so much more ornamental than that of men?

---

helmet, contains in an unusual degree the element of phallic symbolism which, as we have seen, belongs to so many articles of clothing. The removal of the helmet would, like the removal of the sword, constitute a painfully clear symbol of castration: too painful indeed to be tolerated, so that the soldier proudly displays his military glory even in the house of the Almighty, trusting perhaps that the righteous ends for which he is prepared to fight (in the last resort—glorification of the Father [ruler] and protection of the mother [country]—[cf. the present writer's *Psycho-analytic Study of the Family*, pp. 125 ff.]) will induce the Divine Father to take paternal pride in an exhibition in which he might otherwise have been offended.

[1] That this distinction between the sexes goes pretty deep in some directions is shown by the rather strikingly different reactions of men and women to the castration complex so far as clothes are concerned (cf. Flügel, 36). In men, castration itself is symbolised by the removal of garments, while the possession or display of the corresponding garments serves, in virtue of their phallic symbolism, as a reassurance against the fears of castration. In women who suffer from the female form of the castration complex (*i.e.* fear that the penis *has* been lost, instead of fear that it may be lost, as in the male), the corresponding reassurance seems more often to be obtained by a removal of certain garments —as if the phallic symbol lay more in the part of the body covered than in the covering itself. The desire to remove the hat at the earliest opportunity is, there is reason to believe, peculiarly diagnostic of this. Here again there is a clear indication of a greater degree of displacement from body to clothes in the male than in the female.

It would seem that in nearly all more advanced civilisations women have for long established a right to equality with men so far as decoration is concerned, though often retaining a somewhat greater modesty, as manifested in more complete covering of the body. From the fall of the Roman Empire to the end of the eighteenth century, there was little to choose between the decorativeness of the two sexes, except perhaps that, whatever style of dress was in vogue, the skirt always conferred a certain dignity that was lacking from the bifurcated nether garments of men.[1] The Church, while not disdaining display for its own purposes, has, as a rule, used its influence against the development of sartorial decoration, especially when used for purposes of allurement by women. Indeed, the Church may be said to have institutionalised the ancient tendency of men to project their sexual guilt on to women; it accepted the general application of the formula, 'the woman tempted me', and endeavoured to oppose sexuality by combating the source of temptation in feminine attractiveness. Nevertheless, the decorative element of female costume continued to increase in spite of the opposition of the Church and its doctrines.

Towards the end of the Middle Ages, a new and daring step was taken in the introduction of the first *décolleté*. Women thereby introduced the principle of the deliberate mutual reinforcement of the attractions exercised by clothes and nakedness, a principle that has, to some extent, guided women's dress ever since, and has further differentiated it from male costume. Man continued to stake all his attractiveness upon his clothing, whereas woman from now onwards possessed the double weapon of exposure and of decoration. Here we have obviously

[1] It seems a gross exaggeration to say, as Crawley does (17), that 'for the last 500 years of European civilisation decorative dress has been confined to women', though it is doubtless true that 'in the latest stage (of the development of dress) woman as a sex has not only gained freedom and the right to fascinate, previously possessed by the courtesan alone, but has also shifted the equilibrium of sex to a more permanent and efficient position. The story of woman's unconscious struggle for a monopoly of beauty in dress thus illustrates an important social movement.'

an important distinction between the sexes, one which certainly constitutes a part of the more general problem of the greater decorativeness of women at the present day, and which perhaps merits investigation before we proceed with the search for other elements in this general problem.

It is a distinction which would seem to depend upon certain ultimate differences in sexual constitution. Psychologists are pretty well agreed that among the most important of these differences is the tendency for the sexual libido to be more diffuse in women than in men; in women the whole body is sexualised, in men the libido is more definitely concentrated upon the genital zone; and this is true both subjectively and objectively, both for showing the body and for looking upon it. Hence exposure of *any* part of the female body works more erotically than exposure of the corresponding part of the male, save only in the case of the genitals themselves.[1] In view of this it is not surprising that women should be at once the more modest and the more exhibitionistic sex, since both their shame and their attractiveness relate to the whole body. It is perhaps also not surprising that they should have more difficulty in a complete sublimation of exhibitionism from body to clothes. Male libido, more definitely concentrated on the

[1] A subtle but important exception must be noted. The phallus being (erotically) the most important part of man, there is a tendency for the whole body to become the symbol of the phallus (the symbolism of the 'little man', etc. Cf. Ernest Jones' *Papers on Psycho-Analysis*, 2nd ed. pp. 135 ff.). The formation of this symbolism is perhaps helped by the phallic significance of many of the individual garments that cover the body. At any rate, in virtue of this symbolism, any unusual exposure of the male body may be unconsciously looked upon as equivalent to exposure of the phallus, and arouse an affect that would be more appropriate to the latter. In comparison with this, exposure of the female body may seem relatively harmless.

Women, however, have suffered a somewhat corresponding disadvantage in the past—in this case physiological as much as anatomical. The fear and disgust of menstruation, so widespread, especially among primitive communities, has made the female body subject to vast numbers of superstitions and taboos, and has undoubtedly contributed immensely to the immodesty associated with its exposure (cf. Daly, 19). On the anatomical side, also, women suffer from having two highly sexualised (and therefore highly unrespectable) zones instead of one. The conventional insistence on concealment of the breasts is a great difficulty in the way of the fuller exposure of woman's body, as can be readily seen by a visit to almost any bathing-beach. Possibly the next stage in the fight for women's emancipation may be connected with this very matter.

phallus, can more easily find, in various ornaments and garments, a symbolic substitute for this one organ; it is more difficult to symbolise, in a similar way, the whole body ; even though it be entirely covered, there must remain some consciousness of the real flesh underneath the vestments. Hence perhaps the main reason why, in women, the displacement of exhibitionism on to clothes is less complete, and why there is always a greater readiness to combine displaced exhibitionism with actual exposure, as in the *décolleté*.

Female Exposure and the Charge of Immodesty.—If, on the one hand, it is more difficult for woman completely to sublimate her exhibitionism on to clothes, it is also, for much the same reason, easier for her to tolerate a certain amount of erotic exposure and to harmonise it with her sexual morality. Her sexuality, being more diffused, can more easily escape recognition as such, and it is doubtless possible in some cases for women to exercise a good deal of sexual attraction in this way without conscious realisation of the fact. Even in so far as a sexual motive is acknowledged, it may still appear to be a relatively harmless and permissible one, because the skin-muscle erotism and the exhibitionistic impulses (which are the chief components involved) are, to a considerable extent, satisfying in themselves, and do not press forward with any irresistible urgency towards a genital goal; whereas in man, with his more concentrated sexual organisation, the ultimate genital aim of the whole sexual process is usually nearer to consciousness. In witnessing female exposure, man is often more acutely conscious than woman herself of its sexual intention; moreover, he cannot consider the exposure to be 'harmless', since it seems to him a direct incitement to more definitely sexual conduct. Now, as it is against genital sexuality rather than against the more exhibitionistic and auto-erotic elements that the chief inhibitions in both sexes are directed, these inhibitions are more readily put into action when the participation of the genital elements is realised; hence, in man, who more readily apprehends this genital participation, there is apt to be a greater inhibition of the sexually arousing display than in women. Men may, therefore (rightly from their own standpoint), accuse women of being immodest; and women (also rightly from theirs) may reply, either that sexuality was seen where none was present (*i.e.* consciously recognised), or that they—the women—have a more 'natural' and 'healthy' attitude to the body (*i.e.* that they can enjoy the pleasures of exposure without apprehending or intending any concomitant genital desire).[1]

Both sexes have some right upon their side in this dispute. On the one hand, the men have a clearer view of the ultimate biological end of all sexuality, including the decorations and exposures of female dress. On the other hand, the women are undoubtedly right in implying that there is a certain reciprocity between genital sexuality and those other 'component instincts' (to use again the psycho-analytical term) which are more especially operative in the relatively harmless pleasures of exposure. The women's argument about their own 'natural' and 'healthy' attitude is very much the same as that used by the supporters of 'nude culture', who are never tired of maintaining that nakedness tends powerfully to diminish 'sexuality' (*i.e.* the more directly genital impulses of sexuality). The—by now extensive—experience of the 'Friends of Nature' would seem to show that this contention is correct, the chief reason probably being that the increased pleasures of exhibitionism and of skin and muscle erotism have drained off a certain quantity of sexual energy which might otherwise have taken a purely genital channel.

Women have also attempted another line of defence against the male charge of immodesty; they have said that, if their own sex is immodest, it is only because men have made them so; it is only in response to an insistent

---

[1] Recently in a number of students' discussion circles, this difference of attitude between the sexes actually led to what has been described by those present as a 'sex war'.

male demand that women consent (as they pretend, reluctantly) to expose their persons. The charge of immodesty is admitted, but the real guilt is thrown back upon the other sex. This is indeed a reversal of rôles; it means that woman is refusing to accept the part of the guilty temptress which man, in the endeavour to protect his own sex guilt, is ever ready to thrust upon her. It is one sign, among others, of women's objection to play the traditional scapegoat. In so far as it pierces the pretence involved in the male projection of guilt, this tendency helps to a clearer view of the situation; it is, of course, true that female exposure would have little point or meaning but for man's response thereto. But, while clarifying from this standpoint, the tendency in question only confuses the issue in another direction. For, if it correctly diagnoses the presence of masculine desire, it incorrectly endeavours to hide the presence of a corresponding feminine wish to excite and 'play up' to this desire, and only substitutes one projection for another; in virtue of this tendency, women endeavour to project their own guilt on to men, in much the same way as men have, in the past, projected theirs on to women. According to such information as I have been able to gather, this line of defence is mostly adopted by women who, in virtue of inferior personal attractiveness, are likely, themselves, to receive less than the usual amount of male attention. This itself is of interest because it indicates that this particular projection is probably only an instance of a more general tendency to the projection of sex desire by sexually unsatisfied women (such as is seen, for example, in a clearer and more pathological form, in the sexual delusions of 'old maids').

The Great Masculine Renunciation and its Causes.—If, from the point of view of sex differences in clothes, women gained a great victory in the adoption of the principle of erotic exposure, men may be said to have suffered a great defeat in the sudden reduction of male sartorial decorativeness which took place at the end of the eighteenth century. At about that time there occurred one of the most remarkable events in the whole history of dress, one under the influence of which we are still living, one, moreover, which has attracted far less attention than it deserves: men gave up their right to all the brighter, gayer, more elaborate, and more varied forms of ornamentation, leaving these entirely to the use of women, and thereby making their own tailoring the most austere and ascetic of the arts. Sartorially, this event has surely the right to be considered as 'The Great Masculine Renunciation'. Man abandoned his claim to be considered beautiful. He henceforth aimed at being only useful. So far as clothes remained of importance to him, his utmost endeavours could lie only in the direction of being 'correctly' attired, not of being elegantly or elaborately attired. Hitherto man had vied with woman in the splendour of his garments, woman's only prerogative lying in *décolleté* and other forms of erotic display of the actual body; henceforward, to the present day, woman was to enjoy the privilege of being the only possessor of beauty and magnificence, even in the purely sartorial sense.

What were the causes of this Great Renunciation? Those who have duly considered the matter seem to be in the main agreed that these causes were primarily of a political and social nature, and that, in their origin, they were intimately associated with the great social upheaval of the French Revolution. One of the purposes of decorative dress was, as we saw in Chapter II., to emphasise distinctions of rank and wealth—distinctions which, in the fifteenth, sixteenth, and seventeenth centuries, the aristocracy had often endeavoured to preserve by means of special sumptuary laws. But distinctions of this kind were among the chief of those that the French Revolution, with its world-echoing slogan of 'Liberty, Equality, Fraternity', aimed at abolishing. It is not surprising, therefore, that the magnificence and elaboration of costume, which so well expressed the ideals of the *ancien régime* should have been distasteful to the new social tendencies and aspirations that found expression in the Revolution.

There were, in particular, two ways in which these new aspirations tended to produce a simplification in the dress of the male sex. In the first place, the doctrine of the brotherhood of man was obviously incompatible with garments which, by their very nature and associations, emphasised the differences in wealth and station between one man and another. The new social order demanded something that expressed rather the common humanity of all men. This could only be done by means of a greater **uniformity** of dress, a uniformity achieved particularly by the abolition of those distinctions which had formerly divided the wealthy from the poor, the exalted from the humble; since these distinctions consisted largely in a greater elaboration and costliness of aristocratic costume as compared with that of the lower classes, the change in question implied at the same time a greater **simplification** of dress, by a general approximation to more plebeian standards that were possible to all. This tendency to greater simplification was powerfully reinforced by a second aspect of the general change of ideals which the Revolution implied—by the fact that the ideal of work had now become respectable. Formerly, all work connected with economic activities of any kind —the production or distribution of useful commodities —was considered degrading to the dignity of those classes who chiefly set the fashion. There were relatively few activities—the practice of arms, together with that of political or amorous intrigue, being perhaps the most important—that were considered worthy of a gentleman. The really significant moments of life were those that were passed on the field of battle or in the drawing-room, for both of which tradition had decreed a costly and elegant attire. With the new ideals of the Revolution (ideals which, in the main, became more and more consolidated as the nineteenth century progressed) a man's most important activities were passed, not in the drawing-room, but in the workshop, the counting-house, the office—places which had, by long tradition, been associated with a relatively simple costume. As commercial and industrial ideals conquered class after class, until they finally became accepted even by the aristocracies of all the more progressive countries, the plain and uniform costume associated with such ideals has, more and more, ousted the gorgeous and varied garments associated with the older order, until now it is only in such archaic features of social life as are represented by Court ceremonies, that anything resembling the former brilliance and variety is to be seen. The process of democratisation in clothes is one that is still going on. The most advanced countries, so far as political and social conditions are concerned, exhibit, on the whole, the greatest uniformity and consistency; in these countries there are the smallest sartorial distinctions between class and class, and, such as they are, these distinctions seem about to disappear.

If the causes that have produced the very remarkable change here in question may be conveniently considered as primarily social, it is of course true that such a change can only have been brought about by the operation of very powerful psychical inhibitions. It is, indeed, safe to say that, in sartorial matters, modern man has a far sterner and more rigid conscience than has modern woman, and that man's morality tends to find expression in his clothes in a greater degree than is the case with woman. Hence it is not surprising that, as we saw in Chapter V., modern man's clothing abounds in features which symbolise his devotion to the principles of duty, of renunciation, and of self-control. The whole relatively 'fixed' (cf. Chapter VIII.) system of his clothing is, in fact, an outward and visible sign of the strictness of his adherence to the social code (though at the same time, through its phallic attributes, it symbolises the most fundamental features of his sexual nature).

Social Nature of the Sex Differentiation Implied.— The world has undoubtedly become aesthetically the poorer for this change, as the result of which brightness and contrast have been replaced by drabness and similarity; but there can be little doubt that the drastic reduction of the decorative element in male costume has really, to some extent, achieved its aim. Greater uniformity of costume has really been accompanied by greater sympathy between one individual and another, and between one class and another; not so much, it would appear, because the wearing of the same general style of clothes in itself produces a sense of community (this is strongly marked only in cases where a particular costume or uniform distinguishes a particular body of persons from the population as a whole—as with a military uniform), but because it removes certain socially disintegrating factors that are liable to be produced by differences in clothes. How severe these disrupting influences may be can be readily seen by comparing woman's and men's clothes at the present day. Take any ordinary social function. The men are dressed in a dull uniformity of black and white, 'the very embodiment of life's prose', as one writer has it (though this same sombre costume is not without its admirers). But if there is a lack of romance, there is also absent the envy, the jealousy, the petty triumphs, defeats, superiorities, and spitefulnesses engendered by the—doubtless more poetical—diversity and gaiety of the women's costumes. One woman can seriously hurt another, even to the point of making a permanent enemy of her, by being better or more fashionably dressed upon some significant occasion. As long as individuality is permitted, women struggle with one another for wearing the 'latest' or most costly frocks. The snobbery of wealth may even take a purely quantitative form, and it may—and often does—become a point of honour to wear a different dress each day (or several different dresses each day, according to the varying occasions of morning, afternoon, and night). The more wealthy women have thus a great advantage over their poorer sisters, who can often ill afford so long a sequence of costumes. With men the superiority of this kind conferred by wealth is obviously much reduced; a man can, for instance, safely wear the same dress suit for months or years in succession. The richer man, who could afford to wear a different smoking jacket every night, would have little gain, since only the closest inspection would reveal such differences as there might be between one jacket and another.

If such be, indeed, the chief influences that have led to the abandonment of all serious attempt at the ornamental rôle by the male sex, two questions naturally present themselves to us. In the first place, why did not these influences affect women's costume in the same way as that of men? In the second place, how have men been able to bear the sacrifice that the new order has imposed upon them? What has happened to the psychological tendencies (Narcissistic, exhibitionistic, etc.) which formerly found expression in the decorative aspects of their dress? To answer these questions fully would require a deeper knowledge of certain fundamental psychological and sociological processes than we at present possess. We must content ourselves here with indicating the nature of such provisional answers as the knowledge at present available seems to justify.

With regard to the first question, we may perhaps regard the fact that the Great Renunciation was confined to one sex as a particular consequence of a more general difference between the sexes. Taking the history of humanity as a whole, there can be little doubt that men have played a greater part in social life, and have been more easily influenced by social factors, than have women. Whether we seek evidence from the secret societies of primitive peoples or the corresponding associations—political, social, or economic—of the present day, we find almost everywhere that the male sex takes a greater interest and plays a more active part in group life than does the female. Whether this is due, to some extent, to an innate greater susceptibility to group influences in the male, or whether it is entirely a consequence of the natural division of labour between the sexes and the traditions that have arisen in consequence, is a point on which we have no exact knowledge[1] and which we have fortunately no need to discuss here. But if we grant, as we surely must, the general fact of the greater sociability of men, and their greater participation in group life, it is not surprising that if social and political influences have been the chief factors in bringing about the greater uniformity and lesser decorativeness of men's clothes, these factors should have produced a lesser effect on the costume of women; such lesser effect would be only one consequence among many others of the smaller rôle of social influences in the life of women. It is interesting to note, too, that the tendencies which have undoubtedly constituted formidable obstacles to the standardisation and simplification of women's costumes on the lines adopted by men (obstacles which might conceivably have prevented the social factors having these effects on women's costume, even if these factors had been equally strong in both sexes) are those which elsewhere have proved highly antagonistic to social influences, *i.e.* Narcissism and sexual competition. Women are, perhaps by nature and certainly in virtue of our social and sexual traditions, more Narcissistic than men,[2] and these traditions have at the same time imposed upon women—in many societies at any rate—a somewhat keener sexual rivalry than among men.[3] Here, as elsewhere, a high development of social feeling may demand some sacrifice of Narcissism and of sexual jealousy; the adoption of sober clothing by men has undoubtedly meant such a sacrifice, and it would seem that the more active part now being played in social life by women may demand, and indeed is demanding, some very similar sacrifice on their part also. For there can be little doubt that women are in certain respects now following in men's footsteps, and

[1] The whole question is discussed elsewhere by the present writer, 'Sexual and Social Sentiments', *British Journal of Medical Psychology*, 1927, vol. vii. p. 139.
[2] Cf. Freud, *Collected Papers*, vol. iv. p. 44. The wearing of more distinctive and decorative clothes in its turn, of course, fosters this relatively greater Narcissism of women, so that a vicious circle is usually established.
[3] Cf. Flügel, *op. cit.* p. 155.

are themselves tending to adopt a more uniform and less decorative costume, at any rate for the working hours of life.[1]

Effects on Male Psychology.—The second of the two above-mentioned questions—the question as to how man has been able to tolerate the giving up of display—is one that is less easy to answer by simple reference to a general tendency. It is a question that has, of course, much in common with all problems concerned with the renunciation of a source of satisfaction—problems which have figured largely in the psycho-analytic studies of neuroses that have, of recent years, contributed so greatly to our understanding of all mental change and mental development. In general, it would seem that, when a satisfaction is denied, the desires connected with the satisfaction are either inhibited or displaced (*i.e.* find some other outlet); often both inhibition and displacement play a part. Such would seem to be the case with the clothes renunciation here in question. Recent investigations by the present writer[2] have corroborated the impression which may be gained from the daily press, that many members of the male sex are indeed profoundly dissatisfied with their own costume, and compare it very unfavourably with women's. It is probable, indeed, that further more intensive study would reveal deep-lying psychological difficulties and inefficiencies that are the indirect consequences of these dissatisfactions.

On the other hand, the energy that formerly expressed

---

[1] The fact that those women who have entered the active walks of life are now, on the whole, less differentiated in dress from other women than were their predecessors of, say, forty years ago, is due partly to the fact that the ideal of work is now common to far more women than it was then (in this respect women have undoubtedly approximated to men); partly to the fact that, owing to economic circumstances and to the spread of this ideal, a sexually more 'normal' type of woman is adopting work as a 'career'; partly, again, to a general change of attitude towards sex and, in particular, to a lessening of the apparent incompatibility between the ideals of work and of sex (an incompatibility the former strength of which is well brought out in Reginald Berkeley's play, *The Lady with a Lamp*, where the heroine, Florence Nightingale, conceives that the due performance of the work to which she is called demands the sternest repression of her sex life and of all hopes and ideals associated therewith.   [2] Flügel, 35.

itself in clothes has probably, to some extent, been successfully employed in other directions. A greatly increased interest in the external world has been made possible by the fact that work in many new forms has, during the last 130 years, become respectable to members of the fashionable world. 'Work', with all its attendant preoccupations, has thus, to some extent, ousted interest in 'showing off'. But it is also possible to point to changes more intimately connected with the exhibitionistic love of self-display. Although we are still largely ignorant of the real dynamic relations involved, we know that it is often easier to deal with a particular impulse by certain subtle modifications of object or attitude than by a change in its ultimate goal or nature. Thus we can see that, in the case of the exhibitionistic desires connected with self-display, a particularly easy form of conversion may be found in a change from (passive) exhibitionism to (active) scoptophilia (erotic pleasure in the use of vision)—the desire to be seen being transformed into the desire to see. This desire to see may itself remain unsublimated and find its appropriate satisfaction in the contemplation of the other sex, or it may be sublimated and find expression in the more general desire to see and know. It is perhaps no mere chance that a period of unexampled scientific progress should have followed the abandonment of ornamental clothing on the part of men at the beginning of the last century.

Another subtle psychological change may consist in the projection of the exhibitionistic desire on to a person of the opposite sex. A man will usually feel proud when he appears in public accompanied by a beautiful or well-dressed woman, and, although this pride is itself of complex structure, one important element certainly lies in the vicarious display which he is thus permitted (just as he may feel a vicarious shame if his companion is ill-dressed).[1] In such cases there is clearly some element of

---

[1] In certain cases this tendency may take the extreme form of a husband demonstrating the beauties of his wife's naked body to his friends, as in the classical story of Candaules and Gyges, as told by Herodotus (i. 10). Sadger (82)

identification with the woman. That there should be such a tendency to identification is not surprising. We incline in general to identify ourselves with such persons as we admire or envy, and it is natural that men with strong exhibitionistic desires should, vicariously as it were, admire women and at the same time envy them their opportunity for bodily and sartorial display. The identification in question may be one in which the projection of the exhibitionistic desire on to the woman is complete. In other cases, however, the projection is only partial, and here the man may consciously seek to identify himself with a woman by wearing feminine attire. This latter desire may itself vary from a slight affectation of 'effeminacy' to the full adoption of women's dress in all its details.

Eonism.—This last consideration has brought us to the phenomena of transvestitism, or Eonism, as Havelock Ellis has recently called it, after the Chevalier d'Eon de Beaumont,[1] a striking eighteenth-century example of this anomaly. As is well known, a certain proportion of individuals of both sexes desire to wear (and often do wear) the full or partial costume of the opposite sex. This desire (as is also well known) has an intimate relation to homosexuality, but the relation is not in every case a simple one; complete Eonism, for instance, does not necessarily coincide with active homosexuality, or even with a tendency towards the physical characteristics of the opposite sex. Hercules himself, as the myth tells us, spent some time dressed as a woman, and—as the writer has been informed by a most reliable authority—a well-known modern athlete of Herculean build has done the same. This is a tendency of much psychological interest and is indeed worthy of a volume to itself. But as, unlike most of the other matters treated in

---

is of opinion that in such cases there is usually a repressed homosexual component, the husband only exhibiting his wife (in words or in deed) to men towards whom he feels a personal attachment.

[1] Whose portrait (in female attire), painted by Sir Joshua Reynolds, is to be seen in the Kaiser Friedrich Museum in Berlin.

this chapter, it has been made the subject of considerable specialistic research, we shall not dwell upon it here. Probably Havelock Ellis is right in considering that the Eonist presents an example of extreme development in a certain direction, of tendencies to identification that play some part in every normal sexual life. Every lover must to some extent 'enter into' and sympathise with his sexual object, and to that extent identify himself with it. To the Eonist this identification is of abnormal importance, and he achieves it by clothing himself in the dress associated with his object, a process which has something akin to aesthetic 'empathy'.[1]

Closer psychological study will, no doubt, reveal in more intimate detail the nature of the process of identification here at work. Psycho-analytic studies, so far as they have yet been devoted to this subject, show, for instance, that here, as elsewhere, the phallic symbolism of clothes is of great importance. Thus, in a communication to the International Psycho-Analytical Congress in July 1929, Dr. Fenichel suggested that there were two chief stages in the psychological development of the male Eonist: (1) an unconscious refusal to accept the lack of the penis in women, (2) an unconscious identification of the self with the imaginary penis-possessing woman.

Turning to anthropological evidence, we find that temporary or permanent dressing in the garments of the opposite sex may be indulged in for other than directly sexual purposes. In every case there is probably the desire for some kind of identification with the opposite sex, but the specific and superficial reason for this desire may vary greatly.[2] In some cases the change may magically symbolise some other desired change, often of an apparently quite unconnected character—*e.g.* in the

[1] Havelock Ellis, *Eonism and other Studies*, ch. i.
[2] Cf. Crawley, *The Mystic Rose*, and (17). In a private communication, Mr. Geoffrey H. White, who has made a special study of boys' clothes, enumerates no less than twenty-eight superficial reasons why boys have at various times and places been dressed as girls. He rightly insists upon the desirability of a more systematic investigation of the psychological causes and effects of such juvenile transvestitism than has yet been made.

weather; in other cases the direct transfer to one sex of some experience or characteristic of the other may be the end in view, as when in the couvade the magical transference of labour pains from the mother to the father is helped by some exchange of garments, or when young male initiates are dressed as girls, or captured soldiers dressed as women—the motive in the last two cases being pretty clearly connected with the ideas of deprivation of virility that are associated with the castration complex.[1] This same complex is probably active too in the desire to deceive demons or fairies by exchange of dress; if a boy or man already appears as a woman, he will escape the threatened unmanning. Finally, the exchange of dress may be only a particular example of the general exchange of rôles (*e.g.* between master and servant and slave and free-man) that characterises special holidays. As such it probably serves much the same purpose as a mask or disguise in relieving the wearer from the duties and responsibilities of everyday life. Indeed, this whole subject of the motives and effects of the exchange of dress is one which, in spite of some study, is clearly capable of rendering further rich harvests to the anthropological and psychological investigator.

[1] Cf. too the curious custom of dressing as girls the young boys of the island of Marken, in Holland, a custom which Jelgersma (51) considers was due to the desire of the fathers to be free of male rivals while they were themselves away fishing. White, however (104), combats this view, and considers that this and certain other isolated instances of a similar character are merely relics of a once more general habit of dressing boys as girls.

CHAPTER VIII

TYPES OF DRESS

I will clothe thee with change of raiment.
Zechariah iii. 4.

HITHERTO (except for a few incidental considerations, mostly in the last chapter) we have dealt with dress from what might be termed the static point of view; we have taken it as it existed at any given moment, and examined its causes, nature, and effects, the needs to which it ministers, the satisfaction that it brings, and, generally, the factors in the human mind to which it corresponds. We must now adopt a more dynamic or evolutionary standpoint, and turn our attention to the changes and developments of clothing. In approaching this vast theme it is well to bear in mind the limitations of our own present modest undertaking. It is not our business here to examine in detail the history of dress; so far as historical considerations go, we must be content with the briefest and vaguest outlines of certain general principles and of such specific examples as may be necessary to illustrate them. We are, strictly speaking, here concerned only with the mental causes and effects of the changes that human covering has undergone; and such historical background as we shall present will be only that which appears necessary in order to envisage correctly the more distinctly psychological problem of sartorial evolution.

In contemplating the whole dazzling gamut of dress throughout the ages and the climes, it is natural in the first place to make certain major classifications, with the help of which we may hope to reduce the vast array of different styles of costume to some kind of order. Of the various systems of classification that have been proposed, we will deal with two only, as being perhaps the most useful and illuminating for our present purpose.

Fig. 14. The beginning of costume

From C. H. Stratz, *Die Fraunkleidung* (by permission of Herrn Ferdinand Enke)

The first system—one which has been adopted by a number of authors and has therefore made its mark upon the literature—is that which we owe to Stratz,[1] who divides all human costume into three main classes, which he calls respectively the primitive, the tropical, and the arctic. This is a classification which depends upon the nature (and in particular the extent and form) of the clothes themselves. It might be said to be in the strict sense a sartorial classification. Our second classification we will adopt (with a modification) from Müller-Lyer. It is one for which there is as yet no quite satisfactory or recognised terminology. It divides all dress into two classes, for which we may propose the terms 'fixed' and 'modish' (or 'fashionable') costume.[2] It is essentially a sociological classification, and relates not so much to the nature of the clothes themselves as to their psychological, historical, and social implications.

Let us deal first with the 'sartorial' classification into primitive, tropical, and arctic costumes. The essential feature of **primitive** costume is that the only, or at any rate the most important, covering or ornament is placed about the loins. The most characteristic garment (if it can be called such) consists of a ring worn round the hips—a form of adornment which may be found among very many primitive peoples, and which has even in some cases persisted in relatively high cultures; it is depicted, for instance, in certain bronze figures of female dancers in ancient Egypt.[3] The low female waistline of recent years (though of course complicated by

---

[1] H. Stratz, 93.
[2] F. Müller-Lyer, 67. Müller-Lyer himself proposes three classes—'natural,' 'national', and 'modish'. We have modified this system because: (1) It appears to partake of the nature of cross classification. The 'natural' category is distinguished from the others by the fact that the clothing in question is formed of simple natural products, such as fat, oil, leaves, skin, grass, flowers, or the bark of trees. Such a category would be more logically distinguished from the 'artificial', in which natural products are treated by some special process before being worn (a dual classification which is, of course, of great importance from the point of view of cultural anthropology). (2) The 'national' seems to be so closely allied to certain other kinds of costume that it may conveniently give way to a wider class with a broader designation. Hence the substitution of the new term 'fixed', a term which seems to apply to all costumes belonging to this wider class, whether 'national' or otherwise. [3] Stratz, 93, p. 114.

factors not present in the more exiguous primitive costume) may too in some ways be looked upon as a return to the aesthetic standard implied in this earliest stage of human dress.

The hip band is sometimes worn alone, though it is usually supplemented in one or both of two directions: (1) the wearing of rings or other forms of 'circular' decoration on other parts of the body, particularly the arms, the legs, and the neck; (2) the addition of some material which is made to hang from the hip ring itself. This material may be at first almost vanishingly small in quantity (see, for example, Fig. 14); so small indeed that, though usually placed in front and near the genitals, it cannot possibly be credited with the function of concealing these organs (another argument in favour of the view that decoration is more primitive than modesty). Nevertheless, it is from this scanty appendage to the hip ring that clothing itself, in the narrower sense of covering, as distinguished from mere ornamentation, seems to have had its origin. In its further development this appendage grows bigger, extending sometimes from the front right round the body, sometimes becoming elongated so that it may reach almost to the knees (cf. Fig. 9). It then becomes something in the nature of an apron. In the simpler forms of primitive costume, natural materials alone are used, for the most part flowers and leaves. Such floral decoration can be very tasteful (cf. Fig. 15), though its individual constituents have of course to be constantly renewed. At a higher level of sartorial development, more permanent artificial garments may be prepared from bark, cotton, flax, or leather. This implies the arts of plaiting, weaving, and of treating skins. It would seem as though animal substances are in the beginning more often used by men (probably in their capacity as hunters) than by women; women, on their part, tend to make greater use of floral ornamentation—a sex distinction which has been maintained until the present day, and which probably to some extent depends upon the deep-lying psychological

Fig. 15. 'Primitive' costume from Samoa, showing circular floral decoration and necklace of white whale's teeth

From E. Selenka, *Der Schmuck des Menschen* (by permission of Vita Deutsches Verlagshaus)

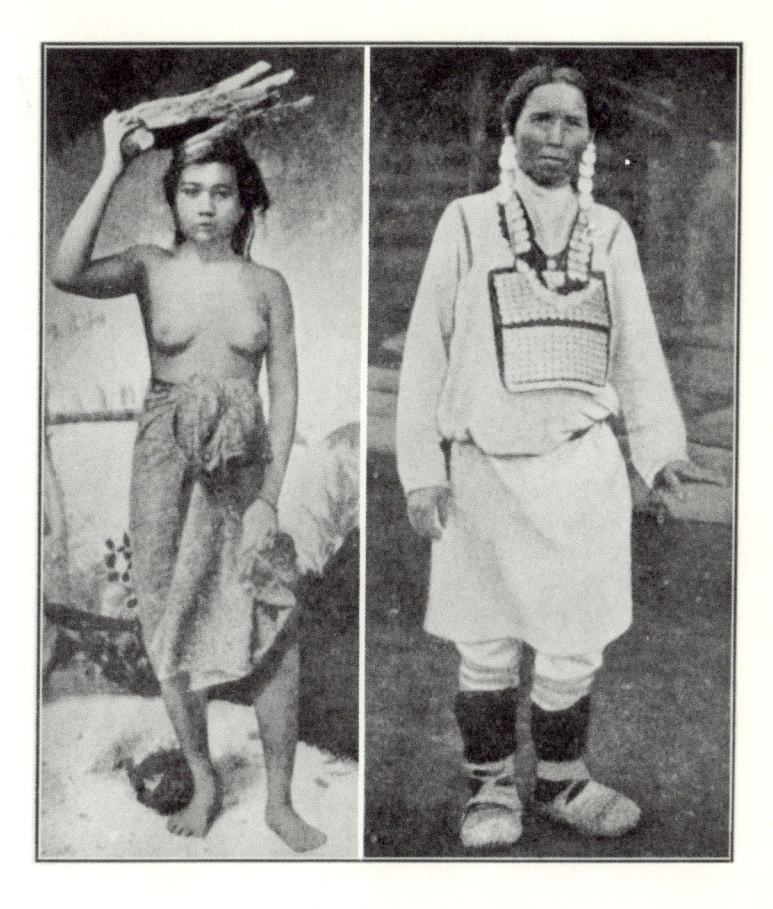

Fig.16. Typical forms of (a) 'Tropical' and (b) 'Arctic' costume from Java and Siberia respectively

From C. H. Stratz, *Die Frauenkleidung* (by permission of Herrn Ferdinand Enke)

identification of flowers and womanhood (as exemplified by the fact that women—but not men—often bear the names of flowers, that we frequently present flowers to women, and but seldom and in the smallest quantities to men, that we talk of the physiological process of 'defloration', etc.). Although (in all but the modern world of fashion) men are sartorially more progressive than women, primitive costume is still occasionally used by men in some places for certain definite purposes, mostly of an occupational character. Thus a loin cloth is sometimes the only garment of workmen in Japan, China, India, and even parts of Egypt, where women—whatever their occupation—are as a rule more amply clad. The reason for this distinction is probably to be found in the greater diffusion of the erotic value of the female body (a matter which we discussed in the last chapter) and the consequent greater, or at least more diffused, modesty of women.[1] We may note that primitive costume as worn habitually by both sexes is practically confined to dark skin races enjoying a relatively simple form of culture.

The transition from primitive to **tropical** costume comes about through the increase in size of the garments originally suspended from the hip ring. The loin cloth or apron then becomes a skirt, which is indeed the characteristic and essential garment of tropical costume. When the material of the skirt becomes sufficiently extensive to have an appreciable weight, it necessitates the raising of the hip ring to a higher portion of the body, from which the weight can be more securely suspended; the hip ring thus gives place to a waist ring or girdle. A typical example of the simplest form of tropical costume is shown in Fig. 16. In this form it consists of nothing but a skirt and perhaps a girdle. In its further elaboration it may be supplemented by some light

---

[1] It will perhaps help us to appreciate the difference in question if we remember that, in the last century in England, men were permitted to enter the sea in bathing-drawers at a time when women wore bathing-dresses of a most voluminous character, which covered almost the whole of the trunk and a considerable portion of the limbs.

covering on the upper part of the body, or the skirt itself may be raised so as to cover the chest; but the garments themselves usually remain loose and light, and are not closely moulded to the form (except in so far as the girdle may increase in size and gradually develop into a corset, bolero, or jacket).

Tropical costume is, for the most part, made from vegetable rather than from animal products, and is associated with the further development of the art of weaving. It is worn in very many of the warmer parts of the world and, in its more complicated developments, forms the basis of the costumes of many higher peoples, particularly those of India. Its greatest sociological and anthropological importance, however, is connected with the fact that from it is derived the clothing of European women—and hence of Europeanised womanhood throughout the world. Western female attire is of course greatly complicated in comparison with the simpler forms of tropical costume; in particular by the addition of garments covering the upper portion of the body, garments that are in some cases tightly fitting. Nevertheless, historical considerations, which show that women's modern dress has undergone no fundamental change of principle from the early classical forms (which themselves clearly belong to the tropical group), together with certain present details of this dress, permit us to regard it as essentially tropical in its origin and nature. Among these modern details, the most important is the very general tendency to lighter and less complete covering of the upper body among women as compared with men. The tendency, so constantly recurring during the last few hundred years, to bare the bosom and some portion of the back and arms, may be said to represent a return to the true spirit of tropical costume. This tendency, the psychological aspects of which were dealt with in the last chapter, is here seen in its historical and anthropological background. Another feature of women's costume which points in the same direction is the lesser strength, thickness, weight, and amplitude of their foot-covering as compared with men's; for elaborately protective boots and shoes are associated with arctic rather than with tropical costume.

The peculiar feature of **arctic** costume is that the garments fit tightly to the body and cover it more or less entirely. This involves a departure from the principle implied in the skirt, which, by its very nature, is incapable of fitting closely to the lower limbs. If these limbs are to be securely encased, bifurcated garments are essential; hence the development of trousers. Both in its origin and in its further history, arctic costume seems to be associated especially with the Mongolian race. This may well be, as Stratz suggests, because the early home of that race being northward of the Himalayas, expansion to the south was blocked by that most formidable of natural barriers, so that migrations were of necessity towards the north. As already indicated, there is evidence that warm clothing is not essential to man's existence, even in quite cold climates; but physiology shows clearly that, to say nothing of their comfort, clothes have an economic function in diminishing the heat loss to be made good by food. Hunger, it has been said, is not only the best cook, but the best tailor and the best shoemaker besides; and it may well have been that those people who reduced their need for food by more amply covering their skins, achieved a very great advantage in the struggle for existence in the colder parts of northern Asia and Europe. The most efficient way of diminishing heat loss is to cover the body closely. Loosely hanging garments, however thick, are of comparatively little use for such a purpose. In this way was born the tailor's art; sleeves, trousers, and hats (as distinct from merely ornamental head-dress) came into existence, and, at the same time, the trunk itself became more snugly fitted.[1] As long as no effort was made to enclose the body tightly and completely, tailoring, in the strict sense (as understood in Savile Row)

[1] According to another classification, which we shall not treat in detail here, clothing at this point from being *gravitational* became *anatomic*.

was not required, but, with the development of arctic costume, clothes had to be accurately fitted to the body, if the body was to be completely protected and at the same time retain reasonable freedom of movement. Hence the emigration to a colder climate would seem to have led to a greatly increased skill in the preparation and fitting of clothes. It also led to a change of material, for in colder places vegetable fibres are both less suitable and less easily obtained than in the tropics. The skins and furs of animals thus became the essential elements of dress, and the arts of preparing them for clothing were developed as necessary preliminaries to the work of the tailor himself.

If, as the name implies, arctic costume owes its origin to the influence of northern cold, it is in its extent by no means actually confined to colder climates. With the exception of Japan, it is almost universally characteristic of the Mongol race, for both sexes and in all parts of the world.[1] It is also found among those Semitic races which have been subject to the influence of more northernly populations; for, as is well known, trousers form an important element in the costume of many Mohammedan women (though in some Islamic peoples these are replaced by the tropical skirt). The most important triumph of arctic costume, however, has been with European men, with whom it has ruled almost continually and universally from the fall of classical civilisation to the present day. With the exception of kilts (such as those of Scotland and Greece and a few lesser-known varieties), of special ceremonial robes (doubtless owing to the superior impressiveness of the skirt), and of clerical and monkish garb (probably as indicative of a renunciation of the symbols of virility), for the last 1400 years or more the European male dress has contained nether garments of a bifurcated type, each leg being separately encased in a covering of its own.

---

[1] According to Stratz (93, p. 256), trousers are worn as a workaday garment by women in Europe just in those parts where ethnographers are in doubt as to whether the racial elements are of purely white origin.

Historically this characteristic feature of western male attire seems to have been brought into our civilisation, on the one hand, by the northern invaders who broke up the Roman Empire, on the other hand, from the peoples of the East. With the overthrow of the Empire there was a strong movement in favour of the general adoption of the thicker and more close-fitting costume appropriate to the colder climate from which the conquerors came, and this movement was reinforced by Christian asceticism, which regarded with disapproval the exposure of the body incidental to the loose costume of classical times. Women in Europe seem nearly always to have had their legs more or less covered, so that, in their case, increased general clothing of the body brought no need for a revolution in the essential lines of their costume, such as that which happened in the case of male dress.

Corresponding to this most characteristic feature of arctic costume, the bifurcated nether garment, the other parts of European male clothing are likewise constructed on arctic principles, as is shown in the use of thicker and stiffer materials (both for outer and inner garments) more complete and constant covering of all parts, including neck and arms, together with heavier and more solid footwear. Once again, as in the case of the predominantly tropical clothing of women, we can here view from the historical side what we have already studied from the different standpoint of psychology.

Let us now examine the second, and more sociological, classification of clothing into the **'fixed'** and **'modish'** (or 'fashionable') types. The distinctions here implied are not so much matters of race, sex, or cultural development, but depend rather on certain differences of social organisation. In their actual manifestations, the differences between the two types become most clearly apparent in the opposite relations which they have to space and time. 'Fixed' costume changes slowly in time, and its whole value depends, to some extent, upon its permanence; but it varies greatly in space, a special kind of dress tending to be associated with each locality and with each separate social body (and indeed with every well-defined grade within each body). 'Modish' costume, on the other hand, changes very rapidly in time, this rapidity of change belonging to its very essence; but it varies comparatively little in space, tending to spread rapidly over all parts of the world which are subject to the same cultural influences and between which there exist adequate means of communication. It is this latter type of costume which predominates in the western world to-day, and which indeed (with certain important exceptions) has predominated there for several centuries; a fact that must be regarded as one of the most characteristic features of modern European civilisation, since, in other civilisations, both of the past and of the present, fashion seems to have played a very much more modest rôle than with ourselves. Outside the sphere of western influence, dress changes much more slowly, is more closely connected with racial and local circumstances, or with social or occupational standing—it exhibits, that is, to a much greater degree, all the distinguishing features of the 'fixed' type.

Within this sphere, however, the exceptions to which we referred reveal also the essential characteristics of 'fixed' clothing, and thus serve to define these characteristics very clearly by bringing them into sharp contrast with those of the co-existing and predominating 'modish' type. The exceptions in question seem to fall into two main groups, each of which can be subdivided into three further groups as follows:

Geographical costumes . { National. Local. Family.

Uniforms . . . { Military. Occupational. Associational.

In the geographical costumes it is the topographical rather than the social element that is important. Tradition has associated certain costumes with certain races or with certain countries. Within each **racial** or **national** group (which, as a rule, presents some essential common element distinguishing it from other groups) there are minor variations corresponding to particular localities. Thus there are essential differences which enable us to distinguish almost at a glance between the 'national' costumes, say of Sweden, of Holland, and of Switzerland. But within each of these larger groups there are numerous minor variations corresponding to different **localities,** differences which in some cases (*e.g.* in Sweden) may be so closely associated with a given area as to distinguish two adjoining villages. In other cases the differences may distinguish **families or clans,** as with the Scottish tartans, although, in such instances, there are usually present certain secondary local associations also.

In the group of **uniforms** the **military** (which for our purpose must include the naval) stand out, both because of their unique social and historic importance and also from the fact that they exhibit an extreme development of the hierarchic features of dress. Not only are differences of nationality and differences of locality (these latter corresponding in general to particular regiments) indicated by distinctive differences of uniform, but within each group distinctions of rank are very clearly indicated, generally according to the primitive method of marking each successive rank, from below upwards, by an increase in the decorativeness of the corresponding costume.

Were it not for their altogether exceptional significance, the military should perhaps be regarded as constituting only a particular sub-group of the occupational uniforms, for fighting is only one particular kind of professional activity among many others. Indeed, there are certain kinds of **occupational** costume which exhibit a hierarchical development only second in complexity to that of the military group—such, for instance, as the ecclesiastical or the academic. In fact, throughout the occupational group there tends to be some indication of rank by distinction of sartorial detail, though these distinctions do not so regularly take the form of quantitative differences of decoration (*e.g.* the uniform of the matron or police inspector is scarcely more elaborate or ornamental than that of the ordinary hospital nurse or constable).

Associational costumes are those which distinguish special societies formed for private ends within the larger social groups. As already indicated in an earlier chapter, such costumes are to be found among peoples of all degrees of culture, and they play an important part in many of the secret societies of primitive peoples. Among the corresponding modern societies distinguished by special uniforms, we think naturally of the Freemasons and the Ku-Klux-Klan. In many instances, however, associational insignia take the form of special garments or of local decorations rather than of complete costumes. In masculine attire the tie, which so often indicates the wearer's school, college, or sporting club, is especially important in this connection. In these latter cases there is, as a rule, no attempt at any hierarchical significance, the associations themselves being, for the most part, democratic in nature, so far at least as their official organisation goes. There may, however, be some special form of ornamentation to indicate particular abilities or distinctions, *e.g.* the club initials on the blazer, the 'blue's' tie, the boy scouts' and the girl guides' badges—if we include the last two under the associational group.

In all these 'fixed' costumes—both of the 'geographical' and of the 'uniform' kind—we find the three important elements of relative permanence in time, characterisation of a special group of persons with common social or topographical associations, and of uniformity from one individual to another (so long as the individuals fall within the same hierarchical sub-groups, where such exist). In all these points, the 'fixed' costumes are clearly differentiated from the 'modish' costumes which are simultaneously in use. As regards permanence in time, it is evident, for instance, that the value of a 'national' costume or of a military uniform depends largely upon the fact that it is closely associated with the past history and traditions of the people or regiment concerned. Any innovation is unwelcome, since it seems to constitute a break with these traditions; as is shown by the unwillingness with which a long-established military uniform, however unpractical, is abandoned, even under the stress of modern war. In this matter the psychology of 'fixed' costumes is exactly the opposite of that of 'modish' costumes, whose value lies mostly in their newness, and which are despised at the slightest sign of their becoming 'old-fashioned' or 'out of date'. As regards the second point—the characterisation of a special group of persons—it is evident again that all the various kinds of 'fixed' costume that we have considered have a special (and often valuable) social significance, inasmuch as they indicate membership of a group, and are, in a way, symbolic of the feelings, sentiments, and interests that unite the group; to wear them is a special privilege, which is jealously guarded, and the infringement of which is seldom attempted, or, if attempted, much resented.[1] In this too, 'fixed' costume differs radically from 'modish' costume, where there are no definite distinctions of class or group or nationality, and where imitation is the rule. As to the third point—uniformity between individuals of the same sub-group—here again the value of the 'fixed' costumes described is felt to depend largely upon there being no individual differences

---

[1] The importance attached to particular features of dress that have become symbolic of special social privileges and respect can often be well seen in school life. In the absence of definite uniforms or other hierarchical costumes, items of what is elsewhere 'modish' dress are apt to be treated as 'fixed' dress, to which only certain members of the community are entitled. The following passage from Robert Graves' *Good-Bye to All That*, amusingly illustrates this tendency: 'The social code of Charterhouse was based on a very strict caste system: the caste marks were slight distinctions in dress. A new boy had no privileges at all; a boy in his second term might wear a knitted tie instead of a plain one; a boy in his second year might wear coloured socks; third year gave most of the privileges—turn-down collars, coloured handkerchiefs, a coat with a long roll, and so on; fourth year a few more; . . . but very peculiar and unique distinctions were reserved for the bloods. These included light grey flannel trousers, butterfly collars, coats slit up the back, and the privilege of walking arm in arm' (p. 72). He goes on to describe the deliberate infringement of this convention by three six-formers, who 'slowly walked up the aisle (of the school chapel), magnificent in grey flannel trousers, slit coats, First Eleven collars, and with pink carnations in their buttonholes'. 'It is', he says, 'impossible to describe the astonishment and terror that this spectacle caused.'

whatever, except such as may be necessary to fit the varying shapes and sizes of the members of the group. A 'national' costume, if it is worn at all, must be correct in every detail; if, through ignorance (as sometimes happens at a fancy dress ball, when it is worn by those who have but a superficial acquaintance with its technicalities), some individual modification is introduced, this is felt, by those who know the costume better, to be something of an insult to the social group concerned—of much the same kind as when, for instance, the Union Jack is flown upside-down—and the wearer is condemned as lacking in knowledge or politeness, instead of being admired, as he might well be if he introduced some slight innovation into fashionable costume. The same applies to such isolated local decorations as the club or college tie, as distinguished from the tie that is merely fashionable and which has no special group associations. This is even more the case with military uniforms; it is indeed almost unthinkable that the different members of a regiment should be allowed to exercise their personal taste as regards cut or colour, or even as regards the size or situation of their buttons; here, it is felt, everything depends upon all being dressed *exactly* alike, whereas in fashionable costume individual variation and departure from the style of the majority (so long as it be within certain limits) is of the very essence of success. It is only in the occupational uniforms that there is sometimes allowed some measure of individual variation. Policemen must dress alike, but chauffeurs, chambermaids, waitresses, and butchers may, to some extent, exercise their own discretion (or their employers may exercise it for them). Many of these occupational costumes are, in fact, less 'fixed' than the others that we have considered; they are a matter more often of convention than of rigid rule. Only the main lines are prescribed by custom, and, so long as the costume is clearly recognisable for what it is intended, the minor details are allowed to vary. Such partly variable, partly conventionalised, costume seems to be somewhere near the borderland between the 'fixed' and 'modish' types. Indeed, it has been suggested[1] that, as regards certain types of occupational dress, namely, those of servants, it is possible to formulate something in the nature of a general law to the effect that 'the costume of servants is that of the masters of an earlier generation'. In so far as this holds true, this kind of occupational dress follows the general line of development of 'modish' dress, but at a certain distance. One of the penalties attaching to the very slow development of men's dress in recent years, is that servants are apt to catch up with their masters, as has happened in the case of waiters.

It is clear that some of the 'fixed' costumes that we have considered are in an obsolescent stage; they have for long been fighting a losing battle against 'modish' costume. This applies particularly to these belonging to the geographical group, which are now seldom worn except in remote places, by the lower and more conservative classes (here again woman shows a greater conservatism than man), and for curiosity and quaintness rather than as an ordinary and everyday occurrence. Taking a wider view, we find that during the last century European 'modish' dress has quietly ousted 'national' dress, not only from Europe itself, but from many other parts of the world, so that throughout the vast sphere of predominating western influence Paris now rules the costumes of women, London those of men.

The case of uniforms is rather different. Military uniforms obviously depend on the fate of war itself; and in a number of ways they powerfully influence many other 'occupational' uniforms. In the more military-minded countries, there is generally a greater tendency to distinguish men of different occupations by their uniforms than in countries with more pacific and commercial interests. Apart from this, the extent to which uniforms are employed depends somewhat upon the relative emphasis laid upon group organisation and upon individuality respectively. In England in the second

[1] By Webb, 103, p. 102.

half of the nineteenth century, when individualism was most predominant, the use of uniforms sank to a very low level. Since then the increasing claims of social discipline, group loyalty, and group responsibility are tending, in certain cases, to make uniforms more frequent than they were; so that, for instance, bus conductors and lift attendants now wear uniforms, where formerly they dressed in billycocks or blouses, as the fashion of the moment, or their ability to follow it, dictated. The ultimate fate of uniforms in civil life is an interesting question, to which we can more profitably return in a later chapter, after we have dealt with the more intriguing mysteries of fashion.

CHAPTER IX

THE FORCES OF FASHION

'See'st thou not, I say, what a deformed thief this fashion is? How giddily he turns about all the hot bloods between fourteen and five and thirty....?
All this I see, and I see that the fashion wears out more apparel than the man. But art not thou thyself giddy with the fashion too, that thou hast shifted out of thy tale into telling me of the fashion?—*Much Ado about Nothing*, iii. 3.

'La Mode est la déesse des apparences', Mallarmé tells us. Fashion, we have been brought up to believe (and generations of writers in a myriad of journals have contributed to this belief), is a mysterious goddess, whose decrees it is our duty to obey rather than to understand; for indeed, it is implied, these decrees transcend all ordinary human understanding. We know not why they are made, or how long they will endure, but only that they must be followed; and that the quicker the obedience the greater is the merit. To contemplate in an unprejudiced and scientific manner the nature and activities of this divinity is as difficult as any other psychological investigation in the domain of religion; when one is not a worshipper, one tends all too easily to become a scoffer, and neither attitude befits the scientist. If the writers in the technical journals of La Mode preach as true believers, the small number of outside students resemble atheists rather than agnostics, and can ill conceal their joy at ridiculing the mysteries that others venerate. Mindful of this double danger, it is now our task to approach the goddess without fear or rancour, and to study, so far as we are able, with unbiassed judgment and unclouded vision, her origin, her essence, and her edicts.

In pursuance of this programme we will first investigate *why* fashion exists in the modern world; we must, that is, examine the psychological and social causes that have originated it and that maintain it. We will then pass to the question as to the actual agencies through which fashion works, studying also the psychological functions and limitations of these agencies—in other words the *how* of fashion. Finally, we will contemplate the *what* of fashion by reviewing a few of the concrete ways in which its influence is felt.

The Why of Fashion.—There can be little doubt that the ultimate and essential cause of fashion lies in competition; competition of a social and a sexual kind, in which the social elements are more obvious and manifest and the sexual elements more indirect, concealed, and unavowed, hiding themselves, as it were, behind the social ones. We have already seen that decoration has a sexual and a social value, attractive (according to the prevalent taste) and striking forms of ornamentation being useful both for purposes of sexual allurement and as signs of rank, wealth, or power—following the convention that the more elaborate and decorative the costume, the higher the social position of the wearer. So long as the system of 'fixed' costume prevails, each social grade is content to wear the costume with which it is associated. But when the barriers between one grade and another become less insuperable, when, in psychological terms, one class begins seriously to aspire to the position of that above it, it is natural that the distinctive outward signs and symbols of the grades in question should become imperilled. As we have already had occasion to remark in another connection, it is a fundamental human trait to imitate those who are admired or envied. At the stage of social development in question, those in a given social stratum have learnt not only to admire, but as a rule to envy also, those who are above them; they therefore tend to imitate them; and what more natural, and, at the same time, more symbolic, than to start the process of imitation by copying their clothes, the very insignia of the admired and envied qualities?

If this were all that happened, the significant sartorial distinctions would merely tend to become abolished by a gradual appropriation by the lower social ranks of the styles affected by the wealthy and the powerful (a process which, as certain sociologists—notably Herbert Spencer—have pointed out, tends frequently to take place in the case of titles—as in Spain, where every beggar is a *caballero*). But the higher social classes on their side are naturally unwilling to abandon the signs of their superiority.[1] They can endeavour to retain their sartorial distinctiveness in two ways: either by passing sumptuary laws forbidding to others the use of their own special garments; or else by the abandonment of these garments, which are in danger of losing their distinctive value now that they are being copied, and by the adoption of a new form of dress which shall re-establish the desired distinction. Since the method of sumptuary laws, though often tried, seldom if ever proves effective, recourse must sooner or later be made to the second method. And thus fashion is born. There is now a movement from both ends; one from the lower social ranks in the direction of those who stand higher in the scale, and another from these latter away from their own former position, which has now become fashionably untenable. It is this double movement which essentially constitutes fashion, and is the ground of the perpetual variation to which 'modish' costume is subject.

When the double movement is thoroughly established, it manifests itself not only in the community as a whole, but also within each individual member of the

[1] Some writers on fashion, again following Herbert Spencer, distinguish two motives for the imitation involved in fashion—which may be briefly described as reverence and the desire for equality respectively. It is clear, of course, that some element, if not of reverence, at least of admiration, is always necessary for this imitation; we do not willingly imitate people except on this condition. The imitation of a fashion is always in one sense a compliment to those from whom it is copied. Occasionally, too, the element of desire for (at any rate certain specific forms of) equality or similarity may be almost or quite absent (as, for instance, in the case of wearing a high collar in obsequious imitation of a potentate who has himself adopted one to hide a scrofulous neck). But if this were generally so, the imitated would feel little need to create a fresh distinction for themselves, and fashion (as a continuous movement) would come to an end through the permanent adoption of the imitated style by all concerned. The element of rivalry, therefore, seems essential to the continuance of fashion.

community. For practical purposes it may be said that our view of separate social classes corresponding, so to speak, to the pursued and the pursuing, is little more than a convenient abstraction. Almost every individual partakes to some extent of both characters, the one or the other predominating according to his circumstances, ambitions, and abilities. The paradox of fashion is that everyone is trying at the same time to be like, and to be unlike, his fellow-men—to be like them in so far as he regards them as superiors, to be unlike them (in the sense of being more 'fashionable') so far as he thinks they are below him. Inasmuch as we are aristocratically minded and dare to assert our own individuality by being different, we are leaders of fashion (for we all exercise some influence, however small); inasmuch as we feel our own inferiority and the need of conformity to the standards set by others, we are followers of fashion. Here again, from the point of view of the individual, the essentially unstable nature of fashion becomes apparent.

As already indicated, fashion implies a certain fluidity of the social structure of the community. There must be differences of social position, but it must seem possible and desirable to bridge these differences; in a rigid hierarchy fashion is impossible. But it is of course not necessary that fashion should infect at once the whole of a community. Indeed, in most cases it probably began among a relatively small section towards the top of the social scale, and for long periods its more striking manifestations were found only among the aristocracy, particularly among those whose life was spent in courts and capitals, the common people meanwhile dressing in costume which approximated more to the traditional or 'fixed' type. But with the rise, first of a bourgeoisie and then of a democracy, fashion spreads inevitably downwards, until finally the whole community is more or less involved—as is the case with nearly all progressive countries of to-day. But with the attainment of complete democracy, the conditions become once again less favourable for fashion.[1] When every man is as good as his fellows, there are no superior social strata left to imitate, and it would seem as though the race of fashion must end, since those behind have definitely caught up those in front. Actually, however, the race tends to be prolonged by the fact that the aristocracy of fashion—an aristocracy which is essential to its existence—changes as political and social development proceed. In most countries to-day it is no longer entirely an aristocracy of nobility or wealth. These still furnish in many cases an indispensable foundation, but they are supplemented by further very varied elements, to which the demi-monde, the stage, Bohemia, the world of sport and motoring all furnish contributions. In the case of men's clothes especially, it is perhaps even true that changes occur as much from below as from above, since the upper social circles have become so very wedded to the idea of a more or less stereotyped correctness, which only permits of variation within very narrow limits; thus in London it is the 'bloods' of Whitechapel rather than those of Mayfair who are reintroducing colour, the riders of the humble bicycle rather than of the aristocratic horse who have begun to popularise the 'Byron' collar.

Meanwhile there have come into play a number of fresh influences tending to maintain fashion. Among the most important of these is one of a definitely **economic** order: as fashion has spread downwards into all classes, large and powerful commercial interests have become involved and great industries have been built up to supply the constant stream of novel garments that fashion demands. This again supplies a stimulus at both ends of the fashionable scale. On the one hand, modern means of **mass production** and improved methods of **transport and distribution** have made it possible to supply copies of all the newest and exclusive models rapidly, in great

[1] As they are also in the relatively anarchic state of some very primitive societies. Thus it has been said that Bushmen have no fashions, while Kaffirs have: the presence of fashion among the latter being connected with their well-marked social differentiation (Mustoxidi, 68).

numbers, and at relatively low prices, so that women of moderate means in small provincial towns can wear clothes of practically the same design as those that were introduced by the leaders of fashion in the great cities only a few weeks before. At the same time, increased facilities for rapid locomotion and for travel have brought people in all parts of a country, and indeed in most Europeanised parts of the world, into much closer touch with the great centres than was formerly the case, so that they have far better opportunities of learning at first hand the latest changes of fashion in these centres. Meanwhile, too, a multitude of special journals has sprung up, all aiming at the stimulation of interest in these changes. Thus the movement of fashion is hastened from below. To meet this increased speed of imitation, a constant supply of new models must be produced for the benefit of the leaders, in order that they may preserve their distinction. The whole march of fashion is thus accelerated, and the consequent more rapid turnover in clothes, though perhaps of doubtful benefit to the community as a whole, is of advantage to the clothing industries, which not unnaturally endeavour to maintain it, employing for this purpose all the arts of modern salesmanship; arts which are constantly in use for suggesting that this or that style is out of date and that some new garment of fresh design must be acquired on pain of being hopelessly behind the fashion.

This economic tendency towards rapid change of fashion is assisted by the fact that modern clothes tend on the whole to be less durable than those of many former periods. By some writers this fact has been brought into connection with the better environmental conditions of modern civilised life, and especially of urban life. The shoes, for instance, that we can wear in modern towns with their carefully paved streets would have been quite unsuitable for the street conditions that existed in most towns two hundred years ago; we do not need the thick boots that were then the only safe or convenient form of footwear in which to cross the muddy sewers with which the streets of that period abounded. Nevertheless, our thinner shoes wear out more quickly and have to be replaced the sooner; and since we have in any case to purchase new ones, we may as well gratify our vanity by getting such as are in the latest fashion. This is undoubtedly true of many present-day articles of dress, contrasting, as they do, strongly, in this matter, both with many former fashions and with clothing of the 'fixed' type. (Cf., for instance, the stuff of modern 'modish' dresses with the much more durable materials of which 'national' dresses and uniforms are made.)

The general tendency to rapid change in recent times, though it admittedly depends to some extent upon factors of an economic order, has been philosophised by certain authors, who have seen in it only one particular manifestation of the generally increased rapidity of social and scientific development in modern life. It is a commonplace that human evolution proceeds slowly at first and thereafter with ever greater speed. The earlier inventions, such as the use of stone and metal tools, took many thousand years to be worked out and generally applied. Motoring, aviation, cinematography, the gramophone, the wireless, have all come into general use in the course of two or three decades. Corresponding to this rapidity of change in our environment, we have become less conservative, more intolerant of the old and more enamoured of the new, a mental tendency which can best express itself in changing tastes as regards clothing (which, by its very nature, is in any case less lasting than are most other forms of applied art). The old no longer inspires us with the same sense of veneration as it did; we are inclined to be revolutionary and iconoclastic, and to look forward ever hopefully (though our hope is not always reasonable) towards the new. In so far as there is truth in this view, our changing fashions may indeed be looked upon as symbolic of our changing outlook upon many other things.

We saw in Chapter VII. that, from the beginning of the nineteenth century onwards, men's clothing has been distinguished from women's by its greater uniformity and its relative lack of the decorative element. This difference we regarded as an effort to reduce competition among men. In harmony with this view is the fact that sex differences are nowhere more apparent than in the field of fashion. Almost everything that we have here said about fashion applies in a lesser degree to men than it does to women. Men's fashions change far less rapidly than women's (so great indeed is the difference, that a twenty or thirty years' old suit can easily be worn in public without exciting comment, whereas a woman's dress of equal age would make the wearer an object of universal curiosity and ridicule). Such changes as occur from year to year affect small details only instead of whole designs. The economic interests at work are adjusted far more to a state of relative permanence than to a condition of violent and continual change, and have made little attempt to exploit the advantages of rapid variation; even the materials used are, to a large extent, more durable, so that the need for replacing outworn garments is less often felt. On all these scores, as well as on the ground of its greater uniformity, men's dress is less 'modish' and more 'fixed' than women's. Indeed, in many of their aspects (*e.g.* attire for formal occasions, for the evening, and for many sports) men's clothes occupy about the same position with regard to types as do some of the 'occupational' clothes of which we spoke in the last chapter. As in the case of these latter, there is some small individual choice in minor details (the shape of a collar or the size and colour of a tie), but none at all as regards general cut, proportions, or design.

In the case of men the elimination of competition by means of clothes has thus very greatly reduced the influence of fashion. A question of great interest is whether women are likely to follow in the same course in the near future. Several factors point in this direction, *e.g.*: (1) the relative victory of mass production over exclusive design, a victory which is tending steadily to reduce the difference between the leaders of fashion and the ordinary rank and file, so that the social distinctiveness of dress is becoming as negligible as it is with men; (2) the ever-increasing socialisation of women, a tendency which subjects them to the same influences as those which led to the reduction of clothes-competition among men (one already notices that in some fields, *e.g.* sport, women's costume has become almost as standardised and 'occupational' as that of men). Against this, however, there are at least two other important factors to be taken into consideration: (1) the great influence of the economic interests which stand to lose by a reduction of the rôle of fashion and which can be counted on to combat any tendency to such reduction by all the means within their power; (2) the fact that women's greater participation in social life and undoubted greater sense of social values has not led to any great reduction in their Narcissism. At any rate our traditions still sanction, and indeed approve, a much greater and more open manifestation of Narcissism among women than among men. Now it is true that Narcissism need not necessarily find expression in fashion (since it is only indirectly connected with competition) but, given the present conditions, it is comparatively easy for the commercial influences to exploit Narcissism in the interests of fashion. This matter of women and fashion is, indeed, one of the many fascinating sartorial problems on which it would be rash, even to the point of foolhardiness, to prophesy. We can only point out the chief influences that seem to be at work, and watch their interplay.

The How of Fashion.—But if all this throws at least some rays of light upon the question of why new fashions are produced, it does not tell us how they are produced. This latter question is admittedly one that is extremely difficult to answer. It is indeed the central mystery of fashion. Individual fashions are, in their origin, almost as elusive as some other social products, such as the rumours or jokes that pass from mouth to mouth, and of which it is seldom if ever possible to trace the source. The general notion is that fashions are originated by some mysterious authority resident in Paris; and the investigations of those few economists who have deigned to turn their attention to the subject[1] would seem to show that there is much truth in this idea. For very many years a large proportion of women's fashions have indeed been born in Paris; partly, it would seem, in the studios and offices of a few big firms, and partly in the private workshops of a few independent designers, who may sell their ideas to these firms or occasionally to private clients.[2] It seems, therefore, that on the producers' side the predominant influence lies with a relatively small group of individuals. But though fashions travel quickly, they have to pass through the hands of many individuals before they have reached out to all corners of the earth, and here, as elsewhere (as, for instance, in the case of rumours), each individual tends to be responsible for some small change.

In any case, however, the producers of fashion as a group are not so all-powerful as the writers of the theological literature of fashion, in their more inspired utterances, would lead us to suppose. To create a fashion it is not sufficient to make a new design. For the design to become a fashion, it must be worn, and not merely at a mannequin parade. It is natural, therefore, that the wearers should have some say in the launching of new fashions. Here too, however, a predominant influence would seem to be exercised by a relatively small group of individuals, though a larger and less homogeneous group than that in the case of the producers. In the early days of modern fashion, this influence came chiefly from the members of royal and aristocratic houses. In later years, however, even before the Great War shattered the last remains of kingly power in so many parts of the world, the royal ladies had largely lost their supremacy. The Empress Eugénie is usually considered to have been the last of the long dynasty of royal fashion

---

[1] I have found the most useful to be Sombart, 90.
[2] The most interesting recent description of the intimate working of the dressmaking industry in Paris with which I am acquainted is that of Roubaud, 80.

leaders, and their place has been taken by a much larger number of more varied individuals. Royal influence has lasted longer in the case of men's clothes, and the British royal family has still some power within this sphere. It is probable, however, that any kind of eminence, of whatsoever sort, is capable of being used to mould fashion. In his day Beau Brummell exercised an immense influence by acquiring a reputation for perfect taste. To take a recent instance, one from the field of sport, there can be little doubt that Suzanne Lenglen was very largely responsible for the complete revolution in women's tennis dress that took place after the war, a revolution that was not without important effects on women's costume generally. More recently still (in the summer of 1929) tennis has seen the battle of the bare legs. Feeling ran high, and the authorities at Wimbledon felt called upon to issue a manifesto, though couched in the discreetest terms. Everyone waited eagerly to see what Miss Helen Wills would do. She appeared in stockings, and all others did the same. But, here again, we can scarcely doubt that, had she elected to play without them, many would have copied her, and in the warm summer that followed, the advocates of uncovered calves would have scored a very decisive triumph.

Nevertheless, fashions cannot be entirely accounted for in terms of individuals, either on the side of the producers or the wearers. For a new style of dress to become fashionable, it must in some way appeal to a large number of people. The mysterious dictates of Paris are, as a matter of fact, by no means always obeyed. During the last twenty years quite a number of new designs have been launched which have seldom seen the light of day outside the fashion shops. One was the harem skirt, which was introduced under the very highest auspices but which completely failed. No greater success was met by the attempt to introduce striking asymmetrical effects, such as a décolletage lower at one side than the other. A more recent and interesting instance concerns the length of skirts. If we are to believe

M. Jean Patou,[1] the short skirt cannot boast the illustrious parentage of *La Haute Couture*. 'Born from the brain of some Boeotian', as that master has it, its legitimacy has never been officially recognised, but this did not prevent its triumphal progress through the world.

It is obvious, therefore, that in dealing with fashion, we have to consider not only the individual creators of clothes but the group mentality of those who wear them. This group mentality offers some fascinating problems for the social psychologist. It has often been held that successive fashions express in some way the 'spirit of the age'; but when it comes to describing in detail how this spirit manifests itself in fashion, the explanations offered are often vague and disappointing. Indeed, it would probably require a much more thorough study (with the collaboration of the historian and the sociologist) before we could explain the full social significance of the detailed changes of fashion from one year to another. Nevertheless, the significance of certain main changes over long periods seems fairly clear. Let us consider very briefly a few epochs in modern history.

If we glance, in the first place, at the costumes of the Renaissance, we seem to find the great release of human energy which characterised that period mirrored, as it were, in its fashions. In men's clothing emphasis was given to strength and muscular development by closely fitting garments that exhibited all the play of the muscles. The coverings of legs and arms were, indeed, so tight that they had to be slashed at the joints to permit of freedom of movement; but these slashes were made the means of elaborate ornamentation with the help of multi-coloured cloths and ribbons. The age indulged in an orgy of colour, which was not afraid of crudeness. There was, indeed, no false modesty about that period; the cod-piece worn by men for no less than fifty years is perhaps the most audacious piece of clothing that has ever been invented, while the women

[1] Interview in *La Liberté* (Dec. 12, 1929).

followed suit by endeavouring to produce the appearance of being always pregnant.

Compared with this crude but intensely vital exuberance, the eighteenth century was a period of artificiality and refinement, in which the glittering ceremoniousness of court life held undisputed sway. Vivid colours were banned in favour of pale tints and powder. In its somewhat exotic magnificence costume bore but little resemblance to the actual human form.

At the close of the eighteenth century and the beginning of the nineteenth, we see again a striking change. All artificiality was swept away; the ideal now was to follow Nature. The Empire costumes of the period are strikingly simple, and make no serious attempt to represent the human body as other than it is. Here, as at other periods, democracy had no use for the gorgeous and complicated trappings which had flourished in a preceding age of absolutism and of highly accentuated class distinctions.

As the nineteenth century wore on, the ideas of class superiority and fastidious refinement once again became attractive and found its expression in a relative artificiality and exuberance of clothing (though this time the movement was confined to women). Finally, a return to greater frankness and sincerity, combined with a great upward movement of democracy in recent years, has brought us back to another period of simplicity and exiguousness in costume.

The real existence of some such influence of the *Zeitgeist* upon costume is corroborated if we compare costume with architecture and the internal decoration of houses. As we pointed out in an earlier chapter, there is a certain parallelism, both of function and of psychological significance, between our clothing and our houses, so that we should expect that the psychological influences that guide our fashions in dress would also affect our styles of building and of decoration. Here again we can only draw attention to the general existence of such a parallelism and illustrate it by a few examples.

To deal first with interior decoration: the desire for classical simplicity which showed itself in dress at the beginning of the nineteenth century is mirrored in the severe and classical style of the furniture and equipment of that period—a style which differed strikingly from the more ornate treatment of the classic that was in vogue during the previous century. The return to a greatly increased elaboration of costume in the mid-Victorian period was accompanied by what now seems to us the over-detailed ornamentation of the Victorian drawing-room, whereas our modern preference for simplicity of dress has been followed once again by a taste for relatively simple interiors.

The case of architecture is complicated by the fact that buildings are by their nature much more permanent than dress, so that any given generation has for the most part to live among the architectural products of its fathers or forefathers. Nevertheless, there are some striking correspondences here also. We can scarcely fail to see in the long lines of Gothic a parallel to the elongated shapes of mediaeval dress. The fussiness of the Rococo style in architecture is correlated with the detailed elaboration of dress of the same period. The early nineteenth century, so intensely classical in the spirit of its costumes, bequeathed us many buildings also in the classic style. The Victorian era, it is true, failed to produce or reproduce any distinctive style of architecture, so it is difficult to trace the correspondence here (unless we recognise as such the equal tastelessness—as it now seems to us—of its buildings and its fashions).[1] On the other hand, we may perhaps be justified in seeing a parallel between the plain, wide-windowed, open style of post-war factory or office building and the relatively simple style of modern dress, which has no ornamental complications and seeks to hide no secrets.[2]

---

[1] May it perhaps be that the aesthetic failure, both of Ruskin's Gothic revival and of the subsequent pseudo-Elizabethan style of domestic architecture, was partly because both were utterly foreign to the spirit of the age—a fact that shows itself in the absence of any corresponding sartorial fashions?

[2] Several writers, including among quite recent ones Gerald Heard (48), have drawn attention to interesting parallels between individual garments and parts

After this excursion into group psychology as manifested in the spirit of the age, let us turn once more, in conclusion, to the problem of the origin of individual fashions. We can perhaps now see a little more clearly, at least in general terms, how it is that the influence of the leaders and initiators is limited. We can at least surmise with some show of plausibility that the harem skirt (which doubtless hoped to satisfy the long manifested hankering after a discreet and unobtrusive bifurcated garment) failed because of its associations with a social system that was definitely antagonistic to the aspirations of women at a time when they were fighting for a vote. Were European women to identify themselves with their relatively unemancipated Turkish sisters, just at a period when these latter were beginning to look westwards in envious admiration of the liberty already won in that direction? We can surmise too that such an apparent anomaly as the hobble skirt achieved its temporary vogue by appealing to the ideal of slimness—an ideal that was itself associated with the growing importance of youth and the corresponding growth of a youthful ideal. We can see too (and with much greater clarity) why it was that the war, with its sudden introduction of the ideal of work and activity, swept away the hobble skirt, which so seriously hampered movement. It is easy to understand also that the short skirt was something in the nature of a triumphant gesture of freedom on the part of women (who had achieved an unprecedented self-confidence and an unexampled admiration as workers during the war); and that, at the same time, it represented the final apotheosis of the youthful ideal, now that youth itself had definitely acquired its freedom

---

of buildings, *e.g.* between roofs, spires, and domes and certain corresponding forms of head-dress, between the long factory chimneys of the industrial era and the long tubular trousers of the same period. Entering into greater detail, Mr. Heard reminds us that, as Gothic windows and arches became gradually less pointed until they reached the rather extreme flatness of the Tudor period, the pointed effects in clothes characteristic of later mediaevalism gradually gave place to an increased breadth. The high pointed head-dress was replaced by a low, broad one, and pointed toes by an extremely broad-toed shoe, the Sableton. In fact the whole style of clothing tended to accentuate the breadth of the body.

and come into its heritage; and how that, this being so, Paris was powerless to prevent its progress. It might be, as M. Patou said, 'la négation même de toute véritable élégance', but it has not been elegance, but youth, freedom, and activity that have been the dominant ideals of these post-war years.

New fashions, if they are to be successful, must be in accordance with certain ideals current at the time that they are launched. Women must see in the new fashion a symbol of an ideal that is before them—though of course, as with other symbols, there need be no conscious realisation of its true significance. This does not mean that the personality of the launcher is unimportant. We have already shown good reason to think otherwise. It means, however, that the influence of the initiating personality is efficient only so long as the persons to be influenced can see in what is proposed, so to speak, the incarnation of their own ideals. In the language of psycho-analysis, they must project their own super-ego on to the person who exercises the suggestive influence.[1] The use of suggestion, in the launching of a fashion, as in any other case, depends partly upon the intrinsic prestige of the suggester and partly upon the affective value of what he suggests.[2] Beau Brummell was such an important figure in the world of fashion because he knew better than any other how to create the ideal of unobtrusive elegance and perfect taste—the most satisfactory form of sartorial exhibitionism that was still permitted to men since the right to the more blatant displays of earlier periods had been

[1] Cf. E. Jones, 'The Nature of Auto-Suggestion', *International Journal of Psycho-Analysis*, 1923, vol. iv. p. 293.
[2] Of course there is also such a thing as negative prestige. A fashion may be killed in its infancy by being adopted by persons whom it is considered undesirable to imitate. The classical instance of this was the sudden disappearance of 'bloomers' in 1851, when a London brewery dressed all their barmaids in nether garments of this type. Another (and in a sense more literal) method of killing fashions was by associating them with public executions—in the persons either of the executed or the executioner. In Queen Anne's reign there was considerable pother about women appearing in the street in their nightgowns. But this fashion speedily came to an end when a woman was executed in a garment of this description. In the terminology of the behaviourist, the habit was 'deconditioned' by being thus brought into association with an event of such a painful character.

lost. Miss Wills had far more influence on tennis costume than other women, for another reason—her special ability within the field of tennis itself. She might have created a triumphant bare-legged mode, where others would have failed. But there are obvious limits to her power; she could not have introduced such a mode twenty years earlier, however well she played. The fashions to be introduced must not be too remote from the sentiments and aspirations of the time. But there is a direct relationship between the prestige of the launcher of fashions and the degree of difference that he can bridge in his attempted innovation. The greater the innovation (either in a progressive or a retrograde direction) the greater the personal prestige that is necessary to introduce it. The Prince of Wales succeeded in brightening men's evening attire by the introduction of white waistcoats. He did not succeed in creating a new fashion when he wore a pullover with a smoking-jacket. Popular as he is, the incongruous associations of the two garments caused too big a shock for the new combination to be adopted. Very big changes (and this was a startling change in view of the intense conservatism of men's dress) can only be accepted if at the same time there is a corresponding change in the ideal. The ideal of men's clothes has become so 'fixed' that to produce an innovation of this magnitude is an undertaking of the greatest difficulty.

At the present moment (early in 1930) two bold attempts at the modification of existing ideals are being made; one (relating to men) of an open nature; the other (relating to women) more insidious. The Men's Dress Reform Party in England is trying definitely to induce a relatively big and sudden change by the inculcation of fresh ideals. On the other hand, the *Haute Couture* has embarked on a more subtle campaign to abolish the ideals of youthfulness, activity, and naturalness that have distinguished women's fashions in recent years. Paradoxically enough, men are being urged to imitate certain aspects of women's dress (*i.e.* its lightness, simplicity and freedom) at the same time that women are being induced to abandon these aspects. The situation is not without a certain piquant interest for the psychological student of dress, and we shall have more to say with regard to both movements before we take leave of the reader.

CHAPTER X

THE VICISSITUDES OF FASHION

Il lui entoura les poignets de cercles d'or et, l'ayant fait mettre debout, il lui passa sous les seins et sur le ventre un large bandeau de lin, alléguant que la poitrine en concevrait une fierté nouvelle et que les flancs en seraient évidés pour la gloire des hanches.
    Au moyen des épingles qu'il tirait une à une de sa bouche, il ajustait ce bandeau.
    — Vous pouvez serrer encore, fit la pingouine.—ANATOLE FRANCE, *L'Isle des Pingouins*, p. 53.

THE **What of Fashion.**—Having now examined both the forces that originate and maintain fashion and the actual agencies—psychological, social, and economic—through which it works, we must in conclusion consider the more specific forms through which it manifests itself. We can of course make no attempt to describe and explain in detail the bewildering sequence of actual modes. This has already been done in several sumptuous and erudite histories of dress.[1] Here we can only endeavour to obtain a rather general view of the whole field by considering the phenomena in the light of certain main principles or tendencies. The manifestations of fashion, like those of modesty, can be conveniently described in terms of a certain number of variables; and the more obvious and important of these, together with their interrelations, can be made clear by a simple diagram of the kind we used in Chapter IV. when describing modesty. The general principles which the diagram is intended to illustrate are essentially the same in both cases. The only differences are that: (1) the present diagram gives a less complete enumeration of the variables in question than does that in Chapter IV. Other variables could be added, *e.g.* a variation in the relative preponderance of the masculine (phallic) and

---

[1] For the fashions of more recent times the reader is specially referred to the work of Fischel and von Boehn, 32.

feminine (predominantly uterine) symbolism of clothes,[1] a variation in the historial epoch of the past from which inspiration is sought, the relative importance of the part and of the whole of costumes, etc.; (2) the psychical

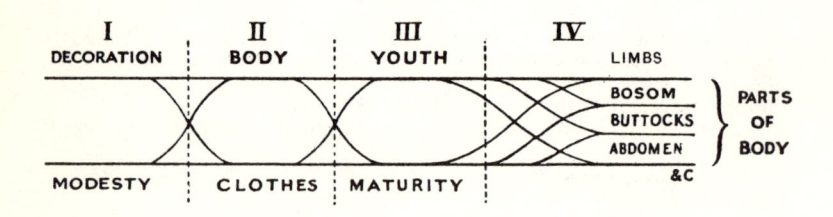

```
  I              II           III          IV
DECORATION     BODY         YOUTH        LIMBS
                                         BOSOM    ⎫  PARTS
                                         BUTTOCKS ⎬  OF
                                         ABDOMEN  ⎭  BODY
MODESTY       CLOTHES      MATURITY       &C
```

energy which we suppose to be flowing along the various lines of the diagram is, in this case, not (as with modesty) of an inhibitory, but of a positive and active kind, corresponding to interest and desire and not to suppression; (3) the different variables are, as we shall see, not quite so independent of one another as in the case of modesty. There tend to be certain correlations between the flow of energy in the different parts of the diagram, I, II, III, and IV (*e.g.*, if the energy flows along the upper line in III, it tends to flow along the top line, rather than along any of the lower lines in IV).

Let us consider now the different variables in turn. There is in the first place a variation in the relative importance of the two fundamental motives of decoration and modesty. There are periods when exhibitionism is triumphant, others when it is sternly inhibited. Consider, for instance, the costumes of the English Restoration as compared with the preceding fashions of the Commonwealth.

In the second place, there is a variation in the amount of displacement of exhibitionistic interest from the body on to clothes. At the one extreme, clothes may be of comparatively little importance on their own account. They only serve to display the body, to throw its attrac-

[1] Cf. Löwitsch, 64.

Fig. 17. Diana, from the Borghese collection of the Louvre. A simple costume which enhances the beauty of the bodily form.

Fig. 18. An elaborate stage costume, which frames rather than covers the body

tive features into better relief, to make it more imposing by the operation of 'confluence' and by the various principles of decoration described in Chapter III.; or to render it more seductively alluring by transparencies and half-concealments. The simple costumes of classical antiquity and their modern reincarnations in Empire dress clearly belong to this category. Thus, to take a concrete example, the draperies of the statue in Fig. 17, in their efficient simplicity so eminently suited to the needs of the divine huntress, attractively reveal the form of the body and give it an additional grace. The modern tennis frock and the simple black-and-white outlines of our waitresses' uniforms illustrate the same fundamental principle. It is possible, however, for the costume to be more elaborate and still serve the same purpose; in this case its essential function is that of a frame, as may be seen from the abundant examples offered by any contemporary Parisian revue, where most elaborate and ornamental accoutrements are so worn as to throw into relief the almost naked body of the wearer; a body which they enframe or encircle rather than cover (see for instance Fig. 18). In all these forms of clothing, whether the body itself is actually covered or exposed (though naturally more so in the former case than in the latter), there must be a certain subordination of colour to form, heavy masses of colouring being in particular excluded. In general, too, this style demands of the wearer a well-proportioned figure and is incapable of hiding any very serious defects of contour.

At the other extreme the body may become little more than (as Carlyle would say) a clothes-horse, the whole effect being achieved by the garments that are hung upon it. This style naturally permits of a greater profusion of garments, greater variation of line, and greater luxuriance of colour. Its main principles are well illustrated in many royal robes of state, where one magnificent garment is piled upon another in the endeavour to achieve the maximum of gorgeousness. The splendid effect of the costume depicted in Fig. 19 is independent of any physical excellencies on the part of the wearer. If, in contemplating this picture, we try to carry out Carlyle's instruction 'to look fixedly on clothes, or even with armed eyesight, till they become transparent', how poor and puny does the royal figure become when deprived of his luxuriant trappings. Indeed, this whole style of dress, in which clothes are everything and the body is little more than a means of suspension, depends upon the assumption, so well stated recently by R. H. Mottram, 'that civilisation is an artificial thing and that man is not beautiful or remarkable but must be made to appear so'.[1]

Between these two extremes (which have been emphasised in order to make clear the principle) there is of course a whole series of continuous gradations, on which fashion rings the changes. During the period of artificiality that distinguished the eighteenth century, the body itself fell relatively into the background; its purpose was largely to serve as a support for gorgeous clothes. With the naturalism that followed the French Revolution, the body once more came into its own rights, and the purpose of clothes became the relatively secondary one of throwing into relief the beauties of the body. Clothing became extremely simple and exiguous (much more so than in recent years), underclothing being almost dispensed with. A fashionable lady's costume had to pass two tests: it must not weigh more than ½ lb. in all (as against 2 lb. or more at the present day) and her dress must be of such thinness and flexibility that it could be passed through her wedding-ring. Not content with this, she damped her dress before putting it on, so that it should cling closer to the figure. The Victorian period was again one of comparative artificiality, in which little attention was paid to the natural form of the body, and in which the quantity, if not the beauty, of the clothes enormously increased. Of late years we have, of course, again laid the accent on the body and indulged in a drastic simplification of dress.

[1] *Daily Mirror*, July 4, 1928.

Fig. 19. Louis XVI, by Callet. An elaborate costume, the effect of which is independent of bodily form

(By permission of Messrs. Levy and Neurdein)

In dealing with the relative importance of the body and of clothes, we have, for the sake of easier description, treated the alternating emphasis from the point of view of decoration only. But the same considerations apply when modesty rather than decoration is the leading motive. Here we need only refer to what we have already said on the subject, and point out that modesty may be directed primarily against the display of the too freely exposed or accentuated body or against too lavish clothing. The Puritans of the seventeenth century were chiefly concerned about the latter point, our modern moralists chiefly with the former.

Recent history has brought into prominence another form of variation—one which concerns the period of life which is most admired. We have already spoken of the tendency to idealise youth, which has been so very much in evidence since the termination of the war. Youth has been granted privileges that it never had before, and maturity has willingly forgone its former dignities in return for the right of sharing in the appearance and activities of youth. As if to symbolise this new ideal, women of all ages adopted some of the principal features of what was formerly the special costume of youth, in particular the short skirt and the simplicity of line and decoration. The differences between girls and grown-up women have further been abolished by an identical style of hairdressing for all ages, and by the endeavour to preserve throughout life a certain immaturity of figure. It was not always so, and even in the early years of the present century girls often looked forward to the privilege of lengthening their skirts and of doing up their hair with much the same ardour as older women now seek to preserve the external signs of adolescence. In past times maturity has often been valued—both sexually and socially—much more highly than it is to-day. Hence the former idealisation of the fuller figure—a feature which now renders somewhat distasteful to us a good deal of the erotic art of former ages, as a visit to almost any picture gallery will show.

But perhaps the most obvious and important of all the variations of fashion is that which concerns the part of the body that is most accentuated. Fashion, in its more exuberant moments is seldom content with the silhouette that Nature has provided, but usually seeks to lay particular stress upon some single part or feature, which is then treated as a special centre of erotic charm. But when modesty predominates, these same centres of potential greater attractiveness become the objects of particular concealment and suppression. During the greater part of the Middle Ages there was a distinct note of asceticism in women's dress, with an attempt to render inconspicuous specifically such feminine characteristics as the breasts; and the corset seems to have been originally worn largely for this purpose. With the greater freedom of emotional life that distinguished the Renaissance, this ascetic trend diminished and a distinctly erotic tinge began to creep into women's costume. The corset, which had formerly been used to compress or hide the breasts, was now lowered, so as to bring them into greater relief, and indeed from that time onwards until close upon the present day, the bosom has always been a centre of special interest in feminine dress. But it was far from being the only one. During the later Middle Ages and the Renaissance, much interest was devoted to the abdominal region, which was made as conspicuous as possible. With the idealisation of pregnancy, to which we have already referred, there tended to be a general adoption of the gait and carriage distinctive of pregnancy. It can be clearly seen in many pictures of the period, as in that by Holbein the Younger on the left-hand side of Fig. 20. In the eighteenth century this abdominal emphasis was abandoned (though it subsequently reappeared in a modified form for occasional brief periods), only to give place to an increasing emphasis on the bosom and the hips. The further accentuation of the bosom was achieved by two means; first, the constriction of the waist, for this was a period of rigorous tight-lacing, and secondly by the adoption of

Fig. 20. The shifting emphasis of fashion

(a) Renaissance dress, with emphasis on the abdomen

(b) Empire dress, giving due weight to the lines of the body as a whole

(c) Crinoline, emphasising waist and hips, and enormously increasing the apparent total bulk of the body

(d) Bustle, emphasising the posterior parts (a tail-like appendage)

From C. H. Stratz, *Die Frauenkleidung*, and Fischel and von Boehn, *Modes and Manners of the Nineteenth Century* (by permission of Herrn Ferdinand Enke and Messrs. J. M. Dent & Sons)

high heels. High heels make a great difference to the whole position of the body when standing. They render impossible the protruding abdomen shown in the Holbein picture; but by the upright carriage that they necessitate they tend to give a corresponding prominence to the bosom.[1]

The Empire style of dress continued to emphasise the bosom (by its abnormally high waist line), but in all other respects it gave expression to the body as a whole rather than to any part of it. In later fashions, however, interest again became centred first on one part and then upon another. The hips soon again attracted interest, and skirts began to billow enormously in order to accentuate them. The extremely scanty clothing that characterised the turn of the century, gave place to a monstrous mass of padding round the legs. Horse-hair was usually employed for this purpose (hence the name 'crinoline' from the French *crin*). It was indeed a godsend when this cumbrous and uncomfortable method gave place to the wire frame that was employed in later forms of the crinoline. Subsequently the accentuation of the hips gave place to that of the posterior parts, and in the seventies, and again in the eighties, women were wearing a creditable imitation of a tail, as will be seen in the right-hand picture of Fig. 20.

At the present time interest has departed from the trunk and is centred on the limbs. Sleeves must be either altogether absent, or else tightly fitting, in order that the long lines and graceful contours of the arm may be fully appreciated. Legs have emerged after centuries of shrouding, and adult woman at last frankly admits herself to be a biped. Indeed, in the last year or two, her ankles, calves, and knees (all the more dazzling in their

---

[1] Nevertheless, high heels have been retained in our modern post-war costumes in spite of an abandonment of the old-time accentuation of the breast. This may well be for four reasons: (1) the desire to reduce as far as possible all accentuation of the abdomen; (2) the desire to increase the apparent height (without increase of breadth) in pursuance of the youthful ideal; (3) an unconscious phallic symbolism attaching to the heel—a factor which would be in harmony with the adoption of the masculine characteristic of short hair and the general 'boyishness' of line; (4) the desire to make the foot seem smaller.

suddenly revealed beauty after their long sojourn in the dark) have been her chief erotic weapons. In this accentuation of the limbs, we can see a natural concomitant of the idealisation of youth. Long slender limbs and an undeveloped torso are typical of immaturity, and, if modesty has departed from the legs, it has now moved upwards to the body, where any display of the (formerly so much admired) characteristics of the fuller figure is discountenanced. The bosom must be small and virginal; and maturity, far from being paraded as at some periods, is concealed as long as possible. Woman, though she has undoubtedly proclaimed her freedom by the present modes, has lost as well as gained. Modesty has not so much been dethroned (as some scandalised elderly persons seem to think) as promoted to a (literally) higher region. In asserting her rights as a human being, woman has lost some of the erotic privileges which she formerly enjoyed in virtue of her specific femininity.

The fashions of the last few years have thus been based upon a certain upward displacement of modesty, an accentuation of the body rather than of clothes, an idealisation of youth rather than of maturity, and a displacement of erotic value from the trunk to the limbs.[1] We shall do well to contemplate this picture while it lasts, for we are perhaps at a turning of the ways which will soon hide it from our gaze. A reaction appears to be imminent, and has indeed already begun. Our fashion journals and our ballrooms have for some little time now been invaded by evening dresses that allow us but fugitive glances of the wearer's calves, which, but a little while ago, were exposed with such ingenuous frankness. The modest and simple bodices characteristic of the evening dress of recent years (another point in which grown women had adopted the fashions of girlhood) are giving place to a more generous décolletage, thus pointing to a return of erotic value to the trunk, corresponding to its withdrawal from the legs; though

---

[1] Perhaps the most illuminating treatment of quite recent fashions from the psychological and social points of view is that of Samson, 84.

the fact that this décolletage is chiefly confined to the comparatively innocent region of the back, shows that this process has to be carried out discreetly, and that the bosom has not yet come back into its own. Not only are skirts longer, but stuffs are more ample, and simplicity of line is disappearing in favour of projections and excrescences in all sorts of odd and unexpected places. In conformity with this, we hear that the managers of revues are looking out for chorus girls with more generous figures than those which have adorned our stages for the last few years. All this points to a powerful reaction in favour of maturity, together with correlated tendencies towards re-erotisation of the trunk at the expense of the limbs and a greater emphasis on clothes as distinct from the body. Curiosity is naturally aroused as to how far this reaction will go, and in particular as to whether we are about to repeat the history of a hundred years ago, when the simple Empire style gradually gave place to the ponderous amplitude and artificiality of the middle of the nineteenth century.

Natural tendencies to reaction might well lead in this direction; the attractions of maturity and 'femininity' must sooner or later reassert themselves as against those of youthfulness and 'boyishness'. But there are certain circumstances which may justify us in doubting whether the reaction will go very far. These circumstances are: (1) an undiminished general activity on the part of women in all forms of work and recreation; (2) a fairly steady democratic and socialistic tradition in the most important countries; (3) an increasing sexual freedom. The first factor is one the importance of which is pretty generally recognised as conducing to a certain simplicity and youthfulness of dress.[1] With regard to the second and third factors, we have already seen reason to believe that they too tend to be associated with simplicity

[1] Though too much confidence must not be placed in the underlying assumption that clothes are reasonably related to activities. Women have trekked across continents in trailing skirts. Men have gone to wars in costumes that made them easy targets for the enemy, and, by way of relaxation, they still dance in overheated ballrooms in stiff shirts and high starched collars.

rather than with artificiality or exuberance of fashion, and with a smaller rather than a larger amount of covering.[1]

That there are indeed very considerable forces working against the new tendency to reaction is clear from the history of this reaction itself, particularly so far as concerns its most essential element, the length of skirts. There is no doubt that the long-skirt movement comes from the dressmakers rather than as a spontaneous revolution in public opinion. The *Haute Couture*, as we have seen, has never really approved of short skirts, and has been fairly consistent in its efforts to suppress them. The more direct attempts to popularise a longer garment having failed, more subtle methods were resorted to. The attempt was first of all confined to evening dresses, which were made to dip at one point, then at several, and finally all round; compensation for the reduced power of *consistent* crural exhibition was moreover provided by the opportunity for *occasional* seductive glimpses of higher parts of the leg that were not ordinarily visible with the skirt of even shortness, and also by lowering the backs of dresses in correspondence with the lengthened skirt (resorting to a general principle which has been involved in several previous changes of fashion). Having achieved this much success with evening dresses, the same principles of lengthening were applied to afternoon dresses, and are here also achieving considerable success. Meanwhile ordinary day dresses were left for a time severely alone, so that for the last year or more two distinct styles of skirt have been in vogue. The wisdom of this step from the tactical point of view has been shown by the comments of women, who have freely asserted that they were willing to be made elegant in the evening, so long as they were allowed to preserve their freedom in the morning. In other words, they walked into the trap that had been

[1] It is interesting to recall that Italy, now the most undemocratic country in Europe, is the only one in which there has been anything in the nature of official measures directed against the short skirt.

prepared for them; and Paris, after some initial defeats, has scored at length a distinct strategical success—and this in spite of the admitted fact that many of the actual designs have in their 'untidiness' shown very little taste. That it is a trap, and that the authorities of the *Haute Couture* have every intention of pushing home their advantage as soon as they can safely do so, is shown by the very cautious attempt that is now being made to lengthen skirts intended for ordinary wear—an attempt that has, however, as yet scarcely begun to affect the rank and file of wearers.[1]

And indeed 'the battle of the skirts', as it has already been christened by the press, is (at the time these lines are written) far from being ended. Considerable alarm has been expressed, as the inroads upon youthfulness and freedom have been realised. Though there is some very real delight in the increased luxuriance of material after the skimpiness of recent years, there is little enthusiasm about the prospect of appearing older and more dignified. There is even some possibility of the opposition becoming organised. It appears that in America a society has recently been founded (under the somewhat cumbrous title of 'The Fashion of the Month Club'), the function of which is to save women from unwelcome fashions and to offer approved monthly suggestions of its own. Still more recently the 'Sensible Dress Society' has been founded in England with much

[1] Even as I write I find the following in the fashion page of a much-read daily paper, under the heading, 'Paris in Petticoats! Height of Femininity reached'. 'Visitors to Paris anxious to know what the summer fashions are going to be are amazed to find that skirts will not only trail on the ground but are fuller than they have been since the days of the crinoline. . . . A typical example of what women may look forward to this summer is a dress of saxe-blue satin that has a large bunch of violets pinned to the cuff. *It has half a dozen petticoats composed of alternate layers of pink shadow lace and snare net*' (italics in the original). It looks as though Paris had grown bolder and were determined to push home its advantage without further delay. Perhaps by the time this appears in print we shall already know whether this confidence is justified or not.

On the other hand, there are also signs that *la Haute Couture* has suddenly grown a little frightened at its own exuberance and is already contemplating a new and simpler line. Thus, in April 1930, at the moment of leaving for America after a tour of Europe, the editress of *Vogue*, in an interview with a representative of an Italian paper, predicted an immediate return to the classical spirit of simple flowing draperies, though of course with long skirts (and with long hair and other 'feminine' characteristics to match).

the same general aims in view. The moment is undoubtedly an unusually thrilling one for the student of dress; and if the psychologist and sociologist can spare a little time from their graver preoccupations, the struggle now taking place in fashion may be well worth their contemplation, for the interesting lesson that it offers of skilful leadership in a cause of doubtful popularity, and of the reactions to this leadership of western womanhood in the first critical years of a new freedom and a new self-consciousness.

CHAPTER XI

THE EVOLUTION OF GARMENTS

Superfluous lags the vet'ran on the stage.
SAMUEL JOHNSON, *Vanity of Human Wishes.*

THERE is still one aspect of the evolution of clothes that we have not considered. We have reviewed in general outline certain main stages or styles of dress—the primitive, the tropical, and the arctic—and have shown the manner in which they influence our present costume. We have seen, moreover, that it is possible to distinguish two principal types of development in dress, the one much more rapid than the other; and that this distinction, though it is in the last resort quantitative rather than qualitative in nature, is yet of value in helping us to realise the varying influence on dress of certain fundamental mechanisms of a psychological and social order. Finally, we have examined somewhat more in detail the rise and fall of certain more specific styles or 'fashions', and have endeavoured here also to indicate the chief social and psychological influences that have been at work. To be complete, a study of the evolution of clothes should descend to a still greater degree of particularity, and should examine the process of evolution as it manifests itself in the development and history of special garments. Our wardrobes, as they exist to-day, consist of a number of garments of fairly well-defined type, each type of a particular shape, size, cut (and often, material and colour). For the sake of convenience we distinguish each type by a special name, and talk, for instance, of blouses, shoes, and stockings, coats, pants, and vests. All the individual garments belonging to a particular type have some essential similarity, chiefly determined by the part and extent of the body which they are destined to cover; at the same time, however, they may, within certain limits, exhibit considerable individual variation as regards shape, colour, material, and size.

Now, in contemplating the changes that human costume has undergone in the course of its development, it is possible to make use of certain of the concepts of biological science, and to compare the evolution of clothes to the evolution of living forms. Appropriately enough it was Sir George Darwin, a son of Charles Darwin, who first drew attention to the analogy that exists between the two developmental series.[1] Unfortunately, with the one striking exception of the work of Webb,[2] the point of view that Darwin suggested does not seem to have been in any way consistently adopted by subsequent writers on dress; nor can we enter upon such a treatment here, since it would engross us in a series of detailed historical problems which would be quite out of place in a small book dealing with the psychology, rather than the history, of dress. Nevertheless, as affording a fitting conclusion to our study of the development of costume contained in the three preceding chapters, it would seem appropriate to indicate, in roughest outline, the general nature of such parallel as can be drawn between biological and sartorial evolution, and to illustrate the nature of the problems with the help of a few specific examples. It is true that the more intimately psychological aspects of development must here remain somewhat in the background. But this does not mean that the problems themselves lack psychological aspects. On the contrary, these aspects must, in reality, be just as important as in the more general questions of development already considered. It is only that our detailed knowledge of the problems is in most cases still insufficient for us profitably to attempt much in the nature of psychological treatment.

In the analogy between the development of living forms and the development of dress, a single individual garment obviously corresponds to a single individual organism, while the corresponding type of garment

[1] Darwin, 20.   [2] Webb, 103.

corresponds to the species. Let us first compare the individual garment to the individual organism. The individual organism comes into the world with certain definite structures of body and of mind which he has inherited from his parents, and, through them, from a long line of remoter ancestors. Similarly, a single garment, for instance a pair of trousers, may be said to have an heredity. Its main lines are determined by the trousers actually being worn at the time that it was fashioned. These latter trousers may be said to be, in a sense, its immediate parents. During its lifetime it is subjected to various external influences which will alter its appearance. If it leads a healthy life, is not overworked, has the good fortune to be worn by a conscientious owner who places it at night within a press or under his mattress, where it can recover from the strains of the day's work, it will long retain its shape and freshness. But if it is allowed to acquire bad habits of sitting, it will (much as a child may do) acquire some permanent defect of figure or of posture. In any case, however, it will, after a time, grow tired and baggy at the knees. Then it will need to take a holiday by going to the tailor's to be pressed and cleaned, and will thus acquire a new lease of life, just as an individual man will recuperate his forces by going for a holiday. The trousers may even meet with an accident, as an individual may. The individual may lose an arm or a leg, and these will need to be replaced by artificial limbs. The trousers also may need to be patched at the knees or in the seat. Ultimately there arrives a time when the trousers are incapable of further service; they die a natural death, just as does the individual. But, during its lifetime, our pair of trousers has, in turn, exercised an influence over other trousers that were being made. It has become, in a sense, the parent of these trousers, and, just as with the individual, parenthood is a function of vigorous maturity rather than of decrepit old age. No tailor will copy these trousers when they have become patched and threadbare and have lost their shape.

Similarly, it is possible to compare a whole type of garments with a species of animal. In this way we might regard trousers as one species, coats as another, shirts as a third, and shoes as a fourth, comparable to, say, men, horses, dogs, and cats. In both cases each individual member of the species bears some resemblance to its immediate forefathers and, in its turn, hands on some of its characteristics to its descendants. In neither case is there any necessary permanent distinction between one species and another. Just as biology has taught us that, in the animal kingdom, one species may gradually develop from another, so there can be no doubt also that one type of garment may have evolved from remote ancestors of quite a different type. It would be a fascinating task, for instance, to trace the development of trousers from the simple shawl tied round the waist, from which they began, through the various loopings and tyings that constituted their earliest attempts at bifurcation, until they gradually attained their present shape.

Just as, in the case of biological evolution, the environment may sometimes be such as to permit of the persistence of living forms over many generations with little if any modification, and may at other times (*e.g.* at periods of quickly changing climate) bring about rapid development by means of rigorous natural selection, so also in the case of clothes. The moulding influences here consist of human desires and human institutions. When these change quickly, the various types of garment in use will be adapted rapidly in accordance with the new tastes and needs, so that within a comparatively few generations the original type of garment may itself cease to exist—that is, it will no longer be easily recognisable as belonging to the same class as its forefathers, and will require expert knowledge to trace its lineage. Such times of rapid change correspond, of course, to periods when the system of 'modish' dress predominates. At its quickest, fashion will probably carry on the evolution of garments at a pace that (if measured in generations) is seldom achieved by natural selection, except in occasional instances of cataclysmic change, or when man himself intervenes to hurry Nature's processes—as in the introduction of a species to a new environment, or in the carrying out of special experiments in breeding. Corresponding also to something in the nature of a cataclysmic change are those moments in the history of dress when not only are the garments in use greatly modified from those favoured in immediately preceding periods, but the actual number of garments is drastically reduced: as occurred most dramatically at the turn of the eighteenth century, and as has happened also in our own day. Such times, when garments are used to outline and frame the body rather than to give an aesthetic pleasure in themselves, correspond to Nature's niggardly periods, when conditions of life become so unfavourable that whole species disappear, and only those who have special powers of adaptation to the new conditions are able to survive (as, for instance, in glacial epochs). But when desire once again becomes directed to a luxurious profusion and amplitude of clothes, then it is as though Nature were again in smiling mood, and in her warm affection had conjured to life a myriad of new offspring to take the place of those that had been lost. The billowing abundance of mid-Victorian times was indeed, from the point of view of clothes evolution, like a period of tropical fertility following upon the arctic chill of 1800, when, at the moment of greatest stress, stockings, shoes, and gowns were the only garments whose existence was assured, and even the most attenuated forms of underwear seemed threatened with extinction. Our own times have constituted another period unfavourable to the development of clothes, both in number, variety, and size. Petticoats have all but disappeared, stockings are perhaps none too safe, the flimsy descendants of the corset are invertebrate degenerates in comparison with their stiff and haughty ancestors, and how puny is the present skirt by the side of its more bulky and imposing predecessors!

Compared with the bewildering variety of fashion, the system of 'fixed' dress provides an environment under which types are relatively stable. Generation after generation of garment is produced, each one differing hardly at all from its predecessors. This resembles natural conditions in those parts of the world (*e.g.* Australia) which, owing to their isolation, are little subject to violent disturbance from outside and in which, consequently, certain relatively primitive types of animal are able to persist unchanged, in a way that would not have been possible elsewhere. Here, where evolution is slower, we may find it easier to study the process of change and development in dress.

The dress of modern men, though far from being entirely 'fixed', approximates, as we have seen, to this condition much more than does that of women. In the remainder of this chapter we propose to use men's dress as a field for the investigation of one particular aspect of clothes evolution—an aspect to which Sir George Darwin drew special attention in his original contribution to the subject.

We know that natural selection, working upon the material provided by the spontaneous variation of living forms, moulds a race by allowing greater chances of survival to those who vary from the parent forms in a certain direction, the survivors then tending, in virtue of the laws of heredity, to hand on their peculiarity to their successors. In this process of evolution, variations in some directions help towards survival, while variations in other directions have no such value, and therefore do not tend to be perpetuated (except in so far as they may be biologically correlated with variations of the first kind). It thus comes about that evolution changes some parts of the bodily structure more than others; those parts which are not subject to essential or to correlated variations in the above sense tend to remain in their original condition. In this way, certain parts of the body may, so to speak, lag behind in the course of evolution, and may even persist when, through changes of other parts of the body, they have lost their original usefulness. They may thus become vestigial organs; and, as is well known, biologists can sometimes explain the nature and original function of a particular organ by reference to the past history of the race, even though this organ appears to have no present use. So it is with clothes. The clothes we wear, especially the clothes of men, have many vestigial features, features which have no utility at present, but which can be shown to have been useful in the past. In some cases it is possible to trace, with a high degree of certainty, how these features originally came about and what purpose they originally served. In other cases their origin is still a matter of conjecture.

Let us consider a few examples, passing gradually from the easy to the more difficult.[1]

Men's tail-coats contain two buttons at the back. These buttons serve no purpose nowadays. They are survivals of a past when horses rather than motor-cars or railways were the principal means of conveyance. When a man was riding, it was often convenient to draw up the tails of his coat so that they did not come into too close contact with the flanks of the horse, and these two buttons are survivals from a time when buttons in this position were actually of use for this purpose. There are many other examples of this kind. Top-boots (other than 'Russian boots') usually have a part that is turned down at the top, this part often being made of different material from the rest of the boots and having a different colour. It is now a part that is purely ornamental, and has no useful function. But it is a survival from the time when the upper part of top-boots could actually be turned up to cover more of the leg when it was so desired. The tags by which top-boots were formerly pulled on still survive, but are again, for the most part, merely ornamental. They can often be seen at the side of the boots, but are now sometimes actually sewn down and are therefore completely useless; so useless, in fact, that in some boots new tags have been inserted in the side of

[1] Most of these examples are taken from the rich collection of Webb, 103.

the boot to take the place of the old ones which have lost their function. There exist several rather similar cases of the transition from the useful to the ornamental. The cuffs that ornament the sleeves of coats are now, for the most part, fixed and serve merely as decoration, but in former times coat-sleeves could often be turned back in order to display the highly ornamented sleeve of an inner garment.

In the case of trousers, we ourselves have in recent years had the opportunity to observe such a transition actually taking place. Men found that it was convenient to turn up the bottom of their trousers to prevent them getting muddy. To begin with, this was only regarded as a temporary measure, and the trousers were turned down again when the wearer came indoors from the muddy streets. But now, for a good many years, trousers have been made of which the ends are permanently turned up and cannot be turned down at all; so that the turned-up portion here has similarly become purely ornamental.

These examples illustrate a very general rule in the evolution of clothes, namely, that what was originally useful was later on retained for the sake of ornament.

Just one more example of this kind. The collars of men's coats usually have a small nick or cut-out portion at the point that divides the collar from the lapels. This obviously serves no present purpose, but it also can be shown to be a survival from the past when it had a function. At one time it was customary to turn up the back of the collar without turning up the lapel. Now the only way in which this could be done was by having a deep nick between the two. The present nicks are not deep enough to serve this function. They have, therefore, lost their usefulness, and are perhaps in process of disappearance, for they have already vanished from the dinner-jacket and have, for the most part, entirely vanished from waistcoats, though these formerly also had small collars with nicks in them.

This last fact, that the waistcoat had a collar and that

this collar has a vestigial feature showing that the collar could be turned up, serves to remind us that the waistcoat itself is the relic of an outer garment, the upper part of which could be raised so as to protect the back of the neck. What was originally an outer garment has, in this case, become an inner garment; and this, in turn, illustrates an interesting feature to which historians of dress have drawn attention, namely, that when a new garment is adopted, there is a tendency for it to be put on over the old garment. This tendency has probably played an important part in the development of dress. Just as particular features of dress are slow to disappear, so also are individual garments themselves, which may persist even under circumstances that one would expect to lead to their disappearance. Sometimes, as here, an older garment is not displaced, but merely covered (a process analogous to that which psychoanalysis has shown to take place in the course of mental development). The significance of this tendency for the history of clothing as a whole lies largely in the fact that it leads to an increase in the number of layers, one above the other, of which a costume may consist.[1]

If in many instances of the development of dress the useful persists as the merely ornamental, in some cases an ornamental feature may be developed in order to hide a utilitarian one. Thus it would appear that the clocks on socks and stockings represent a form of decoration that was originally designed to cover the seams with which stockings were then made, and which were regarded as unsightly. A particularly interesting example concerns the stripes that have in recent years been introduced down the sides of men's dress trousers. This seems to be in the nature of a reversion, such as is sometimes to be observed in the biological sphere also, when a particular individual will revert to characteristics that distinguished the race many generations ago.

[1] Though of course it is very far from being true that all inner garments or underclothes were originally outer garments.

At one time trousers were made so tight that they had to be provided with buttons up the sides, which could be undone when the trousers were drawn on. These buttons later became hidden by a stripe. The stripe persisted after the buttons had disappeared (when no longer needed owing to the increased width of the trousers). In time the stripe itself vanished, but of late years, in an endeavour to make somewhat more ornamental the sombre black of evening trousers, tailors have resuscitated the stripe—thus harking back to a form of decoration which itself arose in the first place to hide a purely useful feature.

In some cases the gradual evolution of a garment may involve very great changes, so that its origin may only be detected in some small vestigial feature. This seems to be the case with that military equivalent of the top-hat, the busby. The busby originally belonged to the Hussars, who were Hungarian soldiers and wore the peasant cap of Hungary that is shown on the left-hand side of Fig. 21. It consisted of a cloth cap with a band of fur round the edge, itself originally, it would appear, part of a fur lining, the bottom end of which was turned up, thus showing the fur. Gradually the fur on the cap became wider and wider and the cloth part grew smaller and smaller. In many forms of the busby, the original shape of the hat, as shown in the left-hand picture, has completely disappeared. The only trace of its origin is to be found in the fact that the top of the busby is (or, at any rate, was) made of cloth instead of fur, but in one form of the busby—that worn by the Honourable Artillery Company—a vestige of the original shape is still to be detected in the small flap that hangs down at the side, as will be seen on the right-hand side of Fig. 21.

Sometimes the retention of a vestigial feature may be due, or at least be attributed (such stories often contain legendary elements) to some particular event, which has given this feature a new value. A striking instance of this is the flash of the Royal Welch Fusiliers. Let Robert Graves, who served in that regiment, tell the story: 'The

Fig.21. Illustrating Evolution in Dress

(a) The red Hungarian cap which was the fore-runner of the busby

(b) A busby (of the Honourable Artillery Company) in which the cap is a vestige only

From W. M. Webb, *The Heritage of Dress* (by permission of the author)

flash is a fan-like bunch of five black ribbons, each ribbon two inches wide and seven and a half inches long: the angle at which the fan is spread is exactly regulated by regimental convention. It is stitched to the back of the tunic collar. Only the Royal Welch are privileged to wear it. The story is that the Royal Welch were abroad on foreign service for several years in the 1830's and, by some chance, never received the army order abolishing the queue. When the regiment returned and paraded at Plymouth, the inspecting general rated the commanding officer because his men were still wearing their hair in the old fashion. The commanding officer, angry with the slight, immediately rode up to London and won from King William IV., through the intercession of some court official, the regimental privilege of continuing to wear the bunch of ribbons in which the end of the queue was tied—the flash.'[1] During the Great War there was a prolonged and obstinate struggle between the regiment and the Army Council, who saw in the flash a distinctive target for enemy marksmen. Nevertheless, the officers and warrant officers continued to wear it—with, it is said, the privately expressed approval of the King himself, who was Colonel-in-Chief of the regiment; and in 1919 the flash was officially sanctioned on service dress for all ranks, together with permission to retain another definite regimental peculiarity, the spelling of the word 'Welch' with a 'c'.

In all these cases the main outlines of development are fairly clear. But, as I said, there are other cases in which we can only surmise the course of evolution. The ornamental markings on boots and shoes, especially those markings which take the form of small perforations through a portion of the leather, have given rise to much conjecture. These markings are of great antiquity and can be traced to Roman times and even earlier. It has been suggested that the earliest shoemakers contented themselves with tying a piece of leather roughly round the foot. This would necessarily give rise to awk-

[1] *Good-bye to All That*, p. 119.

ward puckers in the leather, puckers which could perhaps best be dealt with by the simple process of cutting them away. This would of course leave open slits in the shoe of a kind that are actually observable in some primitive examples to be found in museums; slits which probably became ornamental and gave rise to the vestigial features that still adorn so many of our own boots and shoes.

We saw in a previous chapter that ornaments loosely hung round the body were probably worn earlier than actual clothes. When clothes were adopted they tended to cover these ornaments; and in some cases the ornaments themselves, so that they should not be unnoticed altogether, have come to be symbolically represented on the clothes (an example of the fact that 'sartorial' decoration only copies the other forms of decoration mentioned in Chapter III. Cf. p. 52). This may possibly be the case with the stripes that ornament the sleeves of military and naval uniforms, stripes which perhaps originally represented bracelets such as were conferred on Roman soldiers as a reward for valour.

Interesting problems arise in certain cases as to why a given article of clothing or adornment should be worn on one side of the body rather than on the other. Plumes and feathers in hats are, I believe, nearly always worn upon the left side. This has been thought to be connected with the fact that plumes were often worn when fighting, and that a plume on the right side of the head would be likely to interfere with, or be damaged by, the free play of the sword.

A more difficult problem is presented by the fact that the buttons on men's garments are usually on the right-hand side, those of women's on the left. The true origin of this difference seems to be shrouded in obscurity. It has been suggested, however, that the practice may be connected with the desire to leave the right hand free in the case of the man, in order that he might hold his sword or implement, and the left hand free in the case of the woman. A woman, when buttoning up, would, it is supposed, grasp her attire with her right hand and push it over to the left, leaving her left arm free to carry a child. It is usual to carry children on the left arm (doubtless to leave the stronger right arm free for other purposes), and among many peoples children are, it is said, allowed to suck the left breast more than the right. The left side of a bodice could, if the right lapped over it, be pulled back without exposing so much of the person as would be necessary in the opposite case, and the garment could be afterwards replaced more easily with the right hand if this alone were free. These last explanations are, as I have said, little more than surmises. It is quite possible that the difference between the sexes in this matter of buttons has some other and more general meaning: for in folk-lore and superstition one very often finds that the right side has a masculine significance and the left side a feminine one, and it may very well be that the factors underlying these superstitions have played a part also in this particular instance of sex differentiation.

These examples of the detailed problems presented by the evolution of dress will suffice to show that, not only in its general lines is our costume determined by its past history, but that its smaller and more insignificant details also are, in many cases, in the nature of vestiges, comparable to the organs of similar nature that we carry in our body. To produce a new design or a new form of ornament is always a matter requiring thought and inspiration. It is easier and more comfortable to fall back upon conventional patterns, and tailors have no exemption from the laws of mental inertia. In sartorial evolution, as in the evolution of living forms, it often happens that only the more essential features are changed in the process of adaptation to fresh conditions; the others may remain unchanged, as witnesses to a state that is long past. The degree of antiquity may, as we have seen, vary very greatly. In some cases the ancestry of a sartorial detail is a relatively short one: in other cases our ornaments may still bear testimony to man's first fumbling efforts to encase his body; or, again, they may imitate decorations which, in their original form, were not strictly sartorial in type at all. Always, however, it is the fact that the products of such efforts have become conventionalised as ornaments that has allowed of their survival long after their utilitarian value had disappeared. Analogous cases of an organ acquiring a new function in the course of its vestigial history are not perhaps unknown to biological science. Certainly, they are common enough in anthropology, which teaches us that ancient rites and customs may be continued for new reasons when the old ones have been lost.

In other cases we see the exemplification of a further important general tendency, namely, that many ornamental details are, in their origin, not so much the successors as the accompaniments of utilitarian features. Here, as in other fields of applied art, human beings are seldom contented with the merely useful. Students of aesthetics may point out that the useful in itself tends also to be beautiful; but mankind as a whole, especially at the more primitive levels of development, has but little realisation or understanding of this principle. Men consequently seek to disguise the purely useful by ornamental features, and, as before, these features may persist long after the natural death of the originally useful features which they were designed to hide or mitigate.

We have seen also how conservatism may lead to the multiplication of actual garments; the old is not necessarily discarded or displaced, but may be merely covered. Finally, we have seen that the details of our clothes sometimes undergo reversions to a more primitive type. Even when we seek the new it is often easier to retrace old paths than to track out new ones. As in the sphere of biology (as cases of atavism show) or in that of psychology (as is shown by the phenomenon of regression, the importance of which has been so startlingly revealed by psycho-pathology), we seldom completely outgrow our own past, which is always ready to reassert itself if opportunity should offer.

CHAPTER XII

THE ETHICS OF DRESS—ART AND NATURE

> In all these circumstances I'll instruct you:
> Go with me to clothe you as becomes you.
> *The Taming of the Shrew*, iv. 2.

WE have now examined both the statics and the dynamics of costume, so far as the modest scope and purpose of this volume will allow. In so doing, we have tried to the best of our ability to be impartial, to study the phenomena of dress and their psychological implications objectively and scientifically, and to refrain from introducing any judgments of value into our considerations. If here and there this endeavour may have failed, we may remind the indulgent reader that this exclusion of the categories of good and bad is unusually difficult in the case of costume, if only for the reason that it demands a totally different attitude from that which we mostly adopt towards the subject. In ordinary life we scarcely ever refer to, or even think of, clothes without in some way or other evaluating them; nearly always the clothes in question are beautiful or ugly, modest or immodest, healthy or unhealthy, cheap or expensive, suitable or inappropriate, fashionable or dowdy, well or ill designed and executed. It has indeed been somewhat difficult for the writer (and perhaps also for the reader) to refrain so long from this habitual attitude. But if the need for evaluation so imperiously asserts itself that it requires a special effort to look at clothes impartially, we may reasonably be permitted, having completed our survey, to look back upon our subject—this time from the more familiar point of view—and allow ourselves the relaxation of considering, in the light of this survey, what in clothes is good and bad, which tendencies we approve and which we deprecate. Perhaps we may reap some reward, if not of clearer insight, at least of greater relish, from having thus long refrained from this indulgence.

But in setting out upon this task, it will be well to bear in mind from the beginning that this changed attitude is not without its own perils and perplexities. To search for what is true without subjective bias is difficult enough; to determine what is good is an undertaking that is still harder to free from individual prejudice. The reader must therefore be prepared for the possibility of parting from the writer, even though he may (doubtless not without some protests and some reservations) have followed him thus far. Not that the prejudices of the one are greater (or smaller) than those of the other, but merely because they happen to be different.

Indeed, some preliminary understanding will be necessary, if we are to go any way at all together. Let us therefore start with some first tentative definition of the 'good' in clothes, one that we will, in a moment, try to render more precise. Clothes, as we saw in our first chapter, are intended to have certain functions—and about the gross nature of these functions there is fortunately little disagreement. May we not say then that the 'good' of clothes is to fulfil these functions, and that the better these functions are fulfilled the better are the clothes? The best clothes will then be those which minister most satisfactorily to the needs of decoration, of modesty, and of protection.

Unfortunately, this general statement does not get us very far, for, as we have seen, these three ends cannot always be made to fit together; more especially, decoration and modesty have aims that are contradictory rather than complementary. An ethical survey of clothes must, therefore, evaluate not only the clothes themselves, but also their functions; before we can proceed, we must decide how far these functions *ought* to be fulfilled, and, in particular, how far one function should give place to another when they clash.

But in this matter it is obvious that we cannot consider individual cases merely on their merits; we have need rather of some principle that we can apply to all such cases as they arise. Here our difficulties begin in earnest, for it seems impossible to adopt some sufficiently specific principle, without making certain far-reaching ethical, or even metaphysical, assumptions. To cut discussion short (for this is a treatise upon clothes and not on ethics) I propose—briefly and dogmatically—to adopt a principle compounded from hedonistic ethics and from Freudian psychology, and to say that *the aim of clothes should be to secure the maximum of satisfaction in accordance with the 'reality principle'* [the principle, that is, of basing our satisfactions upon a fundamental recognition of the real world, and not upon a distortion of it, or a denial of its less pleasant aspects]. Such a principle seems to have at least three great advantages. In the first place, it allows of an extensive agreement on most practical points between those who, in the last resort, see the 'good' in 'pleasure' and those who see it in 'function' or 'development'. Secondly, it is a principle that seems to admit of use in relation to all applied art, so that in employing it we are, at the same time, bringing sartorial art into ethical relation with its sister disciplines. Thirdly, it is a principle that has, in recent years, been generally adopted (often, it is true, only implicitly) in psychological medicine, and has been well tested and used within this sphere. The principle, we may add, has a corollary that is of some importance, a corollary that is derived from psycho-analytic assumptions and technique, namely, that *conscious investigation and assessment* constitute the ultimate test as to whether or not a given tendency is in harmony with the reality principle. If it fails to pass this test, we cannot give it our approval, however greatly it is buttressed by tradition, or however strongly it appeals to the potent but dimmer forces of intuition and emotion.

Before we proceed, it will be well to state clearly what seems to be the weakest point in this principle. In adopting it the writer has been guided by a certain parallelism between the arts of designing, preparing, and wearing clothes upon the one hand and certain further applied arts, such as architecture and the making of furniture upon the other. But the assumption of such parallels is apt to play us false. In reality there is no hard-and-fast distinction between applied art and applied science; there is rather a continuous gradation between the creation of objects that are primarily ornamental and only secondarily useful (like the vases that in some cases still decorate our mantelpieces) and of objects that are primarily useful and only incidentally beautiful (such as water towers or bridges). In the former case a greater departure from the reality principle can be permitted than in the latter; and it might be argued that the function of clothing is primarily aesthetic or at least psychological, and need take but little account of 'reality' other than that of a purely psychological order. I believe it might be possible to show that such a view, which approximates clothing to pure art rather than to applied art, and which, therefore, holds that it is a legitimate field for such neglect of external reality as is implied in the 'pleasure principle', would lead in the last resort to conclusions not very different from our own. But such a demonstration would take time and trouble, and, since the more pressing concrete problems of our clothes are awaiting our attention, we must admit that—superficially at any rate—those who take the view just indicated will be justified in dissenting from our principle and, consequently, from many of the conclusions also that we shall derive from its application. Here then there is, perhaps, a parting of the ways with a number of our readers. But even to such readers our further considerations may not be without value, inasmuch as they will at least furnish a statement of certain problems, though the answers may seem to lie in different directions from those which are here indicated.

With this much settled, let us pass to the actual business of evaluation. It will perhaps be most convenient if we deal with individual questions in the order in which they have been treated in this book. Naturally, however, the amount of consideration which we now have to give to any matter will bear no necessary relationship to that which we before devoted to it—since in any given case the facts may be complex and the ethics simple, or vice versa. We shall also find it necessary to supplement our review of the ground already covered by a few further considerations, both general and specific, of matters that seem of special interest and importance from our present standpoint.

The questions of **decoration** dealt with in **Chapter II.** need not detain us long. It is pretty universally agreed that the sexual aspects of decoration are fundamental and must inevitably remain of primary importance, whether we would or no. Our principle, too, requires the frank recognition of the sexual element in decoration and (subject to any subsequently mentioned restrictions) the due enjoyment of the satisfactions that it can give.

The use of decoration to signify **rank** and **locality** obviously depend upon the ethical value of 'fixed', as compared with that of 'modish', costume (since 'modish' costume is in its very essence hostile to associations with place or social status). We can, therefore, safely leave these points for the present.

The connection between **wealth** and costume is also one that must be judged according to our view of fashion. We have seen, however, that modern life is tending to abolish the sartorial distinctions of wealth, as it has done those of rank, at least so far as general style is concerned (the vast improvements made in recent years with artificial precious stones and pearls is tending to abolish the distinctions even as regards the smaller costly ornaments). Men's clothes have, of course, gone further in this direction than have women's, and it would seem that women might profitably copy men at least in one direction, namely, in the abolition of that particular form of snobbery which demands an unreasonably large number of different costumes. The Empress Elizabeth of Austria very sensibly protested when she found that Court etiquette demanded that she should wear a pair of shoes but once,[1] and our present-day leaders of society would be equally justified in protesting against the convention that an evening dress, however beautiful, should not appear on two successive nights. It is absurd, for instance, that a woman visiting friends for the week-end should feel obliged to include two evening dresses in her outfit; the absurdity arising from the fact that, for all but the really wealthy, the additional expense involved is out of proportion to the additional satisfaction (thereby necessitating the sacrifice of potential satisfaction in other directions).

The **carrying of essential articles** is a matter which is well worthy of some attention, though in general it will be agreed that the utilitarian aspects must here definitely take precedence over the decorative. At the present time men and women employ quite different systems, men carrying what is needful in their pockets, women in bags which are not attached in any way to their persons, but carried loosely in their hands. Both systems have serious disadvantages. Men tend to lose their articles in their multitude of pockets;[2] the pockets themselves are not at all conveniently accessible when overcoats are worn in winter; and when, as so often, they are filled to bulging point, they seriously deform the tailor's handiwork; lastly, the necessity for removing a variety of separate articles from a number of receptacles takes considerable time (often longer than the actual process of changing a suit) and frequently leads to some essential article being overlooked. On the other hand, the system at present in vogue among women has even greater drawbacks, namely, that the loosely carried bag is easily lost or stolen and that it involves the use of a hand that should be

---

[1] Eugene Bagger, *Francis Joseph*, p. 245.
[2] When walking in the street in an overcoat, the writer found that he had twenty altogether—and he believes that this is not exceptional.

free for other purposes. The need for carrying about a number of small articles is one of the graver disadvantages of civilisation, and it is time that the problem of how this need can best be met should be seriously tackled. It may seem to many a somewhat insignificant point, but it is a point that concerns all of us during the whole of our adult lives. Few things really bear better witness to the utter absence of rational thought about our clothing than that this matter should be left to chance or fashion. There is room here for experimental study which should take account of all the practical, psychological, physiological, sartorial, and aesthetic aspects concerned. Meanwhile, it would seem as if the solution would lie in the direction of a combination of the present male and female methods. The advantages of having the loose articles contained in a bag, pouch, or wallet (or at least in a few of these receptacles), rather than in a great number of pockets, is pretty obvious; but so, also, is the benefit of having this receptacle securely attached to the body, thus leaving free the hands. Experiment would seem to be required then, as to how such bags or pouches could be conveniently, comfortably, and withal artistically, carried. Attachment to a belt or girdle round the waist seems the most hopeful method in the case of receptacles containing small articles constantly in use, and some of the bags carried in this way in earlier times were far from ugly. For carrying any heavier articles that are less frequently required, the knapsack surely points to the correct method—though its utility for other than military or tourist purposes is seldom recognised except by members of a very few professions.

With regard to the general principle of the **extension of the bodily self,** nothing need be said except that the clearer and more universal recognition of the principle (and of its limitations), together with its more detailed study by experiment and observation, must surely conduce to a greater aesthetic satisfaction in our clothing.

Turning now to **Chapter III.,** the only form of corporal decoration that need concern us is that of painting. We may note, however, in passing that the practical disappearance of the other categories from western civilisation (except for hairdressing and a certain amount of tattooing) tends to show that the principle of evaluation that we have adopted is in harmony with the general trend of social development, which, as we have already indicated, points to an increasing tolerance of the human body in its natural form and thus an acceptance of 'reality'. With regard to **painting and the use of cosmetics** in general, there is, however, considerable difference of opinion at the present moment. The undoubted increase in the use of paint and powder among Western women in the years following the war is a movement away from reality and should, therefore, in accordance with our general principle, be looked upon with suspicion. Its danger lies in the tendency to cultivate an artificial ideal. As long as it is only used to imitate Nature at her best, the standard aimed at is still that of reality (though the method may be makeshift), but when lips become red with an intensity that Nature never gave even to her healthiest and loveliest daughters, there is a small but definite step backwards towards the barbarism that finds beauty in the constricted waist, the contorted foot, and the lopped finger-joint. Another way in which painting may be said to contradict the reality principle is that it leads to Narcissism rather than to love of others or interest in the outer world. The constant and flaunting use of powder and lipstick in public[1] implies a preoccupation

[1] However, it is only fair to bear in mind that the carrying out of personal embellishment in public has not in all cases been confined to women, as is illustrated by the following account of Ibsen's behaviour at a public meeting held in his honour: "'Esteemed Master', begins the speaker. But Henrik Ibsen, interrupting him with a gesture of the hand, says quite quietly and with a voice of glassy clearness, 'One moment, please'. With this he extracts a large blue handkerchief from the back pocket of his coat and rubs his face with it until it shines all over. He then leisurely replaces the handkerchief, dives into his breast pocket and brings out an immense comb, holds his top-hat in front of his eyes and looks earnestly and attentively at his own image reflected in the mirror which is fixed to the inside of the hat. He then proceeds to a thorough combing of his hair and whiskers, until they stand out like a flame from his head, in the way that is to be seen in all his photographs. We look on at all this, nonplussed and dumbfounded,

with self and a relative indifference to other things or persons (that, of course, is why it is liable to be so irritating[1]), in fact, a withdrawal from the outer world that is hostile to the higher forms alike of work and love and sociality.

But lest we should become reactionary through over-righteous moralising on this subject (it may be remembered in our defence that it is our first serious bout after a long period of abstinence), it will be well to bear in mind the circumstances that have elicited this new exuberance of paint and powder. From such individual investigation as I have been able to make on the subject, it would seem that the defiant use of powder-puff and lipstick is a token at once of triumph and of independence, signalling a victory in the spheres both of sex and of society—a victory over old habits of sexual repression and social subordination. It is a victorious gesture on the part of women and, like other victorious gestures, not always in the best of taste.[2] If it is itself in some ways retrograde, it is nevertheless correlated with a great advance in social status and in sexual freedom. Such a minor evil can well be tolerated and excused for so great a gain. It is probable, too, that it will not be permanent. When a conqueror has grown used to the fruits of victory, he has no need of gestures to express his triumph. Similarly, women may experience no need to proclaim

---

but when Ibsen is ready, he strikes an attitude and says, without the slightest sign of embarrassment, 'Thank you, I'm ready now'." A. V. Winterfeld, *Henrik Ibsen*, Reclam edition, p. 30.

[1] Though another factor in this irritation may come from the auto-erotic elements involved in the practice, in virtue of which 'powdering the nose', like any other manipulation of the person's own body, is apt to be unconsciously identified with (genital or anal) masturbation (sometimes of course correctly, for the identification may unconsciously exist for the manipulator also).

[2] As noted in an earlier chapter, Knight Dunlap, 24, p. 76, thinks that the increased use of cosmetics in recent years is a sort of compensation for the exposure of the legs by short skirts: if the disadvantages of the uncomely must be thus ruthlessly revealed at the lower end of the body, the less well endowed have their revenge by equalising all complexions (in the way that all legs were formerly equalised by the long skirt). The theory is attractive, but I have not noticed any less readiness to resort to cosmetics on the part of those with good complexions, as one might expect if it were true. My own observations point rather to short skirts and artificial complexions being both of them symbols of the new-won liberty of women.

their independence when they feel it is assured. Possibly, too, the very necessity of a gesture indicates that the victory is incomplete; here, as always, excessive Narcissism indicates a failure to attain the stage of 'object love', and this failure is often due to an inhibition of the sexual aims relating to this stage. Perhaps the cure lies, not in less, but in more sexual freedom (in the psychological and not merely the sociological sense). When women have more confidence in their ability and right to satisfy their sexual desires, they may find it unnecessary to bolster up their self-assurance with plastered blobs of red and white, but will show a greater faith by trusting the unaided power of the complexion that Nature has provided.

With regard to **external** decorations, we must admit that all forms are justifiable within their proper sphere. We may note, however, a general tendency, as development proceeds (both in the individual and the race) for ever greater emphasis to be laid upon the whole rather than the parts. This of course is in harmony with the general canons of aesthetics. In practice it means (as noted in Chapter III. itself) a somewhat increasing subordination of all purely local forms of ornament. Probably this tendency will demand also an increasing restraint in the use of all non-sartorial forms of decoration —especially of jewellery. Civilised peoples wear fewer isolated ornamental objects than do savages, and, among the more cultured classes of civilised society, it is becoming bad form to indulge in a very free display of precious stones, except upon a few quite definite occasions. Ultimately, perhaps, our aesthetic taste may abolish these forms of decoration altogether. For the present, however, they clearly give too much satisfaction to make it reasonable or hopeful to ask that they should be abandoned.

With **Chapter IV.** we come to the distinctly difficult question of **modesty.** Our traditional morality, derived from Semitic and early Christian sources, assigns to modesty a high value; in quite recent times, however, we have become somewhat sceptical as to its real worth. Application of the standard that we have ourselves adopted in this chapter would seem to require that we should distinguish between two rather different things that are often included under the single term 'modesty': (1) control of conduct, in the sense of refraining from certain forms of 'immodesty', *i.e.* sexually exciting or socially presumptuous behaviour—behaviour in which our exhibitionistic tendencies, if uncontrolled, might lead us to indulge; (2) an emotion of shame or embarrassment, which tends to prevent us from showing or mentioning certain parts of the body, and which may persist even when real circumstances demand mention or exposure, *e.g.* at a medical examination.

Now it is clear that the reality principle demands some degree of modesty in the first sense; on the other hand, it seems doubtful whether modesty in the second sense is ever of much value in itself, since its tendency is inevitably hostile to a true evaluation of certain 'real' factors. In so far as reference to, or exposure of, certain parts of the body is considered 'rude' or 'immodest' (apart from the purpose of the reference or exposure) and gives rise to corresponding emotions, there cannot but occur an inclination to conceal and distort the true functions and importance of these parts of the body—in fact a tendency to refuse the full recognition of their real existence. Now all recent psycho-pathology tends to stress very strongly the difference between non-indulgence and non-recognition. Restraints on indulgence may often be essential (though they are far from constituting the highest pinnacles of virtue); restraints on the recognition of reality (even though they be undertaken in the interests of morality) we have learnt to look upon as highly dangerous. This is, indeed, one of the most important contributions of psycho-analysis to ethics, one which has already produced a far-reaching modification in ethical thought. In so far, then, as we approve of modesty in the second sense, we can at most allow ourselves a sort of conditional approval, in that a certain amount of shame may be inevitably aroused in connection with the due control of exhibitionistic tendencies. We cannot look upon it as a good in itself and we shall regard as desirable its reduction to the smallest possible dimensions.

Lest it be thought that we are seeking to undermine the whole basis of moral restraint, we must remind the reader that the control of conduct in an ethical sense has but little relation to the feeling of shame, and that the manifestations of the latter are notoriously variable and subject to convention. Recent history has shown, for instance, that shame may be withdrawn from a portion of the body to which it formerly attached (the lower part of the legs in women) without any alarming moral consequences. The much more thorough experiments of 'Nude Culture'[1] point in the same direction. Indeed if, as is often done, we content ourselves with the simple equation of the immoral with the genitally sexual, these experiments show pretty conclusively that nakedness is a potent method of reducing immorality.

The real point to bear in mind is that modesty is essentially correlated with desire. Its purpose is to fight desire, but in so doing it rekindles it, so that a circular process is inevitably set in motion. As Anatole France so well says: 'Il est certain que la pudeur communique aux femmes un attrait invincible'.[2] Nature has, in fact, provided that modesty can never finally attain its end except through its own disappearance. And this disappearance involves also the loss of a certain piquancy in desire, a piquancy that can only come when desire and inhibition are adroitly intermingled. Here is perhaps the real rub—the very justifiable fear that in overcoming modesty we shall deprive ourselves also of the most maddeningly stimulating elements of desire. Thus it is that, hiding under the cloak of modesty, there are

---

[1] Cf. Parmelee, 70, and Seitz, 88.
[2] In the chapter in question (*L'Isle des Pingouins*, book ii. chap. 1) he puts, in his own inimitable way, the whole case that we are here urging.

often to be found certain subtle components of the sexual urge itself; a strange alliance, but one that resembles that which we have already seen to exist in the combined phallic and moral symbolism of certain clothes, and one that psycho-analysis has shown to be thoroughly characteristic of the neurotic mind.[1] Modesty is, therefore, not merely an obstacle to the clear apprehension of external reality; it also fosters something in the nature of internal (albeit for the most part unconscious) hypocrisy, and thus stands condemned on a double charge of distorting the appearance both of our bodies and our minds.

Our treatment of modesty has been in very general terms; inevitably so, considering that the application of our main principle was here so difficult. In practice it seems fairly evident that our principle involves a large further extension of the tendencies towards greater freedom that have been in evidence of recent years. We ourselves look back upon certain manifestations of nineteenth-century modesty—such as the inability to mention the word 'leg', the rigorous segregation of the sexes at bathing, the curtained steps of bathing machines (so that the bather might not be seen before she had reached the protecting opaqueness of the water), the monstrously protuberant bathing dresses—with astonishment mingled with disgust; the latter because, at this distance, we are able to perceive the erotic obsessiveness of the modesty in question. Future generations may one day contemplate with similar emotion the fact that we wear bathing dresses at all. Our principle clearly demands that we

[1] We are here touching the fringe of a very big problem. It is true that over-determinations of the kind in question are characteristic of individual neuroses and of their social equivalents. But our knowledge is, perhaps as yet, insufficient to say whether these over-determinations are, for instance: (a) always pathological, and therefore to be resolved whenever possible; (b) essential stages in development, inevitably to be passed through if certain higher levels are to be attained (essential perhaps because of the stimulation of the libido that they produce — a stimulation that manifests itself sexually as the 'piquancy' we have referred to, but which may also be essential for the higher sublimations); (c) always and throughout essential for the higher sublimations. In the opinion of the present writer the evidence hitherto available is against the third hypothesis. If, however, this hypothesis should prove to be the correct one, the position we have taken up with regard to modesty would require some modification.

should be able to tolerate nakedness where it is obviously called for, as on the bathing beach.

It involves too, to give another example, the abolition of the stimulating obscenity of certain underclothes. Ideally, all layers of which our clothing may consist should be equally presentable; whether we wear more or fewer layers on any given occasion should be determined by considerations of beauty, hygiene, and comfort rather than of modesty. There is here a subtle interaction with aesthetic factors which is deserving of further study. Garments which, through their lack of ornamentation, are clearly not intended to be seen (such as women's corsets and suspenders, the coarser forms of underwear, men's braces, and—most ridiculous offenders of all—the back portions of their waistcoats), when accidentally viewed, produce an embarrassing sense of intrusion upon privacy that often verges on the indecent.[1] It is like looking 'behind the scenes' and thus exposing an illusion. True modesty and true aesthetics should alike seek, either to eliminate such purely useful garments, or else to incorporate them in the total aesthetic scheme of the costume worn.[2]

Passing now to **Chapter V.,** our reality test demands that **protection** should have its due place among the functions of clothing. We must beware, however, of modesty masquerading as protection. In recent years our ideas concerning the necessity for protection from cold have undergone great modifications, modifications which may become still more extensive if, as Ernest Jones[3] maintains, our ideas concerning cold are largely determined by deep-rooted complexes, and if a general realisation of

---

[1] The same applies to men's loose cuffs and detachable shirt fronts, when seen apart from their conventional setting. In England there is such a strong feeling against these detachable garments that they are seldom worn in 'respectable' society, though the detachable collar has persisted. In connection with all these garments there is a disagreeable feeling of pretence or hypocrisy, as is indicated perhaps by the French term *faux col*. It seems probable that feelings derived from the castration complex play a part in the emotions raised by such detachable pieces of male dress.

[2] Their unpleasantness is not so much due to their purely useful character as to the fact that, not being intended for exhibition, no effort has been made to fit them into this total scheme.

the consequent illusory nature of these ideas should come about. There is now a strong tendency in medical circles to emphasise the desirability of light clothing, which will allow the skin to perform its natural functions of adaptation to changing temperatures, in place of the former belief that it was the business of clothes to keep the body as warm as could conveniently be borne (and sometimes warmer) under all conditions. Women's lighter clothing, the earlier examples of which were anathematised as 'pneumonia blouses', is now almost universally approved from the hygienic point of view. Indeed, we find a prominent physician going so far as to say that 'the nearer women's dress can approach nudity, having regard to reasonable decency, the better it will be for them'.[1]

This change of attitude has been accompanied by a relaxation in the ideas of modesty, and a greater freedom towards skin and muscle erotism. Indeed it is probably a relaxation of 'moral' inhibitions that has led to a modification in our views on hygiene rather than the opposite. There has been as yet but little serious attempt to study the protective aspects of clothing from a strictly scientific standpoint; we know, for instance, very little about the relations between the reduction of heat-loss by clothing and the all-important matter of liability to infectious disease. If we were in earnest about the hygienic aspects of clothing, we should study the question seriously and systematically. Similarly with regard to the effects of light. The rays of the sun have fallen on us since our first appearance on this planet, but only in

[1] It is often implied (perhaps the above passage is a case in point) and sometimes explicitly maintained that, owing to her more generous provision of fatty tissue, woman is in need of lesser covering than man. This is a very modern point of view which would have seemed strange to earlier generations, who were so fond of contrasting man's strength with women's weakness, and one suspects that it originates from an attempt to find some hygienic justification for existing practice. Nevertheless it may have some real validity, as is suggested by the recent striking successes of women in long-distance swimming—a sport that makes unusual demands on the ability to withstand cold. Meanwhile those who still seek to emphasise man's superior strength sometimes take refuge in the curiously ascetic rationalisation that man, being muscularly stronger, can and should handicap himself with a greater burden of clothes, insinuating that those who complain of this burden are 'out of condition'.

the last few years have we begun to realise that the exclusion of these rays by clothing may have certain important physiological effects. It is true, however, that in this case the few years in question have been quite fruitful in results, though there has, as yet, been little attempt to make use of these results in actual practice.[1] Indeed the hygienic point of view is really quite a new one—one the possibility and importance of which humanity as a whole has only just begun to realise. It is itself still partially obscured by rationalisations of one kind or another, and is, as yet, utterly incapable of combating the formidable and well-entrenched motives of display, modesty, and fashion, and the various sexual and 'moral' symbolisms. Nevertheless the reality value of this point of view can, of course, scarcely be exaggerated. We see here how very imperfect is the development of our clothes mentality as judged by our adopted standard.

Of most of the other motives discussed in Chapter V. there is no need to speak. One of these motives, that of protection by amulets against the evil influences of magic or of spirits, is present only in a vestigial form in cultured societies; its former influence has largely been replaced by hygienic superstitions. Others, such as the uterine symbolism of clothes in relation to a hostile environment, and the phallic symbolism in relation to unconscious fears of castration, we can scarcely hope to alter (if we should wish to do so) except by influencing their causes. It is, however, of some importance that there should be a realisation of the psycho-physiological relation between sensitiveness to cold and lack of love, and of great importance that there should be clear recognition of the alliance between phallicism and the functions of certain types of clothing as symbolic of duty or moral control. The moral symbolism itself raises some difficult problems, similar in general form to those that we have already considered in connection

---

[1] A few interesting facts that throw light upon the hygienic aspects of clothes will be found in Leonard Hill, 51.

with modesty. The application of our criterion can only result in a refusal to allow ourselves to be edified by this symbolism, except in so far as it may be an inevitable but temporary accompaniment of a certain stage of moral progress. And this for the following reasons: (1) because of its tendency to become unconsciously allied with phallic symbolism—an overdetermination which we have reason to believe is of a primitive and neurotic kind; (2) because it partakes of the general unnecessary harshness of the unconscious and unenlightened super-ego, as revealed by recent psycho-analytic study, thus tending to impose unnecessary asceticisms and restrictions—with consequent loss both of enjoyment and efficiency; (3) because it tends to distort the apprehension of reality by substituting a symbolic morality for an effective one, there being no essential connection between, say, a black coat and tight, stiff collar and the due sense of responsibility and duty for which these garments stand.

CHAPTER XIII

THE ETHICS OF DRESS—INDIVIDUAL AND SEXUAL DIFFERENTIATION

> Sir, I would advise you to shift a shirt.
> *Cymbeline*, i. 3.

WITH regard to **Chapter VI.**, it is clear that our principle demands the recognition of **individual differences,** and a somewhat greater adaptability of clothing than exists at present to meet the variation in individual needs. It should be understood that both the psychological and the physiological factors concerned vary very greatly, and that it is impossible for one system to satisfy all individuals. We must also recognise, however, that many of the types by their very nature indicate an unsatisfactory development of the mental tendencies connected with clothes.

Thus the rebellious type chafes continually under the restrictions that clothes impose; the resigned type still suffers, though it does not chafe; the prudish and self-satisfied types seem to represent reaction-formations that have distinctly neurotic elements in their composition; the same applies perhaps in some measure to the protected type, with its extreme sensitivity to cold and tendency to hypochondria. The unemotional type, if it does not suffer, is not entirely satisfactory, inasmuch as it can make no use of a possible source of gratification. The supported and sublimated types alone get real *positive* satisfaction from clothing; and even here some qualifications as to the adequacy of their adjustments must be made. If the 'moral' elements in the supported type predominate, it becomes liable to the objections that we considered in dealing with moral symbolism. Sublimation is by definition satisfactory, so far as we confine our view to a person's relation to his clothes. But when we take a wider view of his development as a whole and of his social relations, it immediately becomes clear that the amount of libido that is sublimated on to clothes should be kept within certain limits. Beau Brummell, though doubtless an artist in his way, was not among the most valuable members of society.

These facts, indicative of the difficulties of development, should bring home to us the desirability of giving special consideration to the **clothing of young children** —a matter which has been almost totally neglected, so far as the psychological and pedagogical points of view are concerned. In such consideration we must bear in mind that the young child can only gradually acquire the adult point of view. It is probable that all children have, in the beginning, a 'rebellious' element, and great care should be taken that the clothes worn in early life should involve as little restriction of movement, as little pressure,[1] as little scratching[2] as possible. Children's underwear needs very special attention in these respects. In all these matters systematic observation and experiment would be in place.

Later on the chief needs are, in the first place, that the necessity of taking care of clothes should be made as little trouble to the child as may be (since otherwise the attitude which regards clothes as a nuisance, inevitable perhaps to some extent in the earliest days, may well become permanently established); and, secondly, that the child should be given opportunity for the development of aesthetic taste along his own lines—by being allowed and encouraged to choose his own clothes, so far as circumstances will permit. Unfortunately both these methods may conflict somewhat with parents' pride in the appearance of their children, but it is better that parents should make some sacrifice of their vicarious exhibitionistic satisfactions than that children should suffer from permanent maladjustments in this important matter. Besides, parents may hope to be indemnified

---

[1] Cf. Landauer (60) and Chadwick (15).
[2] Cf. Flügel (35) and Macaulay (65).

for their earlier loss by an improved appearance of their offspring in later years.[1]

Let us now pass from the subject of individual differences to that of **sex differences (Chapter VII.).** Logically prior to all other questions in this field is that as to **whether the two sexes should be dressed alike or differently.** The existence of sex distinctions in dress has behind it such a long and almost universal tradition that the desirability of such distinctions is usually taken for granted. Yet it is well to put the question, if

[1] A consideration of the clothing of children might reasonably be held to demand a statement as to the attitude we should adopt towards nakedness in relation to children. Our general principle points clearly to the desirability of perfect frankness in this respect. With regard to children's own nakedness, this will probably be freely admitted in the more enlightened educational circles. But it would seem that in the lower social classes of England an exaggerated sense of shame is often inculcated, and young children (especially girls) will often suffer great embarrassment if they have to undress for medical inspection. The idea is even prevalent that modesty can only be adequately safeguarded by means of a plethora of undergarments (cf. Macaulay, 65).

As regards the question of whether adults (and especially parents) should show themselves naked to children, there is less agreement. In certain more 'advanced' circles this is done on principle, but a query as to its advisability has come from a rather unexpected quarter, namely, from the psycho-analysts, who have been much struck with the great affects that appear to be aroused in children by the appearance of the adult genitals (particularly affects connected with the castration complex). It is admitted that the evidence so far available is far from conclusive; nevertheless, Zulliger, in a recent review of the subject (106), says, 'My personal and provisional view is that it is better that children should not see their parents naked'. In the opinion of the present writer he does not give due weight to the fact that in ordinary households it is in any case difficult to prevent accidental exposures before children. It would seem likely also that such special precautions as might be necessary to ensure that there is no such accident might very likely do more harm than the evil that they were intended to prevent. Altogether it would seem desirable to await further evidence before we agree to such a departure from the general lines of education suggested by psycho-analysis. However, it is undoubtedly true that the castration complex is of the greatest importance, and that everything that is reasonably possible should be done to prevent its exaggerated development (to some extent it is probably inevitable). As Zulliger also points out, adults should bear in mind how difficult it is to be unbiased in this matter, and how liable they are to gratify their own exhibitionism under the pretext of bringing up their children 'naturally'.

Another psycho-analyst (Reich, 78) also argues against 'nude education' on the general ground that it logically implies a very different state of public opinion on sex questions than that which now exists. This argument is in a form that would apply to any departure from conventional taste and morals; if itself logically applied, it would abolish all experiments in education that imply such a departure. The true way out of the difficulty surely lies in the direction of teaching the illogicalities and inconsistencies of human institutions as themselves a part of reality. If, for instance, in the present case, it is decided to bring up children to regard nakedness as natural and ethical, this attitude should be supplemented by the information that nakedness is not everywhere looked upon in the same light. The problem here is, it would seem, exactly parallel to, say, that in the case of agnosticism.

only in order that the implications of the usual system of rigid sex-differentiation may be realised. There seems to be (especially in modern life) no essential factor in the nature, habits, or functions of the two sexes that would necessitate a striking difference of costume—other than the desire to accentuate sex differences themselves; an accentuation that chiefly serves the end of more easily and frequently arousing sexual passion. Nowhere better than in this field does our conventional morality exhibit its fundamentally ambivalent nature; for although nominally opposed to the arousal of sexual feeling, it nevertheless approves (and for the most part even legally insists upon) a system that is calculated to arouse this feeling with the greatest possible degree of frequency. And, if pressed, the upholders of this morality would doubtless endeavour to justify their position on the ground that modesty demands a sex distinction—thereby illustrating what we have already said about the dual nature of modesty itself.

Much more logical is the position of those who advocate the abolition of all unnecessary sex distinctions in costume—as Bousfield, for instance, has done in a recent book.[1] If we disagree, as the great majority of us doubtless will, let us be honest, and admit frankly that we are not in earnest about the undesirability of sexual stimulation, and that, on the contrary, we cannot bear to face the prospect of abolishing the present system of constant titillation—a system which ensures that we shall be warned even from a distance as to the sex of an approaching fellow-being, so that we need lose no opportunity of experiencing at any rate the incipient stages of the sexual response.

There seems to be no escape from the view that the fundamental purpose of adopting a distinctive dress for the two sexes is to stimulate the sexual instinct. But though this view is true, it does not, perhaps, represent the whole truth. There would seem to be a negative, as well as a positive, element in our insistence upon sex

[1] Bousfield, 11.

differentiation. The nature of this negative element can, I think, best be seen from the slight disgust which any unconventional approximation to the costumes of the opposite sex is apt to arouse in the normal heterosexual man or woman—a disgust that is often aroused also in some degree by any proposal to abolish the sartorial differences between the sexes. A little further analysis seems to show that this disgust is a defence against the possible arousal of a sexual attraction towards a person of the same sex. At bottom we are all potentially ambisexual in our inclinations. The great majority have become differentiated—most of course in a heterosexual direction; but the possibility of regression to the ambisexual stage (or even, in the case of many, to a stage at which homosexuality predominated) is always present. One way of guarding against this regression is a somewhat exaggerated or obsessive insistence upon heterosexuality. It is as though a mistake must be avoided at all costs; and this can best be done by a sex differentiation of such a kind that we can see at a glance whether or no a given individual falls within the category of permissible sexual objects.

On this double basis, then—the desire to utilise every opportunity of heterosexual stimulation, and the need to guard against the possibility of homosexuality—would seem to be founded the very strong bias that exists in favour of some form of easily recognisable sex distinction in dress. The bias is indeed so powerful that it would be idle to propose the abolition of this distinction. The fuller and more general recognition of the psychological grounds for the distinction may, however, eventually lead humanity to deal with the question in a more unprejudiced way than is at present possible.

But if we decide that the retention of a sex distinction is, in general, more or less inevitable for the present, recognition of its psychological reasons may help us to adopt a more tolerant attitude to those whose mental make-up impels them to abolish the distinctions so far as their own costume is concerned. Here also individual variations must be recognised. At present we punish the homosexual (especially the male homosexual), because the repressions of our own homosexual tendencies are not secure (in the same way that we punish criminals, for the most part, because they have done what certain of our own repressed tendencies are urging us to do). It is as though we were only too glad of the opportunity to project our own guilt on to others. When this fatal tendency to projection (one of the greatest sources of human cruelty) is realised, there will be greater hope for those whose mentality differs from the conventional pattern. We may then recognise that Eonism is not a sin, but, at the worst, a slight social and psychological inconvenience to ourselves.[1]

So much as regards the existence of a sex distinction. Quite another question concerns **the actual nature of this distinction.** As we have seen, the sex distinction has been greatly emphasised in recent times by the fact that men, not content with a different type, have adopted a completely different style of dress to that of women—a style which renounces all gaiety, exuberance, and beauty, which aims only at correctness, and which permits of only the slowest and most gradual modifications. There is, in fact, as a recent writer[2] has well put it, a 'double moral standard' as regards dress, a standard which demands of men a far more austere morality than it demands of women. This has become specially noticeable in the last few years. Since the war, the moral element

---

[1] It may be that in a more tolerant future we shall freely allow, or even encourage, the tendency that undoubtedly exists to make the degree of sex distinctiveness in dress correspond to the degree of (heterosexual or homosexual) differentiation of the wearer; as in Anatole France's vision of society in the year 2270, in which the young girl electrician, Chéron, herself dressed indistinguishably from her male companions, comments as follows on the differences between her age and our own: 'Nous avons, sur les caractères sexuels, des notions que ne soupçonnait pas la simplicité barbare des hommes de l'ère close. De ce qu'il y a deux sexcs et qu'il n'y a que deux on tira longtemps des conséquences fausses. On en conclut qu'une femme est absolument femme et un homme absolument homme. La réalité n'est pas telle, il y a des femmes qui sont beaucoup femmes, et des femmes qui le sont peu. Ces différences autrefois dissimulées par le costume et le genre de vie, masquées par le préjugé, apparaissent clairement dans notre société'.—*Sur La Pierre Blanche*, p. 301.

[2] Baumann, 3.

in women's dress has been considerably relaxed; men's dress, while it has moved in the same direction, has moved to a much smaller extent. The contrast is therefore more marked, and men are beginning to realise the burden to which their own severer clothes-morality condemns them. The rather sudden realisation of the disabilities attaching to conventional male clothing is all the more unpleasant because, for several generations at least, man has prided himself (often with justice) on the greater reasonableness of his own dress—its greater convenience, the greater freedom it permitted to the body, and the advantages it possessed as being relatively exempt from all the wilder vagaries of fashion. Now, almost at a blow, this superiority has vanished. The capacity for rapid change which women's 'modish' dress possesses—that very capacity which man, in his greater sartorial stability had so long despised—has enabled woman suddenly to become reasonable in her costume, and to adopt clothes that are superior to man's in nearly every respect. So great is this difference that it is worth while to attempt a brief enumeration of the chief points in which women's clothes, as they are at the present moment,[1] allow of greater satisfaction than do men's.

(1) The use of a far greater variety of colour.

(2) The use of a far greater variety of stuffs, including an almost exclusive right to artificial silk—that most useful and attractive sartorial invention of modern science—together with other materials that combine lightness with elegance and that allow some passage of the ultra-violet rays.

(3) Much greater individual liberty as regards choice of materials, cut, and general style of dress.

(4) Much lighter weight of clothes (according to recent measurements in America and Germany, men's summer clothes weigh from three to ten times as much as women's).

(5) Much greater adaptability to varying seasons. Women can wear the lightest clothes in summer and

[1] January 1930. In these matters it is well to be precise about questions of date.

thick fur coats in winter;[1] men's clothes are admittedly much hotter in summer, and it is, in some countries at any rate, considered somewhat unmanly to wear fur coats in winter.

(6) Much more rapid and efficient adaptability to the different temperatures of various environments. Women can adapt by wearing a thin layer of essential clothes, and then putting on other layers over this—jumper, coat, overcoat, etc. Modern convention dictates that man should always wear his coat as an essential outer garment. He sometimes makes surreptitious and inconvenient adjustments by taking off his waistcoat or putting on an extra one—obviously from all points of view an inferior method to that of women.[2]

(7) Greater freedom of movement. Except perhaps in high winds, trousers cause a slightly greater impediment to leg movements than do short skirts, while women's upper garments certainly allow of considerably freer arm and trunk movements than do men's coats.

(8) Much greater cleanliness.

(9) An exclusive right to exposure of parts of the body other than the face and hands.

(10) Greater convenience for putting on and off.[3]

(11) Absence of constriction in parts of the body where freedom is especially desirable for comfort and health (a free neck, whereas men are condemned to the collar-and-tie system, with its threefold, or more usually fourfold, bandage round the neck).

(12) Greater convenience for packing and transport.

(13) An admittedly greater hygienic value in virtue of 2, 3, 4, 5, 6, 8, 9, and 11 above.[4]

Truly a formidable list. And the sting of the whole

[1] It is sometimes said that women's clothes provide inadequate warmth for feet and legs. But in cold weather they are perfectly at liberty to wear Russian boots or leggings or (in some countries at least) over-shoes—a very sensible principle.
[2] In this respect men's clothes offend badly against the principle of equal presentability of all layers that we discussed in connection with the subject of modesty.   [3] Cf. Flügel, 35, pp. 132, 135.
[4] Against all this there would seem to be two small sartorial advantages on the side of men: the absence of stockings, with their troublesome habit of developing ladders and the somewhat uncomfortable and unaesthetic apparatus

matter lies in the last point. For recent changes in our ideas of hygiene have deprived men of what would formerly have been their very obvious retort, namely, that men's clothing was more healthy than women's, because it provided, in most circumstances, for a higher temperature of the air immediately surrounding the body. Up to a few years ago, when women appeared in *décolleté* dresses or 'pneumonia blouses', men might envy them their coolness, but could take comfort in the thought that they themselves were not courting disease and death as were their sisters. Now this consolation has been taken from them just as they most needed it. It is as if the reward of virtue, for which many sacrifices had been made, had been ruthlessly snatched away from the expectant prize-winners and given to those who had broken all the hitherto accepted rules of common sense and morals.

It is not surprising then that men find the present situation galling. Discontent is rampant (as my own investigations, among others, amply show), and has in England crystallised in the formation of the Men's Dress Reform Party, which has issued a preliminary call to freedom.[1] Nevertheless, it is clear that the forces that brought about man's 'great renunciation', as we have earlier called it, are still at work and make it difficult for him to strike out for his own rights. In the light of our previous considerations, it is fairly easy to describe the deeper psychological forces on either side of this conflict. On the side of the reformers, the principal factors are:

(1) The Narcissistic tendencies, in revolt against the suppression to which they have been subject for the last 130 years or so.

---

used for their suspension ('that God-send curse suspenders', as a well-known modern author has called them), and the presence of pockets. Of these we have seen that the latter is by no means an unmixed blessing, while the former could easily be done away with, or reduced, if women would give up wearing stockings (as they have to some extent—bare legs have appeared even in the ballroom) indoors and in summer, and wear thicker rolled-up stockings supported by a garter (preferably below the knee) in the winter.

[1] *Practical Dress Reform*, 75.

(2) The various homosexual and Eonist tendencies, in virtue of which men desire to dress as women (for, of course, as women's dress has nearly all the advantages, any reform of men's must inevitably mean an approximation to women's in certain respects). Since, as psycho-analysis has shown, there is a close developmental relation between Narcissism and homosexuality, there is a certain relation between these two factors.

(3) The auto-erotic elements of skin and muscle erotism which underlie the 'rebellious' type of clothes mentality. This last element is not necessarily connected with any homosexual tendency or lack of virility, except perhaps—(a) in so far as a relatively strong skin erotism (relative, that is, to the genital erotism) tends to produce a general distribution of libido resembling the more diffused sexuality of women; and (b) that a relatively weak genital sexuality can provide the individual concerned with only a relatively small enjoyment of phallic symbolism to compensate for the loss of pleasure from cutaneous and muscular sources.

(4) The fact that nonconformity in clothes tends naturally to express nonconformity in social and political thought. Correctness of male attire symbolises conservative principles (identification with, approval of, and obedience to, society as at present constituted), and there would seem to be a general correspondence between conventionality in dress and in politics. Thus, in London, the members of the Constitutional Club, the National Liberal Club, and the 1917 Club correspond on the average to three steps in the descending scale of sartorial correctness. Owing to this correlation, clothes reform tends to receive support from the generally rebellious, as a welcome symbolic expression of revolt.

Among the forces hostile to reform, the following are probably the most significant:

(1) Man's intense fear of appearing different from his fellows. Clothes reformers and women are wont to

taunt man with his cowardice in this matter. They are amply justified, but it must be remembered that this cowardice is only the vice associated with the virtue of a greater social sensitiveness—a sensitiveness that has made man, rather than woman, the producer and developer of those wider social institutions which have rendered civilisation possible. If we were right in what we said about the origin of man's 'great renunciation' in matters of dress, this renunciation (tending as it did to abolish competition) had as its function the development of a further social cohesion. The social tendencies that produced this have established very powerful traditions against sartorial nonconformity among men, traditions which have not operated in the case of the less socialised, freer, and more individualistically competitive women.

(2) Man's generally greater repression of Narcissism. Our whole social traditions allow a freer manifestation of Narcissism in women than in men, and this difference largely finds expression in their clothes. A masculine clothes reformer is thus, as it were, offending against one of the most fundamental principles of male morality; for even though his costume be of the simplest, he cannot avoid making himself conspicuous, through the very fact of being differently attired.

(3) Closely connected with this is the repression of male exhibitionism. In conformity with the ruling convention that woman is beautiful and man is not, there has grown up a very considerable intolerance of the male body; the characteristic signs of maleness, *e.g.* the greater hairiness, muscularity, and angularity, are in some ways much more apt to arouse embarrassment or repulsion than is the rounder and smoother (and of course much more familiar) female form. As previously suggested, this is perhaps due, at least in part, to a repression of phallicism; the worship of the phallus, so common at an earlier cultural level, has given place to an abhorrence of the male genitals, an abhorrence which has spread to some extent to the whole male body, and

which demands that it be decently hid in thick garments, non-provocative in form and colour.[1]

(4) The repression of homosexual tendencies. As we have seen, homosexual tendencies are apt to be strongly represented in the reform movement. This produces a revulsion against it on the part of those who fear, of course unconsciously, to do anything that would gratify these tendencies in themselves.

(5) The guilt attached to the idea of abandoning traditional male costume, owing to the moral symbolism associated with it. A man is apt to feel that if he dispensed with his thick coat and stiff, tight collar, he would be casting off the moral restraints that keep him to the narrow path of virtue and of duty.

(6) Closely correlated with this is, as we have seen, the phallic value of the very clothes that symbolise morality; hence man feels that the clothes reformers are in effect asking him to perform an act of self-castration.

Both these last motives are illustrated in the greater strictness and correctness of men, when in the presence of women, than when by themselves. Most men of the upper social classes experience a curious feeling of guilt and embarrassment if surprised by a woman without a collar and tie or in their shirt-sleeves. On analysis, this feeling seems to be composed of three principal elements: (*a*) a disagreeable suspicion of having been detected in a condition of moral relaxation; (*b*) the feeling that the man is somehow insulting the woman by appearing without the panoply of chivalry;[2] (*c*) a feeling of being sexually inadequate to the demands of a female

---

[1] There is no real opposition between this and what we have already said concerning the importance of the phallic symbolism of dress. This latter symbolism represents a *displaced* gratification of phallicism—a gratification that is psychologically permissible, because it is unconscious and remote from the original aims and object of the desires in question.

[2] A feeling that is apparently reciprocated by women, as for instance in the case of a Berlin typist who sued her employer for being so disrespectful as to dictate a letter in his shirt-sleeves.

So little respectable is a shirt without a coat on top of it, that, as a correspondent tells me, shirted but coatless men are not allowed to enter the fashionable hotels of a well-known Continental sea-bathing resort where, at the same time, lunching in pyjamas is considered quite in order.

presence—in other words, the feeling that the man is impotent or castrated.

These more individual factors are supported by others of a more social nature, in particular:

(1) The fact that here, as elsewhere, men punish those who dare to do what they themselves would like to do but dare not. The employer, though he admits he is not comfortable, feels that his 'position' does not allow him to take off his coat, and would be prepared to punish (by dismissal if necessary) any employee who dared himself to do so.

(2) The fact that the long period during which men's dress has undergone very little change has induced a most thorough-going orthodoxy and conservatism throughout the makers and retailers of men's clothes. No one engaged in this trade has personally known, or has even been taught by anyone who has known, anything essentially different from the present system, and—in great contrast to the women's clothing trade—the whole circle of ideas in the world of tailors and of outfitters has become almost completely stereotyped.

(3) It is often said that women are opposed to any change in male attire. I am inclined to think, however, that this is only true in a certain limited sense. Women are conscious, of course, of the disapproval and ridicule that other men pour on the isolated reformer (they feel especially, perhaps, the implied taunt that the reformer is lacking in virility), and to that extent dislike associating themselves with him. They also, perhaps, derive some satisfaction from the fact that the moral seriousness of male attire contrasts rather piquantly with the symbolic freedom and irresponsibility of their own. Furthermore, they enjoy the reversal of the rôles that recent conditions have brought about; in the place of men's previous contempt for women's fashions, men have now to admit that women's are superior to their own. It would, indeed, be more than human if women did not indulge in a little triumphant amusement at this

situation,[1] but on the whole this amusement in women is astonishingly small—showing thereby their Narcissistic independence, alike of the past disapproval of men and of their present praise. Women are, moreover, aware that from the heterosexual point of view, they have lost much by men's drabness (as is shown by their much greater susceptibility to uniforms, if these are at all attractive), and that they stand very greatly to gain in this way from an abandonment of men's obsessive Puritanism. On the whole, then, it would seem that women cannot be reckoned as very serious opponents of men's dress reform.

In all this we have been taking stock of moral forces rather than ourselves making an ethical evaluation. This short return to psychology has been worth while, however, as throwing fresh light upon the present dynamic aspect of certain problems that were discussed in more general terms in Chapter VII. Returning to the task of expressing our own attitude to the matters concerned, it seems clear that the ideal that we should have in view is the retention of the peculiar advantages enjoyed by both sexes and the abolition of the peculiar disadvantages suffered by both. In the light of what we have seen in this and previous chapters, our judgment of men's clothing is that it represents an ascetic reaction-formation, into which, however (as in the case of many similar mental manifestations), there have crept—or perhaps we should more correctly say, in which there have persisted—certain surreptitious libidinal elements. Judged both by the satisfaction given and by its ability to adapt to real situations, men's clothing must be pronounced a failure; the wholesale inhibitions that underlie it are so severe that they cannot but cause much suffering and much loss of efficiency. Moreover, the unconscious alliance between the super-ego and the instincts is one that we have reason to believe is opposed

[1] An amusement which perhaps sometimes takes the sadistic form of putting man in the dilemma of being 'stupid' if he continues to conform to the existing conventions, or being 'rude' or 'impossible' if he endeavours to depart from them.

to the ultimate interests of morality itself. Our sympathies must therefore be with the reformers; though we must ask them (even in their own interest) to take account of the psychological factors by which they are themselves impelled. In working for the ends they have in view, it is evident that they have two chief tasks before them: the overcoming of the 'moral' associations of men's conventional clothing, and the provision of alternative outlets for 'manliness'. Men have to be convinced that it is a sign of weakness rather than of strength to need the support of external symbols, and that the choking collar and the clogging coat can be abandoned without any very shocking result either to their respectability or their virility; that, in fact, the truest manliness can be achieved by freedom rather than by a slavish subserviency to convention. This freedom can perhaps only be attained by a reduction in the present amount of the displacement of male libido from body to clothes. We must learn to tolerate the male body, and perhaps even to admire it—if only as a counterpart to the female body, which we already idolise. If we are to have faith in the results of modern psycho-therapy, we cannot believe that wholesale repression is ever a really satisfactory solution of a conflict. Sublimation is a better course, but sublimation can seldom be brought about suddenly, completely, or deliberately; to achieve sublimation we must first have the courage to allow freedom. The freedom required here is a more natural attitude of man towards his own body; and perhaps the easiest and at the same time the best way in which this can be done is for man to allow himself a little more latitude in making use of his bodily attractions for heterosexual purposes—in making, in fact, a somewhat greater sexual appeal to women. Such a course seems both likely to meet with smaller social resistances than, and to be socially preferable to, the other alternative—a greater Narcissism (and consequent tendency to homosexuality).

The only serious objection that could be raised

against such a course concerns the possibility of sacrificing the social advantages of men's present costume to which we drew attention in Chapter VII. Our reply to this objection must be twofold. In the first place, modern psychology has taught us that moral or social inhibitions, when they become excessive, are liable to produce fresh evils as great as those which they aimed at preventing—and in this matter the quasi-neurotic asceticism of men's dress seems to be a social counterpart of the excessive repressions so characteristic of individual neuroses. In the second place, it is undoubtedly possible to devise garments that would be comfortable, hygienic, and attractive without arousing any high degree of sexual jealousy or social emulation; indeed, a general change to looser and lighter clothes would be a democratic move, inasmuch as it would tend to diminish the social differentiation due to expert and expensive tailoring. The present 'suit' requires to be made by those possessing special skill if it is to look at all presentable. A simple and loose-fitting costume consisting, for instance, of blouse, shorts, and stockings would be much less dependent on the expert and would therefore also indicate less clearly the social or financial status of the wearer.

The correlative effect on women of such a solution of the present problems of male costume would, interestingly enough, be of advantage to them also. The exclusive social idealisation of the female body exposes women to enormous temptations in the direction of an exaggerated indulgence in Narcissism. As we have more than once pointed out, our whole social attitude expects women to exhibit a greater Narcissism than men. Some difference of this kind may not be harmful; at present, however, it is really difficult for a beautiful woman to develop to the full her capacities as a lover or a citizen (as a mother it is often easier), her Narcissism being so fostered by the admiration she receives as to impede the growth of object love. If man, in his turn, made himself a little more attractive, woman would be given some more powerful motive of heterosexual object love to compete with her Narcissism. That an improvement in men's aesthetic appearance would really have some such effect is indicated, for instance, by the disappointment that women often express when they see a man in civilian clothes after first meeting him in uniform.

If, on the one hand, it may be suggested that men should dress a little more to please women, and that both their own sartorial conditions and women's social value would be improved thereby, we can even go on to suggest that women should on their part dress more to please men. This may at first sound paradoxical. Have not women, it will be asked, dressed to please men throughout the centuries? This is only true in a very wide sense. From general sociological considerations and from the facts of male and female psychology, so far as I have had the opportunity of studying them,[1] it would seem that, as regards all the details of costume, women dress much more to please their own vanity and to compete with other women than to satisfy the more immediate desires of men. Man is so irresistibly attracted to woman that he will love her in the most outrageous and hideous contraptions—not, however, because of them, but in spite of them.[2] Nor again is man interested in the changes of fashion which seem of such importance to women themselves; all the follies of competition in which woman indulges are absolutely unnecessary for the purpose of attracting man; apart from social and economic implications, a man is content to see a woman in the same dress for many days in succession, if only it befits her. It therefore follows that the disadvantages of excessive 'modishness' in

---

[1] Especially 35, p. 136.
[2] The instinctive attraction that woman possesses for man, in virtue of which she seems to him so lovely and desirable, spreads over to her clothes in virtue of the general law of 'transfer of feeling' (Wohlgemuth, *Pleasure-Unpleasure*, p. 242): and her clothes, if attractive, can even make her more desirable, so long as they form a mental whole with their wearer. But (apart from fetishism) man has comparatively little interest in woman's clothes as such, *i.e.* as dissociated from the wearer.

female dress would tend to be reduced if women paid more attention to the admiration of men[1] (other of course than their dressmakers); and men, on their side, would be rid of the burden of their own austerity, if only they would allow their costume to make a slightly greater sex appeal to women. It is a little more sexual freedom on both sides that is necessary—or, in other words, the predominantly sexual function of clothes should be acknowledged and encouraged. But here it is well to stop this train of thought lest the last reader of this book should be preparing to throw it down with a gesture of horror or impatience. And the writer would be sorry to part company with him so very near the end.

[1] 'It would be mortifying to the feelings of many ladies, could they be made to understand how little the heart of man is affected by what is costly or new in their attire; how little it is biassed by the texture of their muslin and how unsusceptible of peculiar tenderness towards the spotted, the sprigged, the mull or the jackonet.' (Jane Austen, quoted in *The Technique of the Love Affair*, by a Gentlewoman, p. 76.)

CHAPTER XIV

THE ETHICS OF DRESS—THE RATIONALISATION OF FASHION

Id nos maxime nocet, quod non ad rationis lumen
sed ad similitudinem aliorum vivimus.
SENECA, *Octavia*, ii. 454.

THE subject of sex differences, to which we have perhaps devoted a somewhat excessive attention, leads on naturally to that of **Chapter VIII.**; for sex differences, it will be remembered, correlated to some extent with both of the main classifications of dress that were there discussed.

It is scarcely worth while to consider at length the respective advangates of **tropical and arctic** dress. A skirt has the merit of more grace and dignity and has more of the real aesthetic potentialities of dress (cf. p. 35); kilts and present-day short skirts show that it can retain the grace, if not the dignity, even in an attenuated form, a form in which it is for most purposes quite as free and practical as the majority of bifurcated garments. As long as it is considered desirable to have some fundamental distinction between the dress of the two sexes, the retention of the skirt as a distinctively feminine garment would seem to be unobjectionable, provided that the skirt is not made of such amplitude or tightness as to hamper movement, provided too that women enjoy the right of discarding it when the nature of an occupation or activity so requires (*e.g.* riding, mountaineering, some forms of factory work where flopping skirts might constitute a danger).

There is more to be said on the subject of the **'fixed'** and **'modish'** types of dress. The chief advantages that can be claimed for the 'fixed' type are: (1) it eliminates the socially disruptive element of competition; (2) it saves time and trouble in choice of costume; (3) it tends to improve the appearance of those who have little personal taste, or aptitude for choosing their own dress; (4) by eliminating all rapid change in costume it abolishes the unnecessary expense to the wearer that is often incurred in rapidly changing 'modish' costume—expense which is due in considerable measure to commercial exploitation of the motives underlying fashion; (5) for the same reasons it tends to stabilise economic conditions in the clothing trade, which are inevitably disorganised—with much attendant individual hardship—whenever fashion undergoes a sudden change.

As against these advantages, it suffers from two drawbacks: (1) its very uniformity must prevent it from adequately expressing individuality or being freely adapted to suit the demands of various complexions and physiques. It thus removes a legitimate source of artistic pleasure (a sublimation, of course, of exhibitionism) from those who are capable of enjoying this pleasure; (2) its dependence upon tradition prevents it from being adequately adapted to changing needs, standards, and ideals. It was only with some difficulty that military uniforms were adapted to changed conditions, even under the urgent stimulus of war. When travel or migration takes the wearers of 'fixed' costume to another climate, much the same difficulty arises. Englishmen in tropical countries have been extremely loth to exchange their frock-coat of ceremony (which we are beginning to think unduly stuffy, even for a temperate zone) for a more convenient and hygienic dress, because they felt that their traditional garb had, by its associations, become the natural symbol of what seemed their racial or political superiority—in much the same way, perhaps, as the Romans were unwilling to exchange their own 'fixed' costumes for more adequately protective ones, when their conquests brought them into colder climates.

Still less easy is it to modify 'fixed' costume in accordance with the more subtle changes of 'the spirit of the age'. Hence it comes about that man's clothes have scarcely altered at all in response to the new views of the value of light and air—views to which women have much more easily adapted themselves. Moreover, if fixed costume depends upon traditions, in its turn it tends to foster and maintain traditions, even when the traditions in question are becoming out of date and therefore harmful. Thus the world-wide 'modish' dress, in spite of its drawbacks, has the great advantage of expressing in outward form the social and economic interdependence of all peoples of the modern world, whereas the distinctions of 'national' dress and of military uniform accentuate local patriotisms, which—though they have their own value—must be subordinated to a world-wide, or at least culture-wide, loyalty, if the realities of modern human life are to be duly represented. As we said in Chapter VIII. the 'geographical' group of 'fixed' costumes is pretty clearly obsolescent. We may deplore the disappearance of a certain picturesqueness, but we should console ourselves with an inspiring vision of the future rather than indulge in regretful longing for the past.

What then of the future? It is clearly incumbent upon us to devise some system that shall partake as far as possible of the benefits of both 'fixed' and 'modish' costume, while suffering as little as may be from their respective faults. Costume must be freed, alike from the ruinous competition and commercialism of fashion, and from the unadaptable conservatism of 'fixed' dress. Reasonable consideration of ends and means, together with an appeal to the highest standards of contemporary aesthetic taste, must replace a frantic search for novelty at any cost or a blind adherence to tradition.

It would seem likely that only concerted action can attain these ends; both for social and for economic reasons, the individual is relatively helpless. Perhaps the most essential step will consist in the creation of Advisory Committees or Boards which will issue periodical reports. Signs of a movement in this direction are, indeed, not wanting. Recently the Men's Dress Reform Party in England established a Committee on Designs, which has already issued a preliminary report, to which reference was made in the last chapter,[1] In America, too, as already mentioned, the Fashion of the Month League intends to guide fashions for women by making periodical recommendations to its members.[2] In the English press there have even been proposals for the establishment of a Ministry of Fashions[3] which shall endeavour to bring about desired changes of mode with a minimum of economic upset. Whether such bodies be established by private societies (as seems most likely in the first place) or by public enterprise, they will have a very valuable and important task to perform. They will have to keep in touch with public feeling, and, at the same time, have a receptive mind towards the proposals of individual creators; for, of course, they will not so much replace the work of individual sartorial artists and designers as co-ordinate this work, and utilise it to the best advantage, by selecting for approval a number of models that seem most satisfactorily to fulfil the needs of the moment. Such models will be understood to have 'passed' the Clothing Board (as we may provisionally call such a body as we are contemplating), in the sense of satisfying it as to their practical suitability, their aesthetic tastefulness, their hygienic qualities and their economic reasonableness. If the Board is in touch with the more advanced thought in medicine, economics, and aesthetics, and is also alive to the wider influences at work in the social and political world, it should ensure the adaptation of costume to the 'spirit of the age', while at the same time making full use of the advances of modern science, and insuring against unnecessary economic dislocation. Though it will probably be at first resented by the clothing trades, it will ultimately bring about the same benefits that co-ordination and amalgamation is elsewhere producing. In fact, the establishment of some such Boards is in complete accord-

---

[1] 75.
[2] Even as I write I have received the report of 'The Sensible Dress Society' with very similar aims (and inspired directly by the desire to retain the short skirt) in England.
[3] *E.g. This and That*, Nov. 16, 1929.

ance with the general trend of the social and economic development of modern times. If they worked satisfactorily and showed themselves worthy of trust, they would give to future costume all the desirable elements of progressiveness and all the individual adaptability that are at present found in fashion, while largely eliminating the pernicious element of change for change's sake, from which fashion is so apt to suffer as long as it is at the mercy of unregulated social competition and commercial exploitation. The rate of change under such conditions will probably be considerably slower than during many periods of fashion's reign, if only for the reason that it is less easy to make a good change than to make some change, and because the Boards will presumably only recommend modifications when they are convinced that there is a promise of some definite improvement in convenience, healthiness, beauty, or economy. The Boards will of course not be infallible in their decisions, but they should at least be able to protect us from the fiercer indignities to which we are exposed by fashion; which, in its less happy moments, is only too likely to make us laughing-stocks for later generations.[1]

In this manner (and perhaps in no other) we may hope to combine the advantages of 'fixed' and 'modish' clothes, to obtain for both sexes and all classes the relative stability, freedom from caprice and absence of undue social competition that distinguish men's clothing of to-day, without its discomfort, ugliness, dirtiness, drabness, and general unprogressiveness; the beauty and adaptability of women's without its helplessness in the

[1] Like other art products, really good sartorial designs are, to a large extent, independent of fashion. Changes of fashion no more affect our admiration for the graceful lines of Empire dress than they do our appreciation of a fugue by Bach or a statue by Praxiteles. But with bad designs, when in the course of time (often a very short time) the suggestive influence of fashion is removed, their badness becomes all the more appallingly apparent, and exposes their wearers to merciless ridicule at the hands of posterity. It is difficult for us now to sympathise with the wearers of the bustle and the leg-of-mutton sleeve, and one trembles to think what will be the judgment of future generations on many of the admittedly 'untidy' longer dresses of last year, to say nothing of the dreary stiffness and stuffiness of male costume. We surely owe our self-respect so much consideration as to avoid clothing ourselves in a manner that must inevitably incur the pitying contempt of later ages.

face of every fickle change. The scope of the Boards' recommendations will, of course, depend upon their mandates and their spheres of influence. At first they will probably only deal with the ordinary civilian dress of men and women, but it may soon be found desirable to extend their activities to uniforms. As we saw in Chapter VIII., 'occupational' uniforms show little signs of dying out. For many professions they are a great convenience, either because it is desirable to be able to recognise the members of the profession at a glance (*e.g.* a policeman on point duty!) or because the nature of the activities involved imposes certain special conditions upon costume. The generally increasing respectability of work and decreasing snobbishness, that are as a whole characteristic of our age, may well lead to an increase of occupational uniforms, where these two reasons hold. There are a considerable number of professions (*e.g.* doctors and waiters) for whom 'modish' or the present conventional attire is utterly unsuitable, and whose work and comfort would both profit by the adoption of a really practical and convenient uniform. Another field for uniforms is that of sport, where etiquette and custom are already prescribing the general nature, form, and colour of the garments to be worn. In all cases, however, uniforms may want periodic revision in view of increasing experience and changing circumstances, and a central body, such as that we have been imagining, would be best fitted to consider and introduce such changes as seem desirable. In proposing uniforms such a Board would of course have to bear in mind the same considerations of hygiene, comfort, cost, and beauty as apply to dress in general.

The details of future fashions, in so far as they relate to the relative influence of decoration and of modesty, of youth and maturity and to the relative predominance of different parts of the body **(Chapter X.)**, we may perhaps for the most part safely leave to the deliberations of our imaginary Board. The antithesis of decoration and of modesty is a matter the practical implications of which we have already considered. With regard to the claims of youth and of maturity, our fundamental principle demands that the needs and advantages of both should be duly borne in mind. The youthful form can be very beautiful, but that does not make the more fully developed figure of early maturity any the less lovely. A true appreciation of reality would avail itself as far as possible of the attractions of all ages. Nevertheless, there can be little doubt that a somewhat youthful ideal has, on the whole, many advantages, as leading to the actual prolongation of the period of greatest freshness and activity. With regard to the part of the body that is most accentuated, our principle here demands that the body as a whole should be taken into account as far as possible, since a very predominant erotisation or idealisation of any one part inevitably tends to divorce our aesthetic notions from an harmonious appreciation of reality as manifested in the complete living organism as Nature has created it.

The antithesis between **body and clothes** merits perhaps a somewhat fuller consideration. Here, once again, is a matter in which our general principle points pretty clearly in a certain direction, but as regards which some readers may be well inclined to doubt its validity or at any rate its applicability. In one sense, fashions which emphasise the body might be said to be nearer reality than those which lay the chief accent on clothes. Gorgeous or voluminous clothes, the shape of which departs widely from that of the human frame itself, tend to substitute an artificial sartorial body for the natural corporeal body, and, by disguising the latter almost beyond recognition, to create the illusion that man is different from what he really is. The whole tendency, as we have seen, springs from a distrust of the natural body, if not an aversion to it. Unfortunately, however, from this point of view, it is not possible for us to change our bodies by the mere process of complicating their outer covers. Our bodies, with all their imperfections, persist underneath; and since they constitute a more essential, permanent, and inescapable element of our being than do our clothes, the reality principle demands that we should make our peace with them and live with them on terms, if not of affection, at least of toleration. In so far, moreover, as we have become reconciled to our natural bodies, we shall treat them more respectfully and take steps actually to increase their attractiveness and beauty, rather than—having given up the body as aesthetically hopeless—to concentrate, as it were in flight, upon the elaboration of its vestments. The period of greatest artificiality in dress—the eighteenth century—was one in which bodily cleanliness and hygiene were much neglected. Beneath the scent, the powder, and the gorgeous trappings, the body was often dirty and ill-kempt—a condition well in keeping with the almost total lack of washing or sanitary equipment that distinguished even the palaces of that time. With this example in mind, we shall do well to demand of clothing that it confine its functions to adorning and protecting the body and that it should not arrogate to itself the right to replace the body in our interests and affections. Our modern attitude requires, both for aesthetic and for hygienic reasons, that we should love our bodies, at least so far as is necessary to improve them. To improve them we must, furthermore, have good models; and it is generally admitted that, the more clothing accentuates the actual body, the greater the advantage (and therefore the influence) of those whose bodies are already comely; while, at the other extreme, if the body is of no more value than a clothes-horse, the advantages of the beautiful and of the plain are, within wide limits, equalised. The new science of eugenics, emphasising the importance of sexual selection for future human welfare, adds its own argument to those of hygiene and aesthetics, and demands that we should duly value the body, if not for our own sake, at least for the sake of future generations. From all these points of view, therefore, it seems desirable to allow those whom Nature has endowed with admirable bodies to reap the natural rewards (both social and sexual) of their physical superiority, rather than to devote our energies to the cunning concealment of bodily defects by an elaboration of costume that distracts the eye and leaves anatomy to the imagination. It is doubtless true that (especially in the beginning) the adoption of this principle will involve some sacrifice, inasmuch as it will compel the toleration of ugly forms that, so far as purely aesthetic considerations go, were better hidden. But on the whole the gains will probably outweigh the losses. Our endurance of the ugly, which we can to some extent curtail, is likely to be more than compensated by our appreciation of the beautiful, which we can to some extent prolong—as is actually the case with faces; where we should doubtless be unwilling to lose the right of contemplating comely features, even though we were saved the sight of others that are plain. The shortening of skirts too, though it has revealed much that is unpleasing, has yet amply recompensed us by the opportunity to realise at leisure on what very lovely lines the female lower limbs are (in favourable cases) built; and in general there seems to be no reason why what thus is true of the upper and lower extremities should not hold good of other portions of the body.

It may be pointed out, too, that this general argument is in harmony with certain well-marked tendencies in the development of dress, if we contemplate this development over a sufficiently long period. Carlyle has much right on his side when he says, somewhat disconcertingly as is his wont, 'the first spiritual want of a barbarous man is Decoration, as indeed we still see among the barbarous classes in civilised countries'.[1] Primitive man seems to find relatively little aesthetic pleasure in the body as Nature has created it. He must modify it very definitely out of Nature's mould before he can admire it. It was one of the greatest achievements of the Greeks to perceive that the body had a beauty of its own that, in the best of cases, could be rendered but little more attractive by extraneous

[1] 14, p. 36.

decoration. So it is also with clothing in the strict sense; the simpler notions about clothes have, as a common basis, the belief that the more ample the clothing that is worn, the grander is the effect. In primitive peoples, the chiefs wear more clothing than the commoners, and on ceremonial occasions as much finery as possible is carried, layer being heaped on layer in the effort to become impressive through accumulated grandeur. The same principle holds in 'national' costume, where Sunday or ceremonial dress is always more elaborate and more bulky than the dress of every day. To a lesser extent this holds of most uniforms and of the ordinary male dress of our own times. Though he has eschewed ornament, civilised man still endeavours, rather pathetically perhaps, to make himself look more impressive by donning thicker, stiffer, or more numerous layers of dark grey or black; bodily exposure is, with him, strongly suggestive of the negligé, and must give place to covering—albeit of a sombre hue —if he is to be fit for ceremony or the politer forms of social entertainment. In the discovery of the *décolleté* woman found a subtler method—a method which brings clothing into line with tendencies long manifest in the 'corporal' forms of decoration. Western 'modish' woman, to make herself attractive, does not put on more clothes; she rather takes them off, and relies for her effects upon the subtle interplay of her natural bodily form and such reduced (but decorative) clothing as she still retains. This is a definite step towards increased accentuation of the body at the cost of a diminished and more subsidiary function on the part of clothes. It implies a striking faith in the attractiveness of at least certain portions of the body, and it marks a new attitude to the relations between clothes and body—one that appears to be quite foreign to the primitive mind. Though frankly erotic in its origin, it is an attitude which is in accordance with the various reasons—hygienic, aesthetic, eugenic, and the rest—that point to the desirability of the decorative function of clothes being secondary and adjuvant rather than primary and essential. It may, therefore, constitute a stage in the history and development of dress that will prove to be of very great cultural and ethical importance, inasmuch as it implies an increasing harmonisation of erotic and cultural ideals with the actual realities of the human body.

As regards **Chapter XI.** there is little need of ethical comment, unless it be for a reflection on the inevitable conservatism of human institutions and a reminder that the removal of vestigial features in the realm of clothes is easier than in that of anatomy. To carry vestiges that have long ceased to function usefully, and which could possibly with advantage be eliminated or replaced even from the point of view of ornament, is a sign of unthinking inertia which does not argue well for the alertness or adaptability of tailors.

CHAPTER XV

THE FUTURE OF DRESS

> O fair undress, best dress! It checks no vein
> But every flowing limb in pleasure drowns
> And heightens ease with grace.
> 			James Thomson, *The Castle of Indolence.*

We have completed our ethical review of our previous psychological considerations. Before we finally take leave of the reader, there are two further matters which we must lightly touch upon—the first an indication of a programme, the second at once an apology, an admission, and a query.

With regard to the first of these points, it should be evident that our ethical considerations in the last two chapters have only outlined a policy of sartorial practice, and have in no way attempted to grapple with the detailed measures of its application. These measures will imply much specialist research of a kind that is in some cases only just beginning and in others not begun. It will probably be the duty of our imaginary Board or Ministry of Clothes to initiate such research, or, at any rate, co-ordinate its problems and results. The researches themselves fall into several fields, of which the chief would seem to be as follows:

Aesthetic.—Experimental aesthetics has as yet barely touched upon the subject of clothes, except in an altogether haphazard and unsystematic way. There is here room for a vast amount of interesting research that should aim ultimately at the formulation of general laws concerning the most pleasing forms, colours, and styles to suit the complex physiological, anatomical, and psychological aspects of individual personalities.[1] Such research could appropriately be done in existing psychological laboratories, but would of course imply the closest co-operation between psychologists, designers, dress-

---

[1] Cf. Audsley, 2.

makers, and tailors—and perhaps also with the exponents of certain other applied arts, for, as indicated in an earlier chapter, styles of dress are not unconnected with contemporary styles of architecture and interior decoration and should be considered in relation to them. (It seems obviously inappropriate, for instance, that clerks working in the spacious, light, and airy buildings of the 'new' architecture should be dressed in the same styles as their grandfathers who were housed in offices of the more intimate and secretive type favoured in that period.) Ultimately, too, such investigation would extend beyond the strictly aesthetic sphere and deal with the sociological effects of costumes, as manifesting themselves in the happiness and efficiency of their wearers. They would deal, for instance, with the relative influence of gay and sober costume upon various kinds of work (a point on which there is at present considerable difference of opinion)[1]; with the mental and physiological effects of different colours and different kinds of decoration[2]; with the relative psychological and social advantages of standardisation and individualisation in style and decorative treatment, and with the kind and degree of sartorial differentiation as between persons of different sex, age, and class. Quite generally indeed it may be said that the relation between aesthetics and sociology is seldom if ever closer than in the field of dress.

Hygienic.—We have already (Chap. XII.), indicated the urgent need of scientific research into the hygienic aspects of the various types of materials that can be used for clothing. Such research is already beginning, but requires systematising and extending. It would most naturally be conducted by medical men or physiologists, again working in co-operation with the actual designers and makers of clothes. It would also need co-ordination with the next branch of research, which would be—

Technical and would consist in the systematic investigation into the qualities and potentialities of the

---

[1] Cf. Flügel, 35, p. 123.   [2] Cf. Chap. III.

various materials. It is a branch of research which has actually made very considerable progress during recent years, as a result of which a number of valuable new materials—combining the advantages of cheapness, attractiveness, and healthiness—have become available for general use.

Economic.—We have already referred to the importance of the economic aspects of clothes. Both from the point of view of the individual wearer and from that of the clothing industry, these economic aspects possess a significance that can scarcely be exaggerated. There is here a wide and complex field, in which new problems will be constantly arising as fashions change and new discoveries are made. It will be well, however, if, among the intricacy of individual problems, the more general and philosophical aspects of economic questions should not be altogether lost to sight. There are in this field certain problems that touch on somewhat fundamental questions, both of politics and ethics. The unrestricted reign of commercial competition tends, as we have noticed, by exploiting the elements of social rivalry, to increase as far as possible the expenditure on dress; this being only one aspect of the results of modern advertising methods, which, especially in America, are trying to develop 'salesmanship' into a fine art. Development in this direction clearly has its limits; all the chief social and financial tendencies of the modern world indicate that, sooner or later, the commercial rivals will, even in their own interests, through some process of amalgamation, seek to put an end to unrestrained competition for the contents of the consumer's purse. The greater the amalgamation, the less the struggle between individual firms and industries, and the greater the co-ordination of the clothing trade as a whole. A Clothing Board would of course endeavour to promote such amalgamation and to foster co-ordination of the different interests concerned. It might, however, reasonably go a step further. Since it will be its business to consider the consumers as well as the producers, it will bear in mind that, both from the point of view of individual satisfaction and from that of social welfare, there is—with clothes as with other things—a point beyond which expenditure rapidly brings decreasing returns.[1] There is much to be said for those[2] who advocate a simpler life on the ground that many of the more expensive luxuries of civilisation give little pleasure, compared to the effort and expenditure necessary to obtain them. In many instances such unremunerative effort and expenditure is due to the desire (sometimes perhaps it might justifiably be called the necessity) of conforming to extravagant and snobbish social conventions. In all such cases the Board would endeavour to use its influence (through persuasion, not of course through force) towards a reduction of the unprofitable outlay. Here, as elsewhere, the fostering of individual happiness, social harmony and sound finance, is a higher duty than the protection of the more immediate interests of a certain group of trades.

Convenience.—There remains one other field for investigation—in this case a very much neglected one, but one in which the problems are relatively simple. In order to give the fullest satisfaction, our garments must not only be beautiful, hygienic, cheap, and comfortable; they must also be convenient in use. We have already touched upon this problem once or twice; as when we spoke about the desirability of investigating the best methods of carrying the rather numerous small articles which civilisation compels us to take with us on our daily wanderings; or, again, when we compared men's present clothes unfavourably with those of women, as regards the ease with which additional garments can be

---

[1] Stuart Chase and F. J. Schlink, in their interesting study of American methods (*Your Money's Worth*), quote an advertising authority as saying that at most only twenty-five per cent. of the business transacted in America is done in response to a natural demand, and that it is out of the other seventy-five per cent. that the great country of salesmanship makes its living. The question naturally arises as to whether a good deal of the money corresponding to this seventy-five per cent. could not be used in a way that would ultimately bring more pleasure and profit to all concerned.

[2] *E.g.* E. J. Urwick, *Luxury and Waste of Life*.

put on and off to suit the varying temperature of the environment. This latter example points indeed to a general problem of very considerable importance that has been almost totally ignored by the designers and makers of clothes—the problem, namely, of how garments can be made, so that a person may dress himself with the smallest possible effort and loss of time. If it is worth while for industrial psychologists to make patient and detailed movement-studies of the work in factories—work, each kind of which is carried on by only a small section of the population for a certain portion of their lives—the movements of dressing and undressing that are carried out by the whole population throughout their lives are surely no less worthy of investigation. Such investigation will certainly result in suggestions for improvement, in the one case as in the other. Unnecessarily fatiguing or difficult operations (such as are due to buttons in inaccessible places, buttons of such a kind or arranged in such a way that the tackling of each fresh button threatens to undo the work already done immediately above it or below it) should be eliminated, or as far as possible reduced. All clothes should be made so that they can be easily put on and off by the wearer without calling in the assistance of others. This is especially important in the case of children, who are often severely worried by complicated fastenings; but in these democratic days it is well that dressmakers should realise that valets and ladies' maids are a vanishing race to be found only in a very small minority of houses. Modern inventions, such as the zip fastener, may greatly facilitate the task of dressing. This brilliant little device might appear at first to be limited in use to the heavier and stronger materials. At the moment of writing it remains to see how far, by being attached to a band of stronger material, it can be employed also in connection with the lighter fabrics. Here is one small problem out of many that calls for a little specialised research.

Certain general principles will also come up for consideration—in particular the question of larger versus smaller garments (*e.g.* 'combinations' versus separate vest and drawers), the elimination of all very small, finicky, and easily mislaid articles (the collar, tie, and stud neckwear system of men is a ridiculous offender in this matter as in others), and the general problem of the relative merits of the 'pull-over' versus the 'fasten-up' type of garment. The former has the advantage of dispensing with special fastening processes, and can also (for that very reason) usually achieve a closer, neater, and more comfortable fit. It has the drawback of disarranging the hair (when pulled over the head), of needing some quite appreciable expenditure of energy when the garment is at all tight, and of arousing—in some persons —emotional objections connected with the obscuring of vision and the general helplessness and ridiculousness incidental to this method of putting on.[1] It seems possible that the zip, or some other improved method of fastening may, before long, achieve all the advantages of the pull-over method without its drawbacks.

We have dwelt somewhat long upon this matter of the putting on and off of clothes, because it is both one of the most important and one of the most neglected aspects of convenience in dress. It is of course far from being the only aspect. Another problem concerns the methods by which the protective and decorative elements in dress can be made to interfere as little as possible with freedom of movement and of posture. This applies of course particularly to special working and sporting clothes, but there seems no reason why freedom should not be studied also with reference to the clothes of every day. The savage, greedy for the maximum of uncoordinated decoration, the follower of fashion bent merely on chasing La Mode wherever she may lead, the stickler for correctness or rigid adherence to tradition—all these

---

[1] 'A man's most dangerous moment . . . is when he's getting into his shirt. Then he puts his head into a bag. That's why I prefer those American shirts that you put on like a jacket' (D. H. Lawrence, *Lady Chatterley's Lover*, p. 275). The context makes it seem highly probable that the fear in this case is connected with the castration complex.

care little if their comfort or health should suffer, provided only they attain the standards they have set themselves. Those who approach clothing in a more critical and rational spirit will inquire whether fashion, etiquette, or beauty have, any of them, the right to curtail freedom and efficiency. They will be inclined rather to assume that true ideals, whether social, moral, or aesthetic, would be in harmony with the physiological laws of human movement and that disharmony in this respect indicates the desirability of revising our sartorial standards rather than of sacrificing our liberty of function. It is already a canon of aesthetics that what is most truly useful and efficient is also the most beautiful. The same general law must surely hold of moral and of social values also.

In practice, however, we are still only beginning dimly to recognise these facts. Until the introduction of the recent sweeping reforms, women's dress impeded free movement in very many ways. Man's coat, that 'strange compromise between the gravitational and the anatomic', as Gerald Heard has called it, with its flopping sides, its hanging sleeves, its dragging on the armpit and the elbows, is so ill-suited to movement, except of the slowest and most solemn kind, that, by the restrictions imposed, it must—both psychologically and physiologically—reduce the efficiency of the male portion of the human race to some considerable extent. How much we do not know; but the greatly increased capacity of woman in the last few years, since she has thrown off her trammels, indicates that the loss may be no small one.[1]

---

[1] The possible inhibitory effects of clothing upon character—both for good and bad—may be illustrated from another field by Stella Benson's amusing, but doubtless somewhat exaggerated, account of the effects of the national costume of Korea upon the behaviour of its wearers.

'We have always understood that the Koreans, as a race, were passive to excess.

'The ancient purpose of the Korean top-hat—which was originally made of porcelain, was, I am told, to keep the peace. A man could not well engage in riotous conduct with a small porcelain top-hat balanced delicately upon his top-knot. Penalty for a broken hat was often, in the old days, death, and always involved the loss of honour.

'The result of this wise scheme has been to induce an almost excessive mildness

We must bear in mind, too, that in certain emergencies, convenience of clothing may be of literally vital importance. Long skirts or floppy trousers have caused many accidents, as did also the abnormally tight skirts worn just before the war. Women, it has been said,[1] have perished in shipwrecks through the cumbersome burden of their skirts, when they might otherwise have been preserved. In recent years, on the other hand, there can be little doubt that light coloured stockings have, at night-time, averted many a disaster upon our now so dangerous roads. These too are things that are not altogether unworthy of consideration by the designers of our clothes.

And now for our final matter. It is in the nature of a debt that the reader may have felt has been owing (with accumulating interest) throughout the last three chapters. We will, however, pay it, as all debts should be paid: in full and with as little fuss as possible.

The principle that has guided us in all our ethical and practical considerations was that clothes should provide the maximum of satisfaction in accordance with the full recognition of reality. As we have proceeded it has more and more become apparent that our bodies have, in an important sense, a greater reality-value than have our clothes. The reality principle demands throughout that we consistently allow ourselves an undistorted recognition of our bodies. Thus, aesthetic taste, as it develops, tends to

---

in the Korean character. And even after porcelain hats gave way to shiny, black, horsehair imitations, it is not surprising that a race which was bound in honour to keep—at least—its spiritual hat unbroken, has been the unresisting prey of its two predatory neighbours—China and Japan.

'However, now we see the Korean in a new light.

'A young generation has arisen which has never worn the mystic topper. Just as crinolines kept our grandmothers modest, so the national top-hat kept the Koreans slow to anger—and the disappearance of both crinoline and top-hat has swung the young generation across to the extreme. Young Koreans, to be sure, billow along in the old voluminous Korean quilted robes—turned black side out in winter and white side out in summer—but they crown this orthodox garb with Japanese schoolboys' forage caps.

'And from under this impudent headpiece, the young Korean lends an ear to the hat-breaking theories now abroad in Bolshevik Siberia and Young China' (*Worlds within Worlds*, pp. 221 and 222).

[1] Dearborn, 22, p. 42.

become reconciled more and more to the natural human form and seeks to set off and reveal its beauties rather than to hide its deficiencies, or to substitute other beauties of a kind that are foreign to anatomy. If this process continues, it means that emphasis must tend to fall ever increasingly upon the body itself and less upon its clothes. But we must not shirk the task of following this process to its logical conclusion. Complete reconciliation with the body would mean that the aesthetic variations, emendations, and aggrandisements of the body that are produced by clothes would no longer be felt as necessary or desirable; in fact there would be no need for clothes, except in so far as they might still be required for purposes of pure protection (and even these requirements, as we have seen, are smaller than has often been supposed, and are likely to become less as the control of environment—*e.g.* by the heating engineer—increases).[1]

Other considerations point clearly in the same direction. Modesty, as we have seen, when its essentially ambivalent nature is recognised, can interpose no reasonable obstacle to nudity; nor, in the long run, can economics—for, in so far as clothes cease to satisfy a need, they fall into the category of useless or conventional extravagances that are better done away with, since the effort, time, or money spent on them can be more profitably employed elsewhere. Hygiene, too, applauds nakedness in many circumstances, and is placing more and more faith in the unaided functions of the human skin.[2] Convenience can surely offer no serious objection, so long as some kind of sartorial harness allows us to transport with reasonable ease the instruments required

[1] At an indoor temperature of 70° F. (which is often attained when central heating systems are in use) all but very light clothing is uncomfortable, even for sedentary occupations, while for any kind of bodily activity no clothing whatever is required.

[2] The following passage may be quoted as representative of the doctrines of the skin enthusiasts: 'This admirable organ, the natural clothing of the body, which grows continually throughout life, which has at least four absolutely distinct sets of sensory nerves distributed to it, which is essential in the regulation of the temperature, which is waterproof from without inwards, but allows the excretory sweat to escape freely, which, when unbroken, is microbe-

in daily life. Apart from this, the saving of time and trouble spent in dressing (or perhaps the more profitable employment of this time in the cause of *bodily* perfection) and the facility with which the natural skin can be cleaned if dirty, dried if wet, are all in favour of nakedness rather than apparel.

Here, however, it may be thought, our principle reveals its own inherent suicidal absurdity, since the standard by which we are to judge clothes would be most completely attained by the practical abolition of all clothes. Such a *reductio ad absurdum*, surely, indicates the need of further qualification in the statement of the principle—qualification that would stress the more intrinsic satisfactions of clothes in administering to human needs, that would assert the superior claims of the psychological values of the desire for beauty, modesty, and protection, as against the value of the mere intellectual apprehension of outer reality.

Such an admission, however, would really mean, not the revision, but the abandonment of our principle altogether. The reality principle, as we have understood it, does not deny the existence and value of human desires; it seeks only that these desires should be guaranteed the surest and most permanent satisfaction, namely, through recognition (rather than distortion or denial) of external reality—and it is just this that has led us to face the possibility (or rather the actual desirability) of the ultimate disappearance of clothes, except for occasional protective purposes. There seems no alternative but to abandon the principle or accept the consequences. The former course would mean a new orientation, the formulation of new principles and a fresh discussion of the whole field of clothing in the light of these new principles—in fact the rewriting of our last three chapters; a task that we must leave to others, with

---

proof, and which can readily absorb sunlight—this most beautiful, versatile, and wonderful organ is, for the most part, smothered, blanched, and blinded in clothes and can only gradually be restored to the air and light which are its natural surroundings. Then, and only then, we learn what it is capable of'.
—(C. W. Saleeby, 83, p. 67.)

the consolation that their labours may at least be rendered lighter by our present failure. Here we can only end by facing the consequences with our backs to the wall. The consequences are twofold:

(1) We must admit that the very existence of clothing for purposes of modesty or decoration implies that the conditions of our standard are but incompletely fulfilled, and that, in recommending this or that as a contribution to sartorial reform, we are guilty of striking a compromise, since ultimately our reforms must end by improving clothes out of existence altogether. This conclusion, it would seem, is after all not so very terrible. It is the kind of compromise that is implied in all art, and indeed in nearly all ethical evaluation of behaviour (as in the Spencerian distinction between absolute and relative ethics). Art itself (and with it sartorial art) is a compromise between imagination and reality; it deals with real media but implies an inability to find complete satisfaction with reality, and creates a new world 'nearer to the heart's desire', away from the limitations and disappointments of reality. In this matter, if we are guilty of compromise, we have at least sinned in the most respectable of company; we have, in fact, only shown that toleration of human frailty and of the relativity of human wishes that all art postulates. Of such a compromise there is little need to be ashamed.

(2) We must honestly face the conclusion that our principle points ultimately, not to clothing, but to nakedness. Here also we are not alone, and our company, if less numerous, is at least worthy of consideration. Apart from the (in some countries) very numerous practitioners of nude culture and its semi-official spokesmen,[1] there have been several other writers within the last few years who have anticipated us in this conclusion. The 'men like gods', who inhabited Mr. H. G. Wells' Utopia, were naked. Mr. Gerald Heard,[2] as the result of his philosophical and historical survey, considers that clothing is destined to vanish from the earth. More

[1] Cf. Parmelee, 70, and Seitz, 88.   [2] 48.

recently still, Mr. Langdon Davies,[1] taking Godiva as his patron saint, leads us with much eloquent persuasiveness towards the same view as to the ultimate inevitability of nakedness. The boldest of all prophets is Professor Knight Dunlap,[2] who believes that nakedness will be at first a uni-sexual affair, but holds that 'within a few years' women at least will expose the whole body in public, and will cause but little commotion by so doing.

Encouraged thus, we may with greater equanimity contemplate the possibility that dress is, after all, destined to be but an episode in the history of humanity, and that man (and perhaps before him woman) will one day go about his business secure in the control both of his own body and of his wider physical environment, disdaining the sartorial crutches on which he perilously supported himself during the earlier tottering stages of his march towards a higher culture.

Meanwhile the crutches are still with us. We can, however, at least see to it that our budding science shall enable us to fashion them efficiently and use them well, and so let them help us further along the road. But the first stage of applied science must consist in an honest review of our present position and a reconnoitring of the path of future progress. These are the humble but necessary tasks on which we have been occupied.

[1] 21. [2] 24.

BIBLIOGRAPHY

I HAVE here included all works on clothes that have gone to the foundation of the present volume, together with a few others which I have not been able to consult myself, but which have been largely used by some of the authorities to whom I am myself principally indebted. No attempt has been made at completeness on the historical, medical, or sociological sides.

1. Abraham, Karl. 'Bemerkungen zur Psychoanalyse eines Falles von Fuss und Korsett Fetichismus', *Klinische Beiträge zur Psychoanalyse*, p. 84. Leipzig, 1921.
2. Audsley, George Ashdown. *Colour in Dress*. A Manual for Ladies. London, 1912.
3. Baumann, Erich. *Die Reform der Männerkleidung*. Gettenbach bei Gelnhausen, 1929.
4. Bibesco, Princesse. *Noblesse de robe*. Paris, 1928.
5. Blanc, A. A. P. C. *Art in Ornament and Dress*. New York, 1887.
6. Bliss, Sylvia. 'The Significance of Clothes', *American Journal of Psychology*, vol. xxvii. p. 217. 1916.
7. Bloch, Ivan. *Das Sexualleben unserer Zeit*, ch. vii. Ninth Edition, 1909.
8. Blum, André. *Les Modes au XVIIe et au XVIIIe siècle*. Paris, 1928.
9. Bonaparte, Marie. 'Über die Symbolik der Kopftrophäen', *Imago*, vol. xiv. pp. 100 ff. 1928.
10. Bourdeau, L. *Histoire de l'habillement et de la parure*. Paris, 1902.
11. Bousfield, Paul. *Sex and Civilisation*. London, 1925.
12. Boyle, Frederick. 'Savages and Clothes', *Monthly Review*. September 1905.
13. Calthrop, Dion Clayton. *English Costume*. London, 1907.
14. Carlyle, Thomas. *Sartor Resartus*.
15. Chadwick, Mary. 'The Psychological Dangers of Tight Clothing in Childhood', *National Health*. 1926.
16. Chalmers, Helena. *Clothes on and off the Stage*. New York and London, 1928.
17. Crawley, Ernest. Article 'Dress', in *Encyclopaedia of Religion and Ethics*.
18. Cullis, M. A. 'Farthingale: A suggested derivation', *International Journal of Psycho-analysis*, vol. xi. p. 87. 1930.
19. Daly, C. D., 'Der Menstruationskomplex', *Imago*, vol. xiv. p. 11. 1928.
20. Darwin, Sir George H. 'Development in Dress', *Macmillan's Magazine*. September 1872.
21. Davies, John Langdom. *The Future of Nakedness*. London, 1929.
22. Dearborn, G. von Ness. 'The Psychology of Clothing', *Psychological Monographs*, vol. xxvi. No. 1. Princeton, N.J., 1918.
23. Dewing, M. R. O. *Beauty in Dress*. New York, 1881.

24. Dunlap, Knight. 'The Development and Function of Clothing', *Journal of General Psychology*, vol. i. p. 64. 1928.
25. Earle, Alice Morse. *Two Centuries of Costume in America, 1620–1820*. New York, 1903.
26. Ecob, Helen G. *The Well-dressed Woman*. New York, 1893.
27. Ellis, Havelock. *Studies in the Psychology of Sex*, vol. i. pp. 1–80, vol. vi. pp. 95–117.
28. Elster, Alexander. 'Wirtschaft und Mode', *Jahrbuch für National-ökonomie und Statistik*, vol. xlvi. Folge, 1913.
29. —— 'Kleidung und Mode' in Marcuse's *Handwörterbuch der Sexualwissenschaft*. Second Edition. 1926.
30. Fairholt, F. W. *Costume in England*. 1846.
31. Ferenczi, 'Sinnreiche Variante des Schuhsymbols der Vagina', *Inter. Zeitschrift für Psychoanalyse*, vol. iii. p. 111. 1915
32. Fischel, Oskar, and Boehn, Max von, *Modes and Manners of the Nineteenth Century*, 4 vols. London, 1927.
33. Fischer, Hans W. *Das Weiberbuch*. München, 1923.
34. Flaccus, Louis W. *Remarks on the Psychology of Clothes*. Pedagogical Seminary, vol. xiii. p. 61. 1906.
35. Flügel, J. C., 'On the Mental Attitude to Present-day Clothes'. Report on a Questionnaire. *Brit. Journal of Medical Psychology*, vol. ix, p. 97. 1929.
36. —— —— 'Clothes Symbolism and Clothes Ambivalence', *Inter. Journal of Psycho-analysis*, vol. x. p. 205. 1929.
37. —— —— 'Sex Differences in Dress', *Proceedings of the International Congress of the World League for Sexual Reform* (1929). London, 1930.
38. —— —— 'De la valeur affective du vêtement', *Revue Française de Psychanalyse*, III. 1930.
39. Fred. 'Psychologie der Mode', *Die Kunst*, vol. xxviii.
40. Freud, Sigmund. *Introductory Lectures on Psycho-analysis*, p. 132. London, 1922.
41. —— —— 'Fetichism', *Inter. Journal of Psycho-analysis*, vol. ix. p. 161. 1928.
42. —— —— *Collected Papers*, vol. ii. p. 163. London, 1924.
43. Friedberger, E. 'Männer- und Frauenkleidung', *Die Umschau*. June 1929.
44. Fuchs, Eduard. *Illustrierte Sittengeschichte*, 3 Bände, 3 Ergänzungsbände. München, 1910.
45. De Giafferi, Paul-Louis. *L'Histoire du costume féminin de l'an 1037 à l'an 1870*. Paris.
46. Goya, H. 'Nacktheit und Aberglaube', *Internationale Zeitschrift für Psycho-analyse*, vol. vii. p. 63. 1921.
47. H. R. 'Zur Symbolik der Schlange und der Kravatte', *Zentralblatt für Psychoanalyse*, vol. ii. p. 675. 1912.
48. Heard, Gerald. *Narcissus. An Anatomy of Clothes*. London. 1924.
49. Hottenroth, Fr. *Le Costume chez les peuples anciens et modernes*.
50. Hiler, Hilaire. *From Nudity to Raiment*. London, 1930.
51. Hill, Leonard. *Sunshine and Open Air*. London, 1924.
52. Hollós, Stephan. 'Schlangen und Krawattensymbolik', *Inter. Zeitschrift für Psychoanalyse*, vol. ix. p. 73. 1923.
53. Jelgersma, H. C. 'Eine eigenartige Sitte auf der Insel Marken in Holland', *Inter. Zeitschrift für Psychoanalyse*, vol. x, p. 272. 1924.
54. Jones, Ernest, *Papers on Psycho-analysis*, p. 136. Second Edition. London, 1918.

BIBLIOGRAPHY

55. Jones, Ernest. 'Kälte, Krankheit und Geburt', *Inter. Zeitschrift für Psychoanalyse*, vol. ix. p. 260. 1923.
56. —— —— 'Der Mantel als Symbol', *Inter. Zeitschrift für Psychoanalyse*, vol. xiii. p. 77. 1927.
57. Jordan, Alfred C. 'Hygienic Costume', *Sunlight*. September, 1929.
58. —— —— 'Healthy Dress for Men', *Franco-British Medical Review*. November 1929. (Also in *American Medicine*, December 1929.)
59. Köhler, Carl. *A History of Costume*. London, 1928.
60. Landauer, K. 'Die kindliche Bewegungsunruhe', *Inter. Zeitschrift für Psychoanalyse*, vol. xii. pp. 387–388. 1926.
61. Levy, L., 'Sexualsymbolik in der biblischen Paradiesgeschichte', *Imago*, vol. v. p. 27. 1917.
62. Lorand, A. S. 'Fetischismus in statu nascendi', *Internationale Zeitschrift für Psychoanalyse*, vol. xvi. p. 87. 1930.
63. Lotze, H. *Microcosmus*, book v. ch. ii. pp. 592–595. Fourth American Edition. 1897.
64. Löwitsch, F. 'Raumempfinden und moderne Baukunst', *Imago*, vol. xiv. p. 293. 1928.
65. Macaulay, Eve. 'Some Notes on the Attitude of Children to Dress', *British Journal of Medical Psychology*, vol. ix. p. 150. 1929.
66. Miomandre, Fr. de. *La Mode*. Paris, 1927.
67. Müller-Lyer, F. *Phasen der Kultur*, pp. 122–135. München, 1920.
68. Mustoxidi. *Qu'est-ce que la mode?* Paris, 1920.
69. Norris, H. *Costume and Fashion in England*. Two volumes at present published. London, 1924 and 1927.
70. Parmelee, Maurice. *Nude Culture*. London, 1929.
71. Parsons, Frank Alvah. *The Psychology of Dress*. New York, 1920.
72. Pendleton. 'Philosophy of Dress', *Blackwood's Magazine*, vol. liii. p. 230.
73. Phelps, Elizabeth S. *What to Wear*. Boston, 1873.
74. Poucher, W. A. *Eve's Beauty Secrets*. London, 1926.
75. *Practical Dress Reform*. Report of Committee on Designs of the Men's Dress Reform Party, 39 Bedford Square, W.C.1. London, 1929.
76. Racinet. *Le Costume historique*. Paris, 1888.
77. Rank, Otto. 'Die Nacktheit in Sage und Dichtung', in *Psychoanalytische Beiträge zur Mythenforschung*. Leipzig, 1919.
78. Reich, W. 'Wohin führt die Nackterziehung?' *Zeitschrift für psychoanalytische Pädagogik*. vol. iii. p. 44. 1928.
79. Reik, Th. 'Völkerpsychologische Parallelen zum Traumsymbol des Mantels', *Inter. Zeitschrift für Psychoanalyse*, vol. vi. p. 350. 1920.
80. Roubaud, Louis. *Au pays des mannequins* Paris, 1928.
81. Sadger, J. 'Haut, Schleimhaut, und Muskelerotik'. *Jahrbuch für psychoanalytische und psychopathologische Forschungen*, vol. iii. p. 525. 1912.
82. —— *Die Lehre von den Geschlechtsverirrungen*, pp. 321–458. Leipzig und Wien, 1921.
83. Saleeby, C. W. *Sunshine and Health*. London. 1928.
84. Samson, J. W. *Die Frauenmode der Gegenwart*. Berlin und Köln, 1927.
85. Sanborn, H. C. 'The Function of Clothing and Adornment', *American Journal of Psychology*, vol. xxxviii. p. 1. 1927.
86. Schurtz, Heinrich. *Grundzüge einer Philosophie der Tracht*. Stuttgart, 1891.

87. Scott, C. A. 'Sex and Art', *American Journal of Psychology*, vol. vii. p. 187. 1895.
88. Seitz, J. M. *Back to Nature: An Exposition of Nude Culture.* Dresden, 1923.
89. Selenka, Emil. *Der Schmuck des Menschen.* Berlin, 1900.
90. Sombart, Werner. 'Wirtschaft und Mode', *Grenzfragen des Nerven- und Seelenlebens*, No. 12. Wiesbaden, 1902.
91. Spencer, Herbert. *Principles of Sociology*, vol. ii. part 4.
92. Stekel, W. 'Der Mantel als Symbol', *Zentralblatt für Psychoanalyse*, vol. iii. p. 601. 1913.
93. Stratz, C. H. *Die Frauenkleidung und ihre naturliche Entwicklung.* Stuttgart, 1922.
94. Storfer, A. J. *Marias jungfräuliche Mutterschaft.* Berlin, 1914.
95. Sully, James. *Studies in Childhood*, pp. 202, 319, 320, 371. London, 1896,
96. Surén, Hans. *Man and Sunlight.* Slough, 1924.
97. Sydow, Eckart von. *Primitive Kunst und Psychoanalyse.* Leipzig, 1927.
98. Tertullian. 'Women's Dress', in 'Fathers of the Church', translated by F. A. Wright, p. 52. London, 1928.
99. Thomas, W. J. 'Psychology of Modesty and Clothes', *American Journal of Psychology*, vol. v. p. 246.
100. Tylor, E. B. *Anthropology*, pp. 242 ff. London, 1892.
101. Ungewitter, Richard. *Die Nacktheit.* Stuttgart, 1922.
102. Walford, Walter G. *Dangers in Neckwear.* London, 1917.
103. Webb, Wilfred Mark. *The Heritage of Dress.* London, 1912.
104. White, G. H. 'A Marken Island Custom', *Notes and Queries*, vol. clviii. p. 273. 1930.
105. Wundt, W. *Völkerpsychologie*, vol. iii. pp. 176 ff. and 219 ff.
106. Zulliger, Hans. 'Nackte Tatsächlichkeiten', *Zeitschrift für psychoanalytische Pädagogik*, vol. iii. p. 51. 1928.

ADDENDA

Bradley, H. Dennis. *The Eternal Masquerade.* London, 1922.
Fenichel, Otto. "The Psychology of Transvestitism," *Int. Journal of Psycho-analysis*, vol. xi. p. 211. 1930.

INDEX

ABDOMEN, emphasis on, 13, 160, 161
Ability, special features of costume indicating, 132
Abraham, Karl, 239
Academic robes, 104, 131
Accidents caused by clothes, 234
Adaptability, greater of women's clothes, 204, 205
——, lack of, in 'fixed' costume, 217
Aesthetics and aesthetic factors, 52, 89, 100, 113, 180, 184, 190, 194, 218, 219 ff.
——, need of research in, 227, 228
Afternoon dresses, 164
Age differences, need of studying, 228
Air currents felt on skin, 87, 92, 96
Ambivalence, 20, 22, 201
Amplitude of garments, moral associations of, 76
Amulets, 72 ff.
Anal elements, 92, 189
'Anatomic' costume, 68
Animal products used for clothes, 124, 128
Antiquity, varying degree of, in sartorial 'vestiges', 179, 180
Apes, tendency to decoration in, 18
Applied art and applied science, relation between, 184
—— arts, need for co-operation of exponents of certain, 228
Aprons, 124, 125
Architecture, 149, 150, 228
'Arctic' costume, 12, 123, 127 ff., 167, 216
—— ——, basis of European male costume, 128
Armour, 69, 70
Arms, exposure of, 57, 65, 95, 126, 161
Art, children and, 18
—— and magic, 72
——, compromise involved in all, 237

Artificiality of eighteenth and nineteenth century fashions, 149, 158, 163, 223
Asceticism of men's dress, 211, 213
'Associational' costumes, 130, 132 ff.
Athletes, costume of, 86
Audsley, G. A., 227, 239
Austen, Jane, 215
Australia, native tribes of, 40
——, animals of, 172
Auto-erotism and auto-erotic tendencies, 86 ff., 108, 189, 207

Bach, J. S., 220
Badges, 51, 132
Bagger, Eugene, 186
Bags for carrying essential articles, 186, 187
Bare legs at tennis, 153
Barmaids kill a fashion, 152
Baseball players, costume of, 71
Bath, a garment sometimes worn in the, 60
Bathing dress, 35, 125, 193
Baths, sun, air, and water, 87, 94
'Battle of the skirts', 165
Baumann, Erich, 70, 203, 239
Beauty enhanced by clothes, 21, 86
—— and modesty, 64, 97
——, differences in, diminished by clothes, 65, 223
Belts, 34, 43, 76, 89, 99, 187
Benson, Stella, 233
Berkeley, Reginald, 117
'Best' clothes, 90
Bibesco, Princess, 37, 239
Blanc, A. A. P. C., 239
Blazer, 132
Bloch, Ivan, 26, 239
Bloomers, 152
Blouse advocated for men, 213
Blum, André, 239
Blushing, 21
Boards. See Clothing Boards
Bodily self, extension of, through clothes, 34 ff., 47, 48
'Body Plastic', 40, 42

243

Body and clothes, relative emphasis on, 156 ff., 222 ff.
——, various parts of, emphasised in different fashions, 156, 160 ff., 221, 222
——, right to exposure of, in women, 205, 238
——, desirability of increasing natural beauty of, 222
——, in a sense more real than clothes, 222 ff., 234 ff.
Boehn, Max von, 13, 47, 155, 240
'Bohemia', influence of, on fashion, 141
Bolero, 126
Bonaparte, Marie, 30, 239
Boots, 46, 99, 142, 177
——, Russian, 173, 205
——, Top, 173
Bosom. *See* Breasts
——, exposure of. *See* Décolleté
Bourdeau, L., 239
Bousfield, Paul, 201, 239
Boyle, Frederick, 94, 239
Boy scouts, uniform of, 34, 132
'Boyishness' in women's dress, 163
Boys, longing for colour in, 89
—— dressed as girls, 120, 121
Bracelets, 30, 178
Bradley, H. Dennis, 242
Breasts, 107, 160, 162
British Broadcasting Corporation, 7
Brown, Cecil, 66
Brownlow, Lady, 66
Brummell, Beau, 147, 152, 199
Buckingham, Duke of, 58
Bus conductors, 136
Busby, 13, 46, 176
Bushmen, 141
Bustle, 13, 58, 67, 161, 220
Butchers, 134
Buttocks, 67, 161
Buttons, 173, 176, 178, 179, 231
'Buttons'. *See* Page Boy

Callet, portrait by, 13, 157
Calthrop, Dion Clayton, 239
Candaules, 118
Canzani, Estella, 11
Carlyle, Thomas, 81, 157, 158, 224, 239
——, ——, quoted, 68
Carrying of essential articles, 33, 186, 187, 230, 235, 236
Castration, 105, 196, 209, 210

Castration complex, 28, 30, 42, 74, 102, 105, 120
—— ——, manifestations of, in the two sexes, 105
—— —— and exchange of garments, 121
Catherine II. of Russia, 11, 48
Ceremonial garments, 48, 70, 128, 225
Chadwick, Mary, 199, 239
Chalmers, Helena, 239
Chambermaids, uniforms of, 134
Change, more rapid in modern times, 143
Charterhouse, hierarchical features of dress at, 133
Chase, Stuart, 230
Chauffeurs, uniforms of, 134
Cheeks, holes made in, 42
Children, attitude of, towards clothes, 18, 85 ff., 199
——, need for care in clothing, 199, 231
China, loin cloth used in, 125
Chinese women, deformation of feet of, 43, 44
Choice, greater freedom of, for women, 204
——, elimination of time and trouble of, in 'fixed' costume, 216
Chorus girls, 163
Christianity, influence of, 57, 129, 190
Church, influence of, 57, 106
——, costume worn in, 104. *See also* Clerical *and* Ecclesiastical
Cicatrization, 39, 40
'Circular' decoration. *See* Decoration, Circular
Circumcision, 42
Class differences, need of studying, 228
Classes, social, differences of modesty in, 60
——, ——, relative influence of fashion in various, 140, 141
——, ——, rôle of, in 'modish' costume, 138 ff.
Classifications of dress, 122 ff.
Cleanliness, 90, 205, 223, 236
Clerical costume, 128
Clerks, costume of, 228
Climate, 17, 68, 128
Clocks on socks and stockings, 175

INDEX

Close fitting garments, 59
Clothes as means of judging other people, 15
—— more important than body in certain styles, 157 ff., 163
—— perhaps an episode in human history, 238
Clothes-horse, the body as a, 157, 223
Clothing Boards suggested, 218 ff., 227, 229
—— materials, 123, 124, 127, 128, 204, 228, 229, 231
—— trade, 217, 219, 229
Coat, symbolism of, 27
——, as impeding movement, 38, 88, 213, 233
——, men not respectable without, 209
——, Tail, 173
Cod-piece, 27, 148
Cold, effect of, on clothes, 22, 57, 68, 87, 127, 128
——, excessive fear of, 23, 82
——, and lack of love, 77 ff. (esp. 80, 81), 99, 196
——, sensitiveness to, 77 ff., 98, 99
Collar, metal, 12
——, shell, 12
——, symbolism of, 27
——, bone, 75
——, stiff, 76, 97, 163, 197
——, open, 95
——, Byron, 141
—— of coats, nicks in, 174
——, detachable, 194
——, tight, of men, 205, 212
——, tie and stud system of men, 232
Colours reserved for royalty, 31
——, political associations of certain, 32
——, moral associations of, 75
——, children's taste in, 89, 90
—— reintroduced into men's dress from below, 141
—— in Renaissance dress, 48
—— in eighteenth century dress, 49
——, amount permissible depends on style, 157
——, greater right of women to, 204
—— need of research concerning use of, 227

Colours, mental and physical effects of, 228
Combinations, 232
Combs, 44, 51
Commercial interests as factor in fashions, 141 ff., 217 ff., 229, 230
Commonwealth, English costumes at time of the, 156
Compensation. *See* Reaction Formation
Competition, role of, in fashion, 138 ff., 216, 218, 229
Complexions equalised by cosmetics, 66, 189
' Component instincts ', 109
Compromise, 22
Conations, movements of dress in relation to our, 38
Concealment of bodily defects, 65, 224
Confluence, 11, 36 ff., 41, 157
Conscience more rigid as concerns dress in men, 113
Conscious investigation as reality test, 183
Conservatism of men's clothing trade, 210
Consumer, need for consideration of, in economics, 229, 236
Contrast, 11, 36 ff., 48
Convenience for putting on and off, 205, 231, 232, 236
—— for transport, 205
Coins, 33
Co-operation in research, need for, 227 ff.
Coronation robe, 48
' Correct ' and ' incorrect ' attire, 56, 61, 93, 111, 141, 207, 209, 232
Corset, 43, 89, 99, 171, 194
——, as fetish, 28
——, moral significance of, 75, 76
——, development from girdle, 126
Cosmetics, 188 ff. *See also* Painting
Cost of clothes, 97. *See also* Expenditure
Courts, influence of, 113, 140, 186
Coyness, 20
Crawley, Ernest, 106, 120, 239
Cretan. *See* Minoan
Crinoline, 13, 47, 49, 161, 165, 234
Crown, 31
Cuffs of coat sleeves, 174
——, detachable, 194
Cullis, M. A., 38, 239

Daly, C. D., 107, 239
Damping dresses before putting them on, 158
Dancers, costume of, 86
——, ——, in ancient Egypt, 123
Dandy, the, 101
Darwin, Charles, 17, 44, 68
Darwin, Sir George, 168, 172, 239
Davies, J. Langdon, 238, 239
Dearhorn, G. van Ness, 7, 234, 239
Décolleté, 57, 58, 62, 63, 79, 106 ff., 126, 147, 162, 206, 225
—— and sex differences, 107
—— as feature of 'tropical' dress, 126
——, general significance of, 106 ff., 225, 226
Decoration as purpose of clothing, 16 ff., 25 ff.
——, relation of, to modesty, 19 ff., 156, 221
——, forms of, 39 ff.
——, 'Corporal', 39 ff., 188 ff., 225
——, 'External', 40, 46 ff., 190 ff.
——, 'Vertical', 40, 46
——, 'Dimensional', 40, 46 ff.
——, 'Directional', 40, 48
——, 'Circular', 12, 40, 50
——, 'Local', 40, 51, 132, 190
——, 'Sartorial', 40, 52
——, interior (of houses), 149, 150, 228
——, ethics of, 185
——, need of, a primitive trait, 224 ff.
—— and freedom of movement, 232 ff.
Defects, bodily, influence of, on dress, 65
Defloration, 125
Deformation, 40, 42 ff.
——, relation of, to culture, 44
Deformity, 60
Demi-monde, influence of, on fashion, 141
Democracy, sexual freedom and exposure of female body, 79, 163
—— and fashion, 140, 141, 149, 163, 213
—— better served by simple male garments, 213
Development of clothes morality, 85 ff.

Development, difficulties of psychological, 199 ff.
Dewing, M. R. O., 239
Diana, statue of, 12, 157
'Dimensional' decoration. See Decoration, Dimensional
'Directional' decoration. See Decoration, Directional
Disease, infectious, relations of, to clothing, 195
Disgust, 60, 62 ff., 96, 97
Displacement, 27, 57, 85, 86, 88 ff., 104, 117, 118, 209, 212
Display, tendency to, 18, 57, 104
——, opposed to modesty, 63 ff., 103
——, sex differences in, 103 ff.
Doctors, costume of, 221
——, need for co-operation of, in research, 228
Double moral standard in dress, 205
Drawers, 232
Dressing and undressing, need for study of, 231, 236
Dressmakers, 146 ff, 164 ff., 215, 227, 231
Dressmaking, 90
Duelling, 40
Duk Duk Society, 32
Dunlap Knight, 7, 65, 69, 71, 189, 238, 240
Durability, lesser, of modern clothes, 142, 143

Ear-rings, 42
Earle, Helen G., 240
Ears, holes made in, 42
Ecclesiastical costume, 131. See also Clerical costume
Economic factors in dress, 141 ff., 217, 219 ff., 235
—— —— ——, need for research concerning, 229, 230
Egypt, hip ring in ancient, 123
——, loin cloth used in, 125
Eighteenth century fashions, 149, 158, 223
Elizabeth, Empress of Austria, 186
——, Empress of Russia, 58
Ellis, Havelock, 28, 66, 120, 240
Elster, Alexander, 240
Empathy, role of, in Eonism, 120
Empire dress, 13, 149, 157, 161, 163, 220

INDEX

Employer, attitude of, to dress reform, 210
England, uniforms in, 135, 136
English, dress of, in the Tropics, 217
d'Eon de Beaumont, Chevalier, 119
Eonism, 119 ff., 203, 207
Epaulettes, 48
Ethics of dress, 181 ff.
—— ——, difficulty of excluding discussion of, 181
—— ——, difficulties of, 182 ff.
—— ——, general principle stated, 183
—— ——, absolute and relative, 237
Eugenics, 233
Eugénie, Empress, 146
Evening dress, 78, 114, 115, 153, 162, 164, 175, 186
'Evil Eye', 73, 74
Evolution of dress, 13, 122, 167 ff.
—— —— compared to biological evolution, 168 ff.
Excessive interest in clothes, 100, 101
Exhibitionism, 27, 86 ff., 97, 104, 107 ff., 118, 152, 156 ff., 192, 217. *See also* Display
—— of women, 107 ff.
——, vicarious, 118, 119
——, ——, of parents, 199
——, repression of, in men, 208
Expenditure on clothes, salesmanship increases, 229
—— ——, decreasing returns on, 230
Expense, 'fixed' costume saves, 217
Exposure, principle of, in women's dress, 107 ff.
Extension of bodily self through clothes, 34, 46 ff., 187
Extravagance of costume, 97

Fabrics. *See* Clothing Materials
Face, attitude of Moslems and Europeans to, 67
Faces, toleration of ugly, 224
Fairfax, Edward, quoted, 39
Fairholt, F. W., 240
'Family' costumes, 130, 131
Fashion, changes of, 22, 47, 97, 155 ff., 229. *See also* 'Modish' costume
——, sexual rôle of, 26

Fashion, unnecessary costliness of, 97, 217
—— and social classes, 112
—— a goddess, 137
—— and competition, 138 ff., 216
——, essential causes of, 138, 139
——, the paradox of, 146
—— and evolution of garments, 170, 171
——, good designs independent of, 220
—— problem, how to have its advantages without its disadvantages, 220
—— and freedom of movement, 232 ff.
'Fashion of the Month Club', 165, 219
Fashions, origin of individual, 145 ff., 151 ff., 167
——, commercial aspects of, 141, 217
——, failure of intended, 147
——, men not much interested in, 214
——, changes of, cause disturbance in clothing trades, 217
—— often seem ridiculous to later generations, 220
Feathers, 49
'Feel' of clothes, 87, 88, 92
Femininity, specific features of, emphasis on, 162, 163
Fenichel, Otto, 120, 242
Ferenczi, Sandor, 240
Fetishism, 28, 214
Fig leaf, 25
Figure of wearer, important in certain styles, 157
——, youthful and mature, 159
Finger joints removed, 42, 45
Fischel, Oscar, 13, 47, 155, 240
Fischer, Hans W., 240
'Fixed' costume, 113, 123, 129 ff., 167, 185, 216 ff.
—— ——, contrasted with 'modish' costume, 129, 130, 133
—— ——, transition to 'modish' costume, 134, 135
—— ——, obsolescent examples of, 135, 218
—— —— superseded by 'modish' costume, 135
—— ——, biological parallels of, 172

'Fixed' costume, men's dress approximates to, 172
——— ———, advantages and disadvantages of, 216 ff.
——— ———, advantages should be combined with those of 'modish' costume, 220
Flaccus, Louis W., 7, 34, 37, 38, 50, 77, 240
Flash of Royal Welch Fusiliers, 177
Flies, clothing as protection from, 71
Floral decoration, 12, 124
Flowers associated with women, 125
Flügel, J. C., 27, 74, 77, 82, 83, 87, 90, 105, 116, 117, 199, 205, 228, 240
Foot as fetish, 28
———, deformed, 42, 43, 188
——— covering. *See* Boots *and* Shoes
——— ———, light, a feature of 'tropical' costume, 127
——— ———, heavy, a feature of 'arctic' costume, 129
Frame, costume as a, 12, 157
France, Anatole, 192, 203
——— ———, quoted, 9, 155
'Fräulein Else', 21
Fred, 240
Freedom, sexual, 163, 215
——— of movement, desirability of preserving, 232 ff.
Freemasons, 32, 132
French Revolution. *See* Revolution
Freud, Sigmund, 28, 116, 240
Friang, André, 8
Friedberger, E., 204, 240
'Friends of Nature', 94, 109
Frock coat used even in tropics, 217
Fuchs, Eduard, 8, 26, 47, 58, 78, 240
Fuller, Loie, 11, 36
Fusiliers, Royal Welch, 176, 177

Garments, individual, evolution of, 167 ff.
———, new, put on over old, 175
Garter, symbolism of, 27
Gas, intestinal, 38
Gas mask, 70
Genital sexuality, 108 ff.

Gentlewoman, A, 215
'Geographical' costumes, 130, 131, 218
Giafferi, Paul Louis de, 240
Girdle, symbolism of, 27
——— developed from hip ring, 125, 126
Girl guides, badges of, 132
Godiva, Lady, 238
Gothic architecture, 150
Goya, H., 240
Graves, Robert, 133, 176
'Gravitational' costume, 68
'Great Masculine Renunciation', the, 110 ff.
Greeks, 224
Group, special social, indicated in 'fixed' costume, 132 ff.
——— mentality in fashion, 148
Gyges, 118

H. R., 240
Hair as fetish, 28
———, disarranging of, while dressing, 232
Hairdressing, 44, 45, 159
Hat, as symbol, 27
———, removal of, 30, 104, 105
———, in wind, 37
———, hiding eyes, 52
———, plumes on, 178
Handkerchief, 28, 37
'Haute Couture, la', 148, 153, 164, 165
Hawaii, 11
Head, deformation of, 42
Head-dress, 12, 37, 46, 58, 104, 105
Heard, Gerald, 83, 150, 151, 233, 237, 240
Heat loss, reduction of, by clothes, 22, 127, 195
Heels, high, 46, 161
———, symbolism of, 161
Helmet, 49, 105
Hennin, 46
Hercules, 119
Herodotus, 23, 118
Hierarchic features of dress, 31, 131
Hiler, Hilaire, 11, 240
Hill, Leonard, 196, 240
Hiller, Eric, 8
Himalayas, 127
Hip ring, 12, 123 ff.
——— ———, origin of clothing from, 124

INDEX

Hips, emphasis on, 13, 161
History of clothes, 7, 122, 148, 155, 168, 175
Hoesli, Henri, 8
Holbein the Younger, 160
Holland, national costumes of, 131
Hollós, Stephan, 240
Homosexuality and Eonism, 119, 203, 207
—— and sex differentiation in dress, 202
——, need of toleration towards, 203
——, repression of, 209
—— and Narcissism, 212
Honourable Artillery Company, busby of, 13, 176
Horns as trophies, 29
Hose of the sixteenth century, 59
Hottenroth, Fr., 240
House and clothes compared, 83, 84, 149, 150
Hungarian cap, forerunner of busby, 13, 176
Hunger, 'the best tailor', 127
Hunters, men as, 124
Hussars, uniform of, 31, 176
Hygiene and hygienic factors, 7, 22, 23, 28, 69, 94, 99, 194 ff., 205, 206, 213, 219 ff.
—— —— ——, a new point of view, 196
—— —— ——, need for study of, 195, 228
Hygienic value of light clothing, 69, 94, 195, 206, 213
Hypochondria, liability of 'protected' type to, 99, 198

Ibsen, Henrik, 188
Ideals, natural and artificial, 188
Identification with opposite sex, 118 ff.
Imitation, rôle of, in fashion, 138 ff.
Immodesty of women, charge of, 108 ff.
Improvements, 'resigned' type cannot suggest, 95
India, loin cloth used in, 125
——, 'tropical' costume in, 126
Indians, North American, 49
Individual differences, 85 ff.
Individuality, inadequately expressed in 'fixed' dress, 217
—— and clothes, need of research concerning, 227, 228

Inertia, physical, 35, 38
——, mental, 179
Inferiority, feelings of, 102
Inhibition, 54 ff., 95 ff., 113, 117, 190 ff., 208, 209, 211, 213, 233, 234
——, difference in the two sexes, 108 ff.
Initiates dressed as women, 121
Initiation ceremonies, 42
Italy, attitude of government and Church in, 57, 58, 164

Jacket, 126
Japan, loin cloth used in, 125
Java, costume from, 12
Jawbone as bracelet, 30
Jealousy of husbands and clothes of married women, 61, 62
—— among women, 114, 116
——, desirability of avoiding, 213
Jelgersma, H. C., 121, 240
Jewellery, 33, 51, 73, 90, 185
Jewels, symbolism of, 27
Jews, head-covering of, in Synagogue, 104
Johnson, Samuel, quoted, 167
Jones, Ernest, 23, 82, 107, 152, 194, 240, 241
Journals, Fashion, 137, 142, 162
Jordan, Alfred C., 241
Juvenal, quoted, 25

Kaffirs, 141
Kilts, 128
King, The, reported approval of flash by, 177
Knapsack, 187
Köhler, Carl, 241
Köhler, Wolfgang, 18
Koreans, costume of, 233, 234
Ku Klux Klan, 31, 132

Landauer, K., 199, 241
Lawrence, D. H., 232
'Leg', objection to mentioning the word, 66, 193
Leggings, 205
Legs, exposure of, 57, 59, 65, 66, 67, 95, 97, 147, 153, 161 ff., 192, 206, 224
Lenglen, Suzanne, 147
Levy, L., 241
Lewin, B. D., 92
Lift attendants and uniforms, 136

Light, effects of, 94, 195, 196, 204
Limbs, emphasis on, 161 ff.
Lips, holes made in, 42
'Little man', symbolism of, 107
'Local' costumes, 32, 130, 131, 185
'Local' decoration. *See* Decoration, Local
Locomotion, increased facilities for, 142
Loin cloth, 125
London, leads men's 'modish' costume, 135
Lorand, A. S., 241
Lotze, Hermann, 34, 241
Louis XVI., portrait of, 13, 157, 158
Löwitsch, F., 156, 241

Macaulay, Eve, 8, 80, 89, 90, 199, 200, 241
McDougall, William, 20
Magic, 22, 71 ff., 120
Magical origin of clothes, theory of, 72
Male body, intolerance of, 208
────── ──────, need for greater tolerance of, 212
────── libido, need for less displacement of, on to clothes, 212
Mallarmé, 139
Mantis religiosa, 47
Marken, Island of, boys dressed as girls on, 121
Masks, 16, 31, 121
──────, effect of, 51
Mass production, 141, 142, 144
Masturbation, 189
Materials. *See* Clothing materials
Maturity, valuation of, 159, 161 ff., 221, 222
Mee, Arthur, 81
Men, more concentrated libido of, 107
──────, phallic symbolism of body as a whole, 107
──────, renunciation of beauty in clothes by, 111, 203
──────, greater sociability of, 115, 116, 208
──────, dissatisfaction with present dress of, 117, 206
──────, sartorially more progressive in earlier stages, 125
────── wear buttons on right, 178, 179

Men, repression of Narcissism in, 208
──────, more 'correct', 209
────── should dress more to please women, 212, 215
──────, more severe clothes morality of, 203, 204, 212
────── put on more clothes for ceremonial occasions, 225
Men's fashions change more slowly, 144, 145, 172, 202
────── Dress Reform Party, 153, 206, 218
────── fear of breaking conventions, 208 ff.
────── modern clothing a failure, 211
────── clothes, moral associations of, should be overcome, 212
────── ────── require new outlet for expression of 'manliness', 212
────── present dress as seen by later generations, 220
────── clothes reduce efficiency, 233
Menstruation, 103, 107
Middle Ages, fashions of, 159
Migration from warmer to colder climate, 68, 127
Ministry of Fashions proposed, 219
Minoan civilisation, constricted waist in, 11, 43
Miomandre, Fr. de, 241
Modesty, inhibitory nature of, 19, 55, 62
──────, as purpose of clothing, 16 ff.
──────, fluctuating character of, 19, 58, 66 ff.
──────, relation of, to decoration, 19 ff., 156
──────, ──────, to display, 63 ff.
──────, analysis of, 53 ff.
──────, sexual and social, 55, 56
────── relates to body or to clothes, 57 ff., 159
────── relates to self or to others, 59 ff.
────── directed against both desire and disgust, 62 ff.
────── and beauty, 64
────── relates to varying parts of the body, 66 ff., 160, 162 ff.
──────, house and clothes, relations of, 83
──────, sex differences in, 103 ff.
────── attaches to two zones in women, 107

INDEX

Modesty in women, 108 ff.
——, evaluation of, 190 ff.
——, two aspects distinguished, 191
—— essentially correlated with desire, 192 ff., 201
—— of nineteenth century, in retrospect, 193
—— and nudity. *See* Nudity and modesty
'Modish' costume, 123, 129 ff., 130, 167, 170, 185, 204, 214, 216, 218, 220. *See also* 'Fixed' costume
Mohammedan influence on dress, 61, 79, 83
Mongolian race, associated with 'arctic' costume, 127
Monk, clothing of, 74, 128
Moral aspects of clothes, 97, 113, 198, 203, 211, 212
—— —— more marked in men, 113
—— symbolism of clothes. *See* Symbols, moral
Moslem. *See* Mohammedan
Mother and clothes, 81, 93
'Mother Nature', 93, 94
Motoring, influence of, on fashion, 141
Mottram, R. H., 158
Movement, apparent increase of, through clothes, 35 ff., 48 ff.
——, restriction of, by clothes, 88, 199, 232 ff.
—— studies, 231
Müller-Lyer, F., 123, 241
Mustoxidi, 141, 241
Mutilation, 40, 42
——, relation of, to culture, 44

'Nacktkultur'. *See* Nude Culture
Nails, trimming of, 44, 45
Nakedness. *See* Nudity
Narcissism and Narcissistic tendencies, 86, 88 ff., 101, 116, 145, 188, 206 ff., 211 ff.
——, sex differences in, 101, 116, 145, 211, 213
'National' costumes, 32, 123, 130 ff., 218, 225
Natural body, increasing satisfaction taken in, 45, 46, 224, 225
—— ——, desirability of appreciation of, 223

Natural products used in primitive clothing, 124
—— selection among clothes and living species, 170, 171
—— attitude to body, 108
—— costume, 123
Nature, 93, 149
Naval uniforms, 131
Neck, constriction of, 205
Necklace, 12, 30, 46, 73
Neurosis and neurotic symptoms, 21, 193, 198, 213
New Pomerania, 12
Nightgowns, 152
Nightingale, Florence, in 'The Lady with a Lamp', 117
Norris, H., 241
Nose, deformation of, 42
Nude culture, 93, 94, 109, 192, 237
Nudity of savages, 17, 94
——, display originally relates to, 21, 86
—— and modesty, 57 ff., 86 ff., 102, 109, 194, 235
—— and health, 94, 195, 235
——, disgust at, 96, 97
——, semitic dislike of, 104
—— in relation to children, 200
—— and economics, 235
—— and indoor temperature, 235
——, increasing tendency to, and ultimate triumph of, 234 ff.
——, various writers anticipate a state of, 237, 238
Nurse, uniform of, 97, 132

'Object love', 190, 213
Occupation, clothes and, 31
'Occupational' costumes, 130, 131, 145, 221
Office, clothes as sign of, 31
'Old maids', sexual delusions of, 110
Ontogeny compared with phylogeny, 17
Overcoat, removal of, 105
——, pockets and, 186
'Over-determination', 21, 193, 197
Over-reaction, 21
Over-shoes, 205
Ovid, quoted, 103

Padaung women, collars of, 12, 50
Padding, 48
Page boy, uniform of, 31

Painting of Skin, 26, 40, 41, 45, 66, 97, 188 ff.
Parents, pride of, in children's appearance, 199
——, nudity of, before children, 200
Paris leads women's 'modish' costume, 135, 146, 152, 165
Parmelee, Maurice, 192, 237, 241
Parsons, Frank Alvah, 57, 58, 241
Past, inspiration sought from various periods of the, 156
——, difficulty of outgrowing the, 179, 180
Patou, Jean, 148, 152
Pendleton, 241
Penis, 28, 120. See also Phallus
Permanence. See Time
Personality, 16
—— of launchers of fashion, 152, 153
Petticoats, 70, 165, 171
Phallic symbolism, 26 ff., 48, 74, 77, 92, 99, 100, 102, 105, 107, 118, 120, 155, 193, 196, 207, 209, 212
Phallus, 30, 208. See also Phallic symbolism
Phelps, Elizabeth S., 241
Phobia, 62
Phylogeny compared with ontogeny, 17
Physiologists, need for co-operation of, 228
Plaiting, art of, 124
'Pleasure principle', 184
Pleský, Const., 8
Plumes on hats, 178
'Pneumonia blouses', 195, 206
Pockets, 186, 187, 206
Police, uniform of, 132, 134, 221
Politics and dress, 32, 78, 79, 111 ff., 163, 207
Poucher, W. A., 241
Pouches, 187
Poulaine, 28
Praxiteles, 220
Pregnancy simulated, 149, 160
Pressure on skin, 76, 199
'Primitive' costume, 12, 123 ff., 167
Prince of Wales, The, 153
Priority of various purposes of clothing, 16 ff.
Professional costume, 97. See also Working Clothes

Professional costume, moral aspects of, 97
Projection of exhibitionism from man to woman, 118, 119
—— of guilt on to women, 106, 110
—— —— from one sex to another, 110
—— —— on to homosexual persons, 203
Protection, as purpose of clothing, 16 ff., 22, 68 ff., 235
——, —— ——, evaluation of, 194 ff.
——, as rationalisation of modesty, 23, 98
—— from cold, 68, 79 ff., 98, 99
—— from heat, 69
—— from enemies, 69
—— from accidents, 70
—— from animals, 71
—— from magic and spirits, 71 ff.
—— from moral danger, 74 ff.
—— from general unfriendliness of world, 77 ff.
—— and freedom of movement, 128, 232 ff.
——, need for, may diminish, 235
—— may in future be the only motive for clothing, 235
Psycho-analysis and psycho-analytic findings, 21, 26, 28, 42, 62, 73, 77, 81, 84, 86, 87, 109, 117, 152, 175, 183, 191, 193, 197, 200, 207
Psychologists, attitude of, to clothes, 7
——, need for co-operation of, in research, 227
——, industrial, 231
Psychology of clothes, 7
—— of religion, 7
Psycho-pathology, 180, 183, 191
Psycho-therapy, results of, 212
'Pullover', Prince of Wales wears, 153
—— versus 'fasten up' systems, 232
Puritans, attitude of, 58, 159
Purple, royal, 31
Purposes of clothing, 16. See also Decoration, Modesty, Protection
Pyjamas, 209

Racinet, 241
Rank, clothes as sign of, 31, 138, 185

INDEX

Rank, indicated in uniforms, 131
Rank, Otto, 82, 241
Rationalisation, psychological, 23, 69, 94, 97, 98, 196
——, economic, 216 ff.
'Reaction-formation', 96, 102, 198, 211
'Reality principle', 183 ff., 222 ff., 234 ff.
—— —— conflicts with modesty and decoration, 237
—— —— and nudity, 237
Rebellion against clothes, 83. *See also* Type, rebellious
Recreational garments, as distinguished from professional, 98
Reform of men's clothes, 206 ff.
—— —— ——, reasons for, 204, 205
—— —— ——, factors in favour of, 206, 207
—— —— ——, factors opposing, 208 ff.
Regiments, distinctive uniforms of, 131
Regression, 180
—— to pre-natal state, 85
Reich, W., 200, 241
Reik, Th., 42, 241
Religion, 7, 26, 104, 105
Removal of garments as sign of respect, 30, 104, 105
Renaissance costume, 13, 148, 160
Renunciation, the great masculine, 110 ff., 206
Repression. *See* Inhibition
Research into clothes problems, programme of, 227 ff.
Respect, signs of, in the two sexes, 105
Restoration, costume of the, 156
Reversion, biological and sartorial, 175, 176, 180
Revolution, French, 79, 111 ff., 158
Reynolds, Sir Joshua, portrait by, 119
Riding to hounds, 71
——, back buttons on coats for, 173
Right and left in Folklore, 179
Rings, 50, 73, 123, 124
Rivalry in women's dress, 114
Rococo, 150

Romans, dress of, in cold countries, 217
Rosicrucians, 32
Rossetti, D. G., quoted, 103
Roubaud, Louis, 146, 241
Royal robes, 157
Royalty, influence of, on fashion, 146, 147
Ruffs, 50
Ruskin, mother of, 66
——, Gothic revival of, 150

Sadger, J., 28, 87, 118, 241
Saleeby, C. W., 236, 241
Salesmanship, 142, 229, 230
Samoa, primitive costume from, 12, 124
Samson, J. W., 162, 241
Sanborn, H. C., 241
'Sartorial' decoration. *See* Decoration, sartorial
Savages, 17, 94, 141
——, adoption of European clothing by, 94, 103
—— and fashion, 141
Scalping, 29
Scars as ornaments, 11, 40
Sceptre, 31
Schlink, F. J., 230
Schnitzler, Arthur, 21
School, tie indicating, 132
——, hierarchic costume in, 133
Schurtz, Heinrich, 17, 56, 67, 70, 241
Science as sublimation of scoptophilia, 118
Scoptophilia, 118
Scott, C. A., 242
Seitz, J. M., 192, 237, 242
Selenka, Emil, 7, 11, 12, 46, 242
Semitic dislike of nudity, 104, 190
Seneca, quoted, 216
'Sensible Dress Society', 165, 219
Servants, dress of, 135
Sex differences, 43, 85, 101, 102 ff., 144, 200 ff., 216
—— —— in libido, 107 ff.
—— —— in modesty, 108 ff.
—— —— in social life, 115, 116, 185, 186
—— —— in fashion, 144, 145
—— —— in position of buttons, 178, 179
—— —— in carrying essential articles, 186, 187

Sex differences in dress, question of desirability of, 201
——— ———, relation of, to sexual stimulation, 201
——— ———, relation of, to homo-sexuality, 202
——— ———, need of studying, 228
Sexual elements in dress, 25 ff., 107 ff., 138
——— rivalry, 26, 116
——— attraction, conscious and unconscious, 108 ff.
——— freedom, 163, 189, 190, 215
——— appeal, need for greater freedom of, in dress, 212, 214, 215
——— selection, 223
Shakespeare, quoted, 15, 85, 137, 181, 198
Shawl, effect of, 11, 35
Shipwrecks, women's clothes in, 234
Shirt, not respectable without coat, 209
———, putting on of, 232
Shoe, symbolism of, 27, 28
———, shape of, 28, 43, 58
———, as fetish, 28
———, high heeled, 46, 161
Shoes, thinner in modern times, 143
———, markings on, 177, 178
———, worn but once, 186
Shorts, 95, 213
Shoulders, padding at, 48
Siberia, costume from, 12
Silk, artificial, chiefly used by women, 12
Simplicity of dress, a sign of youth, 159
——— ———, now disappearing, 163
Simplification of men's dress after French Revolution, 112
——— of modern women's dress, 149, 158
Skater, 36
Skin, 38, 40, 41, 87 ff., 195
———, increasing modern admiration of, 235, 236
———, ease of cleaning as compared with clothes, 236
Skin-erotism, 87 ff., 108 ff., 195, 207
Skins, treatment of, 124, 128
———, use of, for clothes, 29, 127
Skirt, 11, 171, 205, 234.

Skirt, as increasing apparent size and movement, 35 ff., 46 ff., 128, 216
———, hobble, 49, 50
———, length of, 65, 97, 147, 148, 159 ff., 161 ff., 189, 219, 224
———, origin of, 125
———, harem, 147, 151
———, right of discarding, 216
Sleeves, 161
——— of coats, cuffs on, 174
———, leg of mutton, 220
Smoking jacket, Prince of Wales wears pullover with, 153
Snake goddess, Minoan, 11
Snobbery and clothes, 185, 186, 230
Social animal, man a, 15
Social problems and clothes, 31, 32, 78, 79, 101, 111 ff., 121, 129 ff., 138 ff., 163, 189, 190, 198, 200 ff., 216 ff., 228 ff.
Social value of clothes interest, 101
——— ——— of men's plain dress, 114
Societies, secret, 31, 32, 115, 132
Socks, 175
'Softness', moral and physical, 76, 98
Soldiers, captured, dressed as women, 121
Soldiers' headdress in Church, 104, 105
Sombart, Werner, 146, 242
Space, relation of 'fixed' and 'modish' costume to, 129, 132 ff.
Spain, Queen of, 'has no legs', 66
———, beggars' titles in, 139
Spencer, Herbert, 7, 29, 139, 237, 242
'Spirit of the age', expressed in fashion, 148, 219
——— ———, man's dress not in keeping with the, 217, 218
——— ——— and Clothing Boards, 219
Stage, influence of, on fashion, 141
Standardisation and individualisation, need of research into, 228
Stanley, 50
Stiffness of garments, moral associations of, 76, 97 ff.
Stocking, as fetish, 28
Stockings, 59, 66, 171, 175, 205, 213, 234
Stone breaker, goggles of, 71
Storfer, A. J., 242

INDEX

Stratz, C. H., 12, 13, 123, 127, 128, 242
Streets, footwear and condition of, 142, 143
Stripes on dress trousers, 175, 176
—— on sleeves of uniforms, 178
Subincision, 42
Sublimation, 87, 92, 96, 97 ff., 108, 193, 198, 212, 217
Suckling, possible influence of, on position of buttons, 179
Suggestion in fashion, 152, 153
Suits, need for expert tailoring of, 213
Sully, James, 18, 242
Sumptuary laws, 111, 139
Sun helmets, 69
Sunday dress, 225
Super ego, 98, 152, 197, 211
——, alliance of, with instincts, 211, 212
Support afforded by clothes, 76, 99, 100
Surén, Hans, 94, 242
'Suspenders' (for stockings), 194, 206
Sydow, Eckart von, 242
Symbols, sexual, 26 ff., 74, 107, 156, 193, 196. See also Phallic symbolism
——, moral, 74 ff., 97, 98, 113, 193, 196, 198, 209
—— of ideals, 152
Symons, N. J., 8
Swaddling clothes, 93
Sweden, national costumes of, 131
Switzerland, national costumes of, 131
Swords, 30, 33, 104, 178

Taboos on female sex, 103
Tags in top boots, 173
Tailoring and climate, 68
——, as an art, 90, 213
——, ——, birth of, 127, 128
——, need for expert, in present male costume, 213
Tailors, conservatism of, 210, 226
——, need for co-operation of, in research, 228
Taste, opportunity for development of, in child, 199
——, 'fixed' costume of advantage for those of little, 217

Technical research into clothing materials, 228, 229
Teeth, in necklaces, 30, 33
——, knocking out of, 42, 44, 45
Temperature, adaptability to varying, 205
—— of air surrounding body, 206
Tennis dress, 147, 157
——, bare legs at, 153
Tierra del Fuego, inhabitants of, 16
Terrorising function of clothes, 30, 31
Tertullian, 242
Thickness of garments, moral associations of, 76
Thomas, W. J., 242
Thomson, James, quoted, 227
Tie, symbolism of, 27
——, associational aspects of, 132, 134
——, constriction of neck by, 205
'Tight lacing', 43 ff., 160
Tightness of garments, strengthening effect of, 76, 88
—— ——, moral associations of, 76, 97
Time, relative permanence in, feature of 'fixed' costume, 32, 129, 132 ff.
Toga, 49
Top hat, 37, 71
——, Korean, 233, 234
Touch, sense of, 37, 38. See also Pressure
Trade. See Clothing Trade
Tradition, associated with 'fixed' costume, 132 ff., 217, 218
Train of Catherine II. of Russia, 48
Trains, 48, 49, 58
Transfer of feeling, law of, 214
Transport, improved methods of, 141, 142
——, convenience for, 205
Transvestitism. See Eonism
Trophies, 29
'Tropical' costume, 12, 123, 125, 126, 167, 216
—— —— as basis of western female costume, 126
Trousers, symbolism of, 27
——, a feature of 'arctic' costume, 127

Trousers, worn by Mohammedan women, 128
——, worn by European women, 128
——, history of, compared to that of a living being, 169
——, evolution of, 170
——, turned up at bottom, 174
——, stripes on dress, 175, 176
——, compared with skirts, 205
——, floppy, may cause accidents, 234
Trunk, emphasis on, 162, 163
Tunis, outdoor costume from, 12, 61, 65, 83, 84
Tylor, E. B., 242
Type, rebellious, 91 ff., 96, 98, 99, 198, 207
——, resigned, 94, 95, 198
——, unemotional, 95, 96, 99, 101, 198
——, prudish, 96, 97, 99, 198
——, duty, 97, 98
——, protected, 98, 99, 198
——, supported, 99, 100, 198
——, sublimated, 98, 100, 101, 198
——, self-satisfied, 101, 102, 198
Types, nature of, in psychology, 90, 91

Ugliness and modesty, 64, 97, 110
Ugly, toleration of the, 224
Umbrella, 83
Underwear, 88, 171, 194, 199
——, should not be indecent or unaesthetic, 194, 205
Ungewitter, Richard, 242
Uniformity, as principle of men's dress, 112
—— —— ——, its social value, 114
——, increasing among women, 117
——, as feature of 'fixed' costume, 132 ff., 217
Uniforms, 97, 98, 130 ff., 221
——, military, 33, 48, 97, 104, 105, 131 ff., 218
——, and group organisation, 135, 136
——, appeal of, to women, 211, 214
Unity of clothes and wearer, 37
Untidiness of recent dresses, 165, 220
Urwick, E. J., 230

Uterine symbolism, 156. See also Womb phantasies
Utilitarian features of dress persist as ornamental, 175 ff.

Variations, in clothes and living forms, 172 ff.
Vegetable products used for clothes, 124, 128
Veil, 52, 67
'Vertical' decoration. See Decoration, vertical
Vest, 232
Vestigial organs and corresponding features of dress, 173 ff., 226
Victorian era, 150, 171

Wace, A. J. B., 11
Wales, Prince of, 153
Walford, Walter G., 205, 242
Waist, emphasis on, 13
——, constricted, 42 ff., 160, 188
—— line, low, 123, 124
—— ——, high, 161
Waist ring, 125
Waistcoats, 174, 194, 205
Waiter, dress of, 135, 221
Waitress, uniform of, 134, 157
War and warriors, 29 ff., 70, 112, 131, 133, 135. See also Soldiers and Uniforms, military
Wealth, display of, 32, 33, 114, 138, 185
Weapons, handing over of, 30
Webb, Wilfred Mark, 7, 12, 13, 31, 135, 168, 173, 242
Week-end, 186
Weight of clothes, 92, 95, 158, 204
—— ——, lighter with women, 204
Wells, H. G., 237
White, G. A., 120, 121, 242
Whole, emphasis on body as a, 13, 161, 222
——, costume as a, 18, 52, 90, 156
Wicket-keeper, pads of, 71
Williams-Ellis, Amabel, 66
Wills, Helen, 147, 153
Wind, effect of, 11, 37, 38
Winterfeld, A. V., 189
Winterstein, von, 42
Wohlgemuth, A., 214
Womb phantasies, 81 ff.

INDEX

Women, more hygienic clothing of, 69, 195, 205, 206
———, freer Narcissism of, 101, 116, 145, 211, 213
———, head-covering of, in Church, 104
———, sartorial emancipation of, 105 ff., 189, 190
———, greater decorativeness of, 106 ff., 204
———, more diffused libido of, 107, 125
———, exposure of body of, 107 ff., 204, 238
———, smaller participation in social life of, 115
———, imaginary penis of, 120
———, greater conservatism of, 125, 135
———, increasing socialisation of, 145
——— wear buttons on left, 178, 179
———, suggested greater resistance to cold of, 195
———, general superiority of modern clothing of, 204, 205
Women, attitude of, to men's dress reform, 210, 211
——— should dress more to please men, 214
———, desirability of reducing Narcissism of, 213, 214
———, interference with movement by dress of, 233, 234
———, suggested nudity of, in near future, 238
Work, respectability of, 112, 118, 151, 221
——— and women's fashions, 151, 163
———, effects of costume on, 228
Working clothes, 90, 98
Wundt, W., 72, 242

Youthfulness, ideal of, 151 ff., 159, 161 ff., 221, 222

Zechariah, quoted, 122
Zip fastener, 231, 232
Zulliger, Hans, 200, 242
Zweig, Arnold, 76